surrender

THE CALL OF THE

AMERICAN WEST

Joanna Pocock

ANANSI

Published in Canada in 2019 and the USA in 2020 by
House of Anansi Press Inc.
www.houseofanansi.com

23 22 21 20 19   1 2 3 4 5

Library and Archives Canada Cataloguing in Publication

Title: Surrender : the call of the American West / Joanna Pocock.
Names: Pocock, Joanna, 1965– author.

Identifiers: Canadiana (print) 20190103906 | Canadiana (ebook) 20190103922
| ISBN 9781487007249 (softcover) | ISBN 9781487007256 (EPUB) | ISBN
9781487007263 (Kindle)
Subjects: LCSH: Pocock, Joanna, 1965-—Travel—West (U.S.) | LCSH:
West (U.S.)—Description and travel. | LCSH: British—Travel—West (U.S.)
| LCSH: Environmentalism—West (U.S.) | LCSH: Environmentalists—
West (U.S.) | LCSH: Counterculture—West (U.S.) | LCSH: Climatic
changes—West (U.S.)
Classification: LCC F595.3 .P63 2019 | DDC 917.804/34—dc23

Library of Congress Control Number: 2019939719

Book design: Alysia Shewchuk
Cover and interior photographs: Joanna Pocock

Canada Council   Conseil des Arts
for the Arts   du Canada

ONTARIO ARTS COUNCIL
CONSEIL DES ARTS DE L'ONTARIO
an Ontario government agency
un organisme du gouvernement de l'Ontario

*We acknowledge for their financial support of our publishing program the Canada
Council for the Arts, the Ontario Arts Council, and the Government of Canada.*

Printed and bound in Canada

MIX
Paper from
responsible sources
FSC® C103567

PRAISE FOR *Surrender*

'In *Surrender*, Joanna Pocock follows rewilders, nomads, ecosexuals and a host of outliers who see living with and off the land as the salvation of our species and everything else on the planet. Her candid and beautifully written journey confronts the angst, guilt and grief she experiences while examining the greatest existential crisis of all time – the killing of diverse life on our planet. Pocock's book is deeply researched and broad in its search for solutions. Her deft blending and layering of the personal with the political makes *Surrender* a necessary read for our times.' — Edward Burtynsky

'Joanna Pocock's compelling debut, a tapestry of personal narrative and vibrant reporting, explores the fresh, unconventional and often hopeful relationships with nature that are clashing with the tintype images of the American West. So much more than a memoir, *Surrender* is an important enquiry into the ground upon which we find and establish a home.' — Harley Rustad, author of *Big Lonely Doug*

'*Surrender* is an astonishing book about the fragility of nature, grief, the American West, the consolations of travel and the exquisite agonies of mortal life. Pocock travels widely in time and space, through memories, visions, the deaths of her parents and the birth of her child. Beautiful, wise and deeply moving, this is ambulatory philosophy at its finest – for readers of Rebecca Solnit, Lauren Elkin, Garnette Cadogan and Iain Sinclair.' — Joanna Kavenna, author of *A Field Guide to Reality*

'Written with great narrative richness and an anthropologist's intrepid gaze, *Surrender* is fascinating, urgent and profoundly compelling. It is an important addition to nature's library.' — Chloe Aridjis, author of *Sea Monsters*

'A bewitching and deeply affecting book. Pocock's elegant interweaving of the intimate and the expansive, the personal and the universal, culminates in a work that forces us to consider our own place in, and impact upon, a world that could itself have more past than future.' — *Spectator* (U.K.)

surrender

We all hit the middle of our lives at some point. When my sister Mary turned twenty-six did she have any idea she would be dead at fifty-two? Not a clue. What we call our mid-life crisis often doesn't hit at the mid-point of our lives unless we live into our eighties, nineties and beyond – which many of us won't. A better term for 'mid-life crisis' is the less grandiose-sounding but perhaps more accurate *ennui*. By a certain age, we simply get bored of the rhythm of our days, whatever those may be: the commute to work on a packed train, the rush to get a child ready for school, the smell of car fumes as we sit in traffic, the dog whining for its walk. We tire of our living spaces and how the light hits a certain wall each afternoon. We sicken at the sight of the same smudge of sky from our beds, the piles of laughing gas canisters in the gutter, the seemingly endless whoosh of greasy Styrofoam fried chicken containers blowing down the pavement after the pubs close. And the pubs – even they seem threadbare and dull or loud and violent. We begin to realize that we have more past than future – the known is eclipsing the unknown. We panic and plan our escape, whether that be via psychedelic drugs, taking up a religion, or ditching the one we have, quitting our jobs, taking up a fresh partner, joining a polyamorous community – all in the belief we are heading towards that magical thing: freedom. Whatever form it takes, mid-life often arrives in a package with a bright red 'self-destruct' button attached.

The mid-life crisis package I was handed came in a box marked with one simple word: Montana. Over the years my husband Jason and I had spent time in New Mexico, Nevada, Texas, California, Colorado and Wyoming, either travelling or working on various writing and film projects. Now we were approaching fifty and it was time to leave our small patch of east London. The American West was calling us.

We developed an eccentric but effective process of elimination for finding exactly where in the West we might go. This was partly based on after-school activities for our daughter who was six when the planning began. Who knew that the only club she would be able to join in Alpine, Texas was cheerleading? Through a combination of coincidences and research we settled on the alliterative Missoula, Montana, and cajoled our daughter Eve into thinking this would be a Great Adventure. We packed up our house, filled one suitcase each and left London. I had the idea that we could pare away the superfluities of life, only allowing ourselves the necessities, or what Henry David Thoreau called the 'necessaries', the things that over time become 'so important to human life that few, if any...attempt to do without'.

For Eve, this consisted largely of soft toys. The main player in her menagerie was a large rabbit called Lulu, with a strawberry-scented heart. Lulu's accessories filled half a suitcase. I intervened at times over Eve's choice of clothing. She had never experienced a North American winter, so I surreptitiously stuffed jumpers and warm socks among her swimming costumes and sundresses.

I found the process of deciding what I needed and what I thought I needed to be the first step in liberating myself from the known. I started with my books: Isabella Bird's *A Lady's Life in the Rocky Mountains*, Annie Dillard's *The Writing Life*, Ralph Waldo Emerson's *Nature*, *The Cincinnati Arch: Learning from Nature in the City* by John Tallmadge, *The Significance of the Frontier in American History* by Frederick Jackson Turner and the Moon Guidebook to Montana, which was a last minute gift from a friend.

Jason's packing was quick: his camera, the novels he was reading and very few clothes. To Thoreau the 'necessaries' consisted of food and fuel. Clothing and shelter were only 'half unnecessary'. Among the few implements he had with him at Walden Pond were a knife, an axe, a spade, a wheelbarrow, lamps, stationery and 'access to a few books'.

We landed in Seattle and spent our first night at the Kings Inn, the last downtown motel in a rapidly gentrifying, or some would say, long gentrified city. We hired a car and drove east the next morning to begin our new life. My vision of Washington state as a lush ambassador of the Pacific Northwest with thick, impenetrable rainforests was challenged as we crested the Cascade Mountain Range. For hours our car windows transmitted a sandy blur of desert and sagebrush, which was replaced by deep green forests and rocky buttes as we hit the Idaho panhandle and then it thinned out again as we edged into western Montana.

It was on a sweltering July day that we took the exit ramp off Interstate 90 down into Missoula, a university town of around 65,000 people. The layout from above was puzzling. It looked as though a giant hand had tossed a bunch of buildings into the air, leaving them where they landed. Missoula now sat in the dried bed of an ancient glacial lake – its name means 'place of the frozen water' in the Salish language. I had imagined Missoula to be a pretty town with its ring of mountains and its snaking river, but as we approached, the reality was far from the idyll I had conjured.

My daughter read out 'Five Guys Burgers and Fries', savouring the rhyme, as we passed the fast food joint on a corner next to a towering Conoco petrol sign. After that, I don't remember her saying a word. I think we were both stunned by the intense heat, the hard-edged sunshine, the long drive, by the giant signage, the wide roads, the landscape of objects and buildings at once familiar (trucks, shops, houses, roads) and yet utterly foreign in their details.

We pulled up in our rental car to the Campus Inn, which appeared to be the least run-down of the cheap motels on a strip of highway at the entrance to town. The faux quilted bedspreads gave off a vaguely simulated country aesthetic, quickly undermined by the strong smell of bedbug spray. Faded prints of Canada Geese flying across pastel wetlands hung above the Queen-sized beds.

That night I saw a type of funnel-web spider called a hobo. Its body was the size of a nickel and I watched, terrified, as it crawled along the skirting board. Jason and I kept quiet about the spider and lay in bed with Eve between us, listening to the trains chugging past the motel, their boxcars loaded with coal from eastern Montana. My scant dreams were apocalyptic and seemed to linger through the following day. Despite my better judgement, I gave into Eve's pleas that we go swimming in the motel's wildly overheated pool. A few days later, management mysteriously hung a 'CLOSED' sign on the door. E. coli had found its way into the water, which led to my kidneys becoming infected and a stay in an emergency ward. The hospital bill would take us months to pay off.

As we got into our rental car after that first sleepless night to find somewhere to have breakfast, the sun was coming down hard and hot and I remember thinking, 'What the hell have we done?' The Campus Inn would be our home until the house we had found to rent became free.

Two years on, we are back in London and the American West is on fire. Since the 1970s, the wildfire season has increased from five months to seven. And the acreage is also increasing. Before Europeans arrived in the West, wildfires were less intense, moved more slowly and tended to pass through forests every five to twenty years. Vegetation was able to regenerate itself. Fire is such a natural part of the life cycle here that some species need it in order to propagate: the cones from ponderosas, lodgepoles, jack pines and giant sequoias need very high temperatures for their seeds to be released. From early on, the new settlers in the West decided that the best way to keep their homes and livestock safe was to continually suppress fire. The result of this is unnaturally dense forests which are like giant tinderboxes in these increasingly hot, dry summers.

Over a million acres in Montana are burning in twenty-six separate conflagrations. North of the 49th parallel, in British Columbia, a hundred and forty fires are raging. In Idaho twenty-three are still going, eleven in Washington. Sixteen fires are still blazing in Oregon, one of which has ripped through the Columbia Gorge, dropping ash in Portland. Fifteen fires are still uncontained in California. A firefighter has just been killed by a falling tree in western Montana, and the full effects of smoke inhalation are yet to be seen.

Forests are being wiped out and animals are dying. Sometimes predators can benefit from fires in the short term by preying on animals as they flee but this isn't always the case. Bears, wolves, bison and elk are burning to death. Often it's the young who cannot escape quickly enough. Sometimes an adult will return to the den for safety, only to suffocate. Many animals sense fire before humans can, but their response isn't always lifesaving. Porcupines and squirrels react to danger by climbing trees, which in a forest fire is deadly. Large birds can often escape but smaller, low-flying ones can asphyxiate or die of exhaustion. Probably the most affected species in this new age of giant fires are fish. The water that is used to put out fires or the rain that may finally arrive after months of drought washes ash into creeks and rivers. Particulates in fresh water can work their way into the gills of fish, suffocating them. Bears rely on fish, and the knock-on effect of ash entering the ecosystem is obvious. The centuries-old pattern of animals fleeing fires and finding sanctuary in another part of the landscape is long gone. Where can they go, these animals when their habitats have been parcelled up, paved over, built upon and mined out of existence? They are trapped in these forests waiting to burn.

My friends in Washington state are writing to tell me that their bags are packed in case they are evacuated. A close friend with an asthmatic daughter has left Missoula for the Oregon coast so her daughter can breathe more easily. My Facebook feed is full of questions about the best masks to filter out particulates. My dreams these days are filled with burning trees.

These fires are not unrelated to this book.

In Missoula, my proximity to mountains, lakes and rivers brought me closer to the Earth. I could walk out of my front door and be up Mount Sentinel in less than ten minutes. Every night, I'd look out at it, 'Yup, still there,' and head into bed. You cannot live in the American West without feeling a connection to the land. In London, when I look out my front door, I see blocks of flats, streetlights, walls and pavements. In Missoula, I was confronted with mountains and sky and deer looking in at me through my bedroom window, their eyes parallel to mine.

There were a few problems with our rental house in Missoula, which meant we couldn't move in. We'd signed our tenancy agreement and handed over a large deposit but the house wasn't habitable. Tearful arguments ensued while we convinced our landlords to clean the place. We'd just checked out of the motel and I wasn't keen to play host to the hobo spiders or kidney infections, so we looked at a map and decided to head to Butte, a town of around 35,000 people an hour and a half down the I-90 southeast of Missoula.

I was so mired in details to do with our move that I hadn't really thought about what we would find in Butte. In our travels around the West we had come to know the layout of most towns, with their Main Streets, their false-fronted buildings like the ones in Anthony Mann films, their one-storey mercantiles – those ubiquitous general stores selling shoe laces, dog food, cans of propane, powdered milk and energy bars – the diners with their swivelling stools at Formica counters, the bars with their flashing neon advertisements for Coors and Bud Light, the churches and the clapboard bungalows. I was not prepared for the streets of Butte, lined with tall, handsome nineteenth-century buildings, many of them empty and up for sale or rent. Butte's central district, which contains almost 6,000 buildings, is a National Historic Landmark – the largest in the United States – and looks more like a nineteenth-century Manhattan or Chicago than small-town Montana.

As we wandered over to the Berkeley Pit in Uptown Butte and gazed into the toxic, mile-long turquoise pool of contaminated groundwater left over from an open pit copper mine, we were swiftly reminded that we were thousands of miles from the 'East'. The Berkeley Pit is the town's primary tourist attraction, and also happens to be the country's largest Superfund site – in other words, a place that has been contaminated by toxic waste and identified by the Environmental Protection Agency (EPA) as posing a risk to humans and the environment.

We paid our two bucks to walk through an elevated tunnel to a viewing platform where we stared into this solution of arsenic, cadmium, zinc, sulphuric acid and a bunch of heavy metals. Every now and then sirens blared to deter birds from landing in the appealing blueness of the tainted water. When birds do land, which is not infrequent during migration, their oesophagi corrode and they die a horrible death.

As we gazed out over the Berkeley Pit, a woman on a tannoy told its story against a background of upbeat banjo music. We were in *Simpsons* territory: *Houses were cleared away to make room for more mines! And the people were happy to lose their homes because more mines meant more jobs!*

As you drive into Butte, you are faced with a large stone flowerbox the size of a coffin straddling two stone pillars. It is topped with a sign that reads

WELCOME TO BUTTE
The Richest Hill on Earth

From the late nineteenth to the early twentieth century, Butte was indeed one of the wealthiest places in the United States – the result of two tectonic plates meeting at the Continental Divide and rising upwards to reveal precious underground metals.

In 1882, miners in Butte were bringing over 4,000 tons of copper to the surface. A year later, they were mining over 10,000 tons. Around this time, Augustus Heinze started the Montana Ore Purchasing Company and was selling close to 1,000 tons of copper every month. The timing for the discovery of this precious commodity could not have been better. These giant seams of copper ore were discovered just when telephones and electricity were taking off. In 1896, an eight-square-kilometre section of the town was producing over twenty-six per cent of the world's copper and over fifty per cent of the country's needs. Heinze and his competitors Marcus Daly and William Clark were known collectively as the Copper Kings and between them turned Butte into the biggest city between Chicago and San Francisco, and one of the richest places in America.

Butte's wealth went into the pockets of the Copper Kings, but in order for their businesses to keep expanding, they needed workers. The population grew steadily around the turn of the twentieth century with a workforce from Italy, Finland, Austria, Montenegro, Mexico, China, Cornwall, Wales and Ireland. People from Butte (a writer friend calls them 'Butticians') will tell you how the 'No Smoking' signs in the mines were written in sixteen languages and how in the early 1900s there were more people speaking Irish under the streets here than in any other part of the world outside Ireland.

Fourteen towering steel headframes still sit atop old mine shafts in Butte. These structures, also called gallow frames, were used to lower and raise workers, mules and their equipment into the mines and back again, laden with the metal ore. Looming over boarded-up brothels, shops, theatres, handsome red brick houses and more recent bungalows, these headframes have become an icon of the town printed on T-shirts and lending their silhouettes to the logo for a local micro distillery.

Because of these rich seams of copper, Butte is a hilly town. Driving uphill to get a sense of its layout, we came across a small piazza overlooking some gaping holes in the earth, the remnants of open cast mines. This monument is dedicated to those killed in the Granite Mountain Disaster, the country's most deadly hardrock mining accident. On 8 June 1917, a group of men descended into the mine to inspect a loose electrical cable. An acetylene gas lamp accidentally touched the oily paraffin wrapping of a wire, sending fire along the cable and turning the mineshaft into a giant chimney. Not all of the 168 men who died here were killed instantly. Some wrote letters to their loved ones as they slowly asphyxiated. This disaster, along with so many others, is very much part of Butte's collective memory. What you sense in Butte is a town that has survived.

There is a toughness to it. It's Evel Knievel's hometown, after all.

Jason and I fantasized about moving here. The cheap rents and the town's lack of pretension were a tonic compared to the more upscale and pricier Missoula. But we were told over and over that the water in the Berkeley Pit was likely to reach the town's water table by 2020. Butte, we could see, was a wonderfully Montanan conundrum of a place: beautiful, desirable, complicated and rife with historic problems.

On our way back to Missoula, we stopped at a diner in Wisdom. Our waitress told us how she'd escaped a 'bad situation' out East and had stopped here for gas. The diner offered her a job and here she was, years later, happier than she'd ever been. This was a variation on a story we were to hear many times over.

Westward expansion has been written about since Europeans first stepped outside the 'civilized' states of the East and crossed into the 'wild', 'barbaric' outposts of the West. It was famously discussed by Frederick Jackson Turner in his 1893 *Atlantic* essay, 'The Significance of the Frontier in American History'. 'The problem of the West,' he wrote, 'is nothing less than the problem of American development...What is the West? What has it been to American life? To have the answers to these questions is to understand the most significant features of the United States of to-day.'

This question and the answers it engenders still

haunt the place. The West has always encouraged personal reinvention. Historically it has been the place where the restless, the dispossessed, the persecuted, the fugitives, the lost, the chancers and the speculators have gone to seek redemption and reinvention. Wallace Stegner, the author and environmentalist who set up the creative writing department at Stanford University, where he taught Wendell Berry, Edward Abbey, Ken Kesey, Larry McMurtry and Thomas McGuane, called the West 'hope's native home ... a civilization in motion, driven by dreams.' But he was also careful to add, 'The West has had a way of warping well-carpentered habits, and raising the grain on exposed dreams.'

Like every region of the United States, the West is culturally, historically and geographically rich. Yet there are specific characteristics that are unique to it: space and aridity. In 1878, the American geologist and explorer John Wesley Powell defined the West as being the part of America that lies west of the 100th longitudinal meridian, a geographical definition which is still used today. 'Passing from the east to west across this belt a wonderful transformation is observed,' he wrote.

> On the east a luxuriant growth of grass is seen, and the gaudy flowers ... make the prairie landscape beautiful. Passing westward, species after species of luxuriant grass and brilliant flowering plants disappear; the ground gradually becomes naked,

with bunch grasses here and there; now and then a thorny cactus is seen, and the yucca plant thrusts out its sharp bayonets.

Those grass-covered prairies, however, have been overcultivated and are no longer luxuriant. And the aridity seen on the western side of the 100th meridian is creeping east. Aridity, in this context, means land that receives less than twenty inches – roughly fifty-one centimetres – of rainfall per year and requires extra irrigation for agriculture. The line is shifting as the West is becoming drier. In the 1870s, Powell saw this aridity as a problem for human habitation. He urged the American government to rethink settlement in the West and to organize water and land-management plans that took into consideration the dryness of the land. Political leaders rejected the idea, seeing it as a hindrance to development. And the West as we know it continues to suck its aquifers dry and live on what seems to be borrowed water.

The complex history, the literature, the geography, the vast array of cultures and the mythology born and raised in this part of the world were not things I had given much thought to. That is, not until I found myself rolling up to the front door of our motel in Missoula, Montana that July day. What reinvention was I hoping for? What interior grain would become exposed? I wasn't here to seek my fortune, to pan for metaphorical gold or to discover that fabled western self-reliance. I was escaping, yet I was also seeking *something*. I just didn't know what it was.

Every day of my two years in Missoula I watched the light touch Mount Sentinel. Sentinel is by definition a mountain, but a small, rounded one. I got to know the way the sun worked its way across this folded hunk of earth in shades of gold in autumn, a pale lilac in winter, buttery yellow in spring and a vibrant orangey-red in summer. Each season seeped into my body via this mountain. In winter the snow would spread its whiteness and then retreat in spring. Yet our two winters in Missoula were mild for Montana and ski resorts struggled to stay open.

When I spoke to those who had lived in Western Montana a long time, they told me that the seasonal rhythms were out of synch. Perhaps I felt it more acutely because being from Ontario – a place with distinct seasons very similar to those in Montana – I remembered the waist-deep snow in the winters of my childhood, having to be shovelled out of our house because the front door could not be pushed open from the inside. I remember the long days of summer and the achingly beautiful fall evenings where the turning leaves, lit by a setting sun, seemed on fire against the pale sky. The melting ice of spring has laid down in my bones the soundtrack to March, April and May. I could feel the dislocation of the seasons, swinging off their axis, in my body.

Every winter the glaciers in the eponymous Glacier National Park in Northern Montana are shrinking. Of the hundred and fifty that existed in the park in the late nineteenth century, only twenty-five remain. And it is estimated that in the next twenty to thirty years all the named glaciers in the United States will have melted. With no glaciers, there will be no spring run-off. With no spring run-off there can be no rivers. With no rivers, there is no irrigation, fish or fresh water. You get the picture. This is only one example of the myriad climatic changes you can see with your own eyes in Montana, and it is not looking to improve any time soon.

Scott Pruitt, the climate change sceptic and briefly Donald Trump-appointed head of the Environmental Protection Agency (who sued the EPA fourteen times when he was Attorney General for Oklahoma) reversed many of the clean air and clean water acts put into law by previous administrations. A statement Pruitt made just after he was hired could have been uttered a century ago by European settlers: 'True environment-alism, from my perspective, is using natural resources that God has blessed us with.' Land is there to be used and exploited, especially in the West where oil, gas and precious metals are just a few boreholes away from making some people very wealthy.

If you even have half an ear to the ground, you will

pick up the debates around land treaties that were made with Native Americans – the true custodians of much of the West. Many of these treaties have been broken and are still being contested – treaties whose illegal terminations deny tribes (and by extension everyone else) access to clean water, the right to hunt humanely, to grow wild food and to breathe clean air.

The American West is a crucible for so many of the issues coming at us from our news feeds. Living here you are constantly confronted with land, wilderness, wild fires, drought, mountains and rivers. In this land-scape, you are made aware that you are both incredibly small and yet indelibly part of the interconnected web of life. This idea of 'everything being connected' has over the years been bandied about by new agers, but back in 1962, the scientist and author Rachel Carson wrote eloquently about it in her groundbreaking book *Silent Spring*, which played its part in launching the global environmental movement. 'The Earth's vegeta-tion is part of a web of life in which there are intimate and essential relations between plants and the Earth, between plants and other plants, between plants and animals,' she wrote. 'Sometimes we have no choice but to disturb these relationships, but we should do so thoughtfully, with full awareness that what we do may have consequences remote in time and place.' Carson's book, despite fierce opposition from power-ful chemical companies, did provide the ammunition needed to ban one of the worst synthetic weedkillers around: DDT.

Although Carson's argument was a new one for mainstream Americans, it was an idea that most Indigenous communities had understood for millennia: that all organisms – however big or small – rely on each other to thrive. The Oglala Lakota chief Luther Standing Bear put it thus, 'Only to the white man was nature a wilderness and only to him was the land "infested" with "wild" animals and "savage" people. To us it was tame. Earth was bountiful and we were surrounded with the blessings of the Great Mystery.' Chief Standing Bear died of flu in 1939 after working as a rancher, teacher, lay minister and shopkeeper on reservations in South Dakota. He witnessed the 1890 massacre at Wounded Knee in which 250–300 Lakota were killed and another 25 soldiers lost their lives. In what seems like a contradictory move, Chief Standing Bear accompanied Buffalo Bill Cody's Wild West Show to Britain. He eventually became a Hollywood actor, later writing two books about his life: *My People the Sioux* and *Land of the Spotted Eagle*.

This interconnectedness he and others speak of is palpable and yet so are the strands severed from it. For instance, invasive saltcedar bushes, with their pale pink flowers you see waving in the wind like puffy magic wands across great stretches of the West, might look pretty to a newcomer until you look a little closer.

Saltcedar plants, also known as tamarisk, were brought to the US in the nineteenth century as ornamentals. They escaped into the wild in the 1870s and have been aggressively spreading ever since. As if sucking up 200 gallons of water a day from the soil weren't bad enough, the tamarisk secretes salt into the ground, making it inhospitable to native vegetation. Only four species of bird use tamarisk for food or habitat, whereas native species can support up to 154 types of bird per hundred acres.

Despite the visibility of non-native species, razed forests, mined earth, and rivers running orange, there are still people clamouring to dig for copper just eleven miles from one of the last pristine rivers in Montana. And there are those who see federal lands as theirs to use as they want – as their God-given right – and whose idea of a National Park is an untapped energy source rather than a place whose remaining scraps of wildness need to be preserved. Montana strikes the newcomer as a sort of Eden – and in many ways it is. But it is also so much more complicated.

For 12,000 years, the land of the American West was viewed as a gift of creation, to be shared in common. In 1810, the Shawnee Chief Tecumseh was asked by Governor Harrison (who became president of the United States for a month in 1841) to place his trust in the white man's parcelling up of land. Tecumseh is recorded as saying:

The way, the only way to stop this evil is for the red men to unite in claiming a common and equal right in the land, as it was at first, and should be now – for it was never divided, but belongs to all. No tribe has the right to sell, even to each other, much less to strangers...Sell a country! Why not sell the air, the great sea, as well as the Earth? Did not the Great Spirit make them for all the use of his children?

It wasn't until the Europeans arrived with their agriculture, domestication of animals and their sedentism that this conscious effort to support human and non-human life sustainably was replaced by the idea of private ownership.

This mastery over the environment and the belief system that justifies it is embodied in the actions of Cliven Bundy, a Mormon rancher from Bunkerville, Nevada, who was in the news a lot when we first got to Montana. Bundy headed the 2014 stand-off with federal and state police over his refusal to pay the required fees to allow his cows to graze on public land – land managed by the Bureau of Land Management or the Forest Service. The fees for this privilege amount to $1.41 per 'animal unit per month' – an 'animal unit' being one cow and her calf, one horse, five sheep or five goats. His failure to settle such a relatively small fee highlights how much of his refusal to pay was driven by ideology rather than solely financial necessity.

Cliven Bundy, his family, and many of his supporters are affiliated with the Sovereign Citizen Movement, a loose but sprawling subculture whose members believe in the illegitimacy of the United States government. They not only reject having to pay grazing fees to a government they do not recognize, but also refuse to file taxes, register their vehicles, or drive with a licence. Some refuse to use US currency. Their desire to live 'free of any legal constraints' is a brand of libertarianism that is rife in the Western states. I see a direct line between the nineteenth-century pioneer homesteaders and the Bundys of today. Their vision is aligned with the idea that you should be able to raise a family, graze your cattle and do whatever you need to in order to protect your guns, your family and your God – in their case a Mormon God – from what you see as a tyrannical government.

Another armed stand-off in January 2016 between militias and federal employees involved the Bundys. This clash between anti-government protesters and law enforcement officers was set against the backdrop of a fragile ecosystem: the Malheur National Wildlife Refuge in Harney County, Oregon – a 760-square-kilometre bird sanctuary established by Theodore Roosevelt in 1908. The desert, dunes and meadows here are carved out by marshes, rivers, ponds and lakes. This rare combination of water and land supports over 320 species of waterfowl, songbirds, shorebirds and raptors.

In the early 1900s, the photographer William Finley began to document birds around Malheur Lake and noticed that their numbers were dwindling. White pelicans, sandhill cranes, trumpeter swans and the snowy egret were being decimated by plume hunters, who were feeding the fashion craze for gigantic feathered hats. It wasn't only the feathers that nineteenth-century milliners craved: entire heads, wings and sometimes whole taxidermied songbirds would end up perched, silent and staring onto hats worn in the drawing rooms of New York and London. In 1910, Finley wrote a piece in the *Atlantic* in which he despaired at a pair of plume hunters wiping out an entire population of white herons in just a day and a half. 'Malheur has seen many such massacres,' he wrote, 'but none so great as that.' It was at Finley's behest that Roosevelt decided to protect the Malheur ecosystem and its bird populations.

The Paiute peoples have been living in and around Harney County for 16,000 years, thriving on the lakes, the land and the diverse ecosystem until they came into contact with Europeans in the late nineteenth cen-tury. The Paiute were forced by aggressive settlers and a government keen to expand its ownership of resources in the West to live on a small parcel of land known as the Malheur Indian Reservation, whose borders were constantly chipped away until the Paiute were eventually denied hunting and fishing rights. In 1878, they were forced from their ancestral lands. That winter, 550 Paiute men, women and children travelled 560 kilometres to their new 'home', the Yakama Reservation, in Washington state. Many died along the way from cold, starvation and disease. In 1883, the surviving Paiute were allowed to leave Yakama and some returned to Harney County. In 1972, a hundred years after their homeland was parcelled off to private interests, the Burns Paiute Indian Reservation acquired just over 771 acres of land near the Malheur refuge in Harney County. As of January 2016, there were 349 registered members of this tribe.

Perhaps because of the ecological and historical significance of the Malheur Wildlife Refuge, Cliven Bundy's son Ammon decided it would be a fitting location for another armed stand-off against the government. The Bundys gathered with several militant groups in Burns, Oregon, a town of 2,800 just fifty kilometres north of the refuge. In a Safeway parking lot, the Bundys whipped up enough anti-government frenzy to mobilize the takeover of the refuge. When asked about his claims to the land upon which sits the Malheur Wildlife Refuge, Ryan Bundy said, 'We also recognize that the Native Americans had the claim to the land, but they lost that claim. There are things to learn from cultures of the past, but the current culture is the most important.'

One of the sparks which ignited the Bundys' anger was the arrest and conviction in 2012 of the Oregon rancher Dwight Hammond and his son Stephen for two counts of arson on federal land. The Hammonds were re-sentenced in 2015, unleashing fury from Sovereign Citizens and their friends. The Bundys saw this as yet another example of an unfair, punitive government. Despite the Hammonds refusing to be part of the protest, the Bundys went ahead on their behalf, claiming that 'The Lord was not pleased with what was happening to the Hammonds.' They felt it was their duty to summon their contacts within the Pacific Patriots Network, a militia umbrella organization which includes a handful of other grassroots militias, to fight against what they saw as an unfair verdict for the Hammonds.

These heavily armed protestors took over the buildings and the surrounding land of the refuge which is run by the Forest Service and the Bureau of Land Management. LaVoy Finicum, a friend of the Bundys and spokesperson for the Malheur occupation, told the *Washington Post* that 'it needs to be very clear that these buildings will never, ever return to the federal government'. He was shot dead by the FBI shortly after making this statement as he allegedly reached for his gun.

The Malheur occupation crystallized for me much of what was going on in my new home in the West.

Ryan Payne, an electrician and army veteran, was one of the occupation's organizers, and lived just outside Butte, in Anaconda. The Bundys, with their mistrust of what they interpret as a tyrannical government, their stubborn refusal to see land as anything other than acreage for grazing their herds, and their self-conscious and often ahistorical myth-making around the idea of the cowboy, lurk in the darker corners of Montana. If I dug a little, I would be able to get at this material. I could mine not for gems but for the less obvious stuff coursing under Montana's shiny, picture postcard surface.

After our trip to Butte, we finally moved in to our rental house in Missoula. I realized soon after unpacking that I had spent most of my energy over the past few months dealing with the physical details and bureaucracy of moving house and relocating a seven-year-old. I had been worrying about my daughter's abandonment of her friends in London, putting scrapbooks of photos together, gathering addresses, organizing pen pals and focusing on how she would settle into a new school, in a town so different from the one she had left behind. Between making the move 'fun' for a child and keeping on top of the minutiae of life, like remembering where I'd filed the inoculation forms which would allow her to go to a Missoula Public School, I had forgotten to think about myself.

After walking Eve to Paxson Elementary School on a sunny September day, giving her a hug and then crossing the road to head to our new house, I turned around to see her standing in the third grade line with her gigantic backpack. She was stock-still, her back perfectly erect. Her body language read: terrified. I felt like shit. What had we just done? I went home and collapsed. Although I had a novel to finish, I hadn't given any serious thought to what else I was going to do here. I wandered around aimlessly for several days, worrying about my lack of focus.

And then this happened: Missoula started reminding me of Ottawa, the town I had grown up in. This was not good. I am told that when I was very small, I would often ask my parents when we would be leaving. My child's mind could not fathom living there. My hometown was stifling, conservative and suburban. I left at seventeen, as soon as I graduated from high school, and only returned for weddings and funerals – and not even for them much of the time. The reasons for my visceral dislike of this city is a whole book unto itself. In fact, that was the novel I was writing while I was in Missoula. I sunk into a very mild depression, more like a dip than a chasm.

I tried to isolate the details of how this town reminded me of the place I had escaped all those years ago. The layout of Ottawa's streets and the horrible things that happened to me there were beginning to

haunt me in a more concrete and present way. I studied Missoula's physical features as if I were looking at a face that reminded me of someone I once knew who had hurt me. The street signs were the same as those in small towns, affixed onto metal poles that slant awkwardly. As kids we would turn them on their axes so that drivers would get lost, thinking how hilariously rebellious we were being. Like many suburban streets in Ottawa, those in Missoula had front lawns stretching to the sidewalk. Then there was another patch of grass between the sidewalk and the road. I had only ever seen such strips in my hometown. It was these patches of perfectly mowed grass that undid me. There was something about their superfluousness that brought home the affluent emptiness of suburban North America. And here was another problem that had plagued me in Ottawa: I did not know how to drive. Despite having chosen to be here, I felt lost and had no real concrete reason to be here.

In this spirit of confusion and self-doubt, I found myself one evening cycling through the rain to a fundraiser for the anti-trapping organization, Footloose Montana, at the Hell Gate Elks Lodge in downtown Missoula. Built in 1911, the three-storey lodge is older than many of the downtown buildings and stands out for its tall classical columns. Inside, however, it was a mash-up of a high school gym and dive bar. I stood on my own sipping a beer in the dark, underground space when a few people approached me and made small talk in that friendly American way. Where was I from? How had I heard of their organization? Did I know there was a raffle for the posters in the lobby? I ended up chatting with a guy in a suit who told me he liked nothing more than being out in the mountains camping, hunting elk and deer. He didn't mind killing animals for food, but he couldn't see the point of trapping them, which was why he was a member of Footloose. I asked if he ever worried about sleeping outside with nothing but a thin piece of nylon between him and the bears and wild cats roaming around. He looked at me like I was crazy: 'I could only ever live in a place,' he said, fixing my eye, 'where I am not the *top predator*.'

I had never thought of myself as prey. This was when a shift began to occur inside me. My relationship to the Earth had just been set on a new course because of a throwaway comment from a complete stranger in the gloomy basement of the Missoula Hell Gate Elks Lodge. Of course I am prey. *We all are.* And so we should be, yet we do everything in our power to rise above the predators around us, to dominate the land and its non-human inhabitants. We need to take on the responsibility, the vulnerability, the inevitable acceptance of our death that comes with being prey. *We are prey.* It was this thought that allowed me to see my new home through a different lens.

Shortly after our move to Missoula, I found myself waking up in a motel room in Gardiner, Montana (population 875) at 4.30 a.m. on a drizzly September day. Jason and Eve rustled in their beds, reluctant to get up. The sister of a friend of mine, the poet and naturalist Ilona Popper, showed up at 4.45 a.m. sharp. Tall with short, greying hair, sensible shoes and an easy, warm manner, Ilona bundled us into her car and drove us along the northern edge of Yellowstone National Park in the pitch black, towards where she thought we might find a pack of wolves known as the Junction Butte Pack.

After about an hour, we parked up in the Lamar Valley behind half a dozen cars, while half a kilometre away twenty or so Gortex-clad wolf watchers were planting their viewing scopes on the crest of a hill. Ilona introduced me to Rick McIntyre, who had just shown up. As the biological technician for the Yellowstone Wolf Project, Rick started working here in 1994, the year before wolves were re-introduced from Canada. Rick, who is revered locally for chalking up more than 5,000 consecutive days watching wolves, nodded in greeting, then pulled his binoculars up to his eyes and got to work. Much of what we know about the Yellowstone packs comes from his observations and the books he has written on the subject.

Since wolves were re-introduced to Montana in 1995, the debate still rages as to the extent of good or harm these animals effect. In Yellowstone, where they hunt and kill prey, the elk population has been reduced, thus invoking the wrath of hunters whose prime target is elk. To conservationists, however, the regrowth of trees, especially willows, which are decimated by an overabundance of elk, now provide food and habitat for other animals in the Park. Some scientists and conservationists think that a healthier balance has been restored by bringing back the apex predator. The doomsayer in me who believes that ecological meddling rarely has a happy ending sees this issue as one that is so complex, with so many variables, that our limited human brains cannot fully comprehend it. Regardless, it feels right for wolves to be in this landscape, where they have always been.

We followed Ilona up a small hill to set up our own scopes just as the sky was lightening and the rain beginning to fall. After observing a few bison grazing lazily, we spotted what Ilona thought might be the alpha female of the pack – the leader and breeder. A mottled charcoal colour, she looked very relaxed, lying nonchalantly on her side while five wolf cubs ran in

circles and jumped on her, every now and then catching a little swat of her paw. As I watched the cubs roll in the grass like puppies, I felt I was watching something forbidden. Their play seemed private, intimate – something between them and the land that I had no place witnessing. I wasn't expecting to have an emotional response to these animals but a kind of awe began to creep over me – the awe of the European on the Grand Tour when confronted with a waterfall or the eruption of Mount Vesuvius. But then something strange happened. I began to be able to tell them apart, to identify these cubs as individuals. 'Look, there's the one who nips ears,' I was saying to myself. The awe shifted from that of observer to participant. The membrane between the wild exterior and our tamed interior is a porous one. I could see, here in this valley, how it could erode or simply fall away.

In the month or two following my trip to Yellowstone, wolves were constantly in the news. Their advocates had enemies. People were angry. A quick Google search affirmed that many Westerners saw the reintroduction of wolves as an assault on their hunting rights, on their cattle, on their families, on their sense of being the top predator, on their whole way of life. It seemed too easy for me, someone who has been living in a large urban centre, thousands of miles from the American West, for the last twenty-five years, to say that killing these animals was wrong. What did I know? There must be good reasons for laying steel in the ground and making war on wolves?

I enrolled in a free wolf-trapping course put on by the Montana Department of Fish, Wildlife and Parks which was open to anyone over the age of eleven. 'When in doubt take a course,' my father used to say as a humorous yet disparaging summary of my life. I read online that the class would 'discuss all aspects of Montana's wolf population and the trappers' associated responsibilities'. I also learned that taking a dead wolf out of its trap is known as 'harvesting' it, a word that takes away any idea that this once-living creature is more sentient than a potato.

On a sunny October day I made my way to Missoula's Rocky Mountain Elk Foundation. From the outside, the building is part ski chalet, part country club. I entered the large open foyer, where I was greeted by what I would soon learn was a Montana speciality: taxidermy. Tons of it. Lynx, cougars, elk, bears, bighorn sheep, antelope, foxes, martens, badgers and whole dioramas populated with stuffed animals chasing plastic grasshoppers and dragonflies dangling from nearly invisible fishing wire.

I followed some deep voices that led me to the room where the wolf-trapping lesson was about to begin. The carpets were gun-metal grey and the chairs had been set up in very neat rows. Montanans, I was learning, are

very tidy. It looked like we might be gathering to pray. I clocked the one other woman and smiled, but she made it clear she was not here to socialize. The men, around thirty of them, wore baseball caps or cowboy hats, and sunglasses placed backwards on their necks – a look I associate with military personnel. Three generations head-to-toe in denim, leather boots with spurs and cowboy hats silently filled the back row. The youngest, maybe four years old, was a miniature version of the adults: same clothes, same stoic expression.

On a table at the front of the room, where we had written our names on a sheet of paper, was an assortment of metal devices, pelts and skulls. If someone had told me these instruments were used in medieval torture, I would have believed them. But these were foothold traps designed to snap onto the limb of an animal. Conibears (which grip the entire body) and snares (which strangle the animal) are illegal in Idaho and Montana. I was madly writing this all down while a guy behind the table talked unofficially to a few attendees who had clearly used a lot of these traps. They handled these clanking contraptions with familiarity.

Then the day started for real, and like all courses it began with introductions. At the front of the room were Mike Thompson, a wildlife manager at Montana Fish, Wildlife and Parks and Jeff Ashmead, who had worked as a government trapper, gunner, and pilot in the state of Idaho. He was now a trapper for hire – the go-to guy if you are experiencing cattle and ungulate depredation at the hands of wolves. Ashmead, who looked to be in his early sixties, wore reflective shades, a baseball cap, a belt holding up a pair of tight-fitting jeans, and sported a badge on his hat and shirt emblazoned with his own personal logo, depicting a fierce-looking wolf and the acronym JAWS: 'Jeff Ashmead Wildlife Specialist'.

With his beard and glasses, Mike Thompson looked more like a geography teacher. He took us through the stack of photocopied pages we'd all been given: *Montana Department of Fish, Wildlife and Parks – Wolf Trapper Education Handbook*. In 2011 it became mandatory for all trappers to take this certificate course. I sensed resentment in the room, expressed in the form of crossed arms, legs akimbo, and faces that seemed to say, 'Can we get this over with quick so I can get back to my traps?' Once we were through with the rules and regulations in the handbook, Mike Thompson stepped aside and Jeff Ashmead rose, slowly, making the most of his six-foot frame.

'I don't speak for the Wildlife Services anymore, although I worked for them for thirty plus years. I'm a rancher, father of five kids, a family man.'

I could feel the room relax. He was one of them.

Jeff Ashmead explained the fallacy of Mother Nature and her 'balancing act'. He spat those last two words out in a way that left no doubt about his views: nature was there for man to use and any idea that there might be a desirable balance between what we take from the Earth and what we give back was a mirage, a fiction dreamed up by the Snowflakes and Liberals. Then he gave us a brief history of wolves in Idaho and Montana, which had been hunted for their pelts throughout the 1880s, set on fire, shot, poisoned, trapped, and had become extinct by the 1930s. Bison had been slaughtered in record numbers as well, and their meat was often injected with strychnine to kill anything that ate the meat. There are accounts of trappers setting up camp, shooting bison, poisoning the meat, going to sleep, and then waking in the morning to a field of dead wolves.

After grey wolves were reintroduced into Montana they remained on the endangered list. Their numbers grew until in 2011 they were delisted. The point Jeff was trying to make is that we've been meddling with Mother Nature since we've been on the planet, so the idea of preserving things in any kind of balance seemed ridiculous to him. He went on, 'I mean what is this paradise people are trying to reach? It was never even there in the first place!' In one respect he is right: humans have always altered the land – often deliberately and at other times accidentally. The question is not whether we should alter the land we live on but for what reasons and for whose benefit are we doing so.

The room fell silent with what I interpreted as agreement.

Then we were made aware that the wolf counts done

by the state of Montana were inaccurate. Apparently, because of the wily nature of these beasts, only a small proportion of them have actually been counted.

Then the anthropomorphizing began. According to Jeff Ashmead wolves try to find territory where they can bring their 'ladies' or 'girlfriends'. Once the pups are 'at their peak, when they're top athletes, they take their girls off to a new territory. They've had enough of their dads' iron fist.' Ladies? Girlfriends? Athletes? Dads?

He went on for some time about the social bonds between wolves and how these creatures differ from the many wild animals out there, like bears, who use bluff as a scare tactic. These guys don't bluff, apparently. They kill.

It is essential for any decent trapper to know how packs function – you can't trap an animal unless you can work out where it's going to be. We were told that the alpha males (the pack leaders) get territorial of their alpha females (the breeders of the pack). 'There ain't no fornication in my group!' he shouted out, in imitation of an alpha male.

These wolves not only had girlfriends and trigger fingers, but they fornicated. I sensed a vein of sexual thrill in his words, as if killing a wolf were somehow linked to an increase in the trapper's virility.

The main reason we were gathered here today was so he could talk to us about ethics. We were taken through the variety of traps before us, which had names like 'Sleepy Creek #4' and 'Livestock Protection Company #7', and Jeff talked through the pros and cons and price options. The proper setting of the various traps was explained carefully.

'Whatever steps in one of these, you're going to have to deal with. A moose, whatever. You don't want to get a cow moose in one of these because she's not going to leave until she's done some tap dancing on you!'

He got a good laugh.

Jeff told the room how important it was to weight the traps so that you don't catch too much of the other 'stuff' such as 'deer, elk, bobcats, coyotes, fishers, and martens'. Especially the last two, which are 'sensitive species'. Fishers are furbearing animals, bigger than minks, with long bushy tails and rounded ears. In a cartoon, fishers would be the 'cute' ones. By the 1930s, they had become extinct in Montana from a combination of trapping, predation and habitat loss, but were re-introduced in 1959. After their rise in numbers, they are no longer considered endangered, yet Montana Fish, Wildlife and Parks have capped the number of fishers each person is allowed to harvest to one. Their pelts have risen in price from 28 dollars in 2004 to 40 dollars in 2018, but have been as high as 145 dollars in recent years, making this decision irksome to trappers. Fur from the smaller, cat-sized marten is known as 'sable'. There are no restrictions on their harvesting. Nevertheless, you wouldn't want to be seen trapping an animal that was historically 'sensitive' when you are trying to catch a wolf.

'You should lay your traplines as if your grandmother was watching you,' Jeff told us, wagging a finger. I glanced down at the handbook open on my lap to see an Aldo Leopold quote: 'Ethical behaviour is doing the right thing when no one else is looking, even when the wrong thing is still legal.'

At break time I wandered down a hallway of the Rocky Mountain Elk Foundation, looking at framed photos of past donors. A trapper came up to tell me that wolves are bloodthirsty creatures who will prey on just about anything, even children. They make a point of going for your pregnant horses and cows – that is how evil they are. He told me about a photo online showing a foetus hanging out of a horse killed by a wolf. 'Uneaten!' the guy emphasized as he smiled with what almost seemed like excitement, titillation. 'Wolves kill *just for the fun of it.*'

Apart from preventing cattle depredation, the other reason people trap wolves is for their pelts, which can fetch thousands of dollars at auction. Even in death though, wolves cause problems: 'Wolves don't give up their hide even when they're dead!' Jeff Ashmead exclaimed. 'I can skin a coyote in under ten minutes, but a wolf takes five to six hours!' Nasty old wolves. Yet despite the fact that wolves are killed in order to reduce cattle deaths and to make money, trapping is often referred to as a sport, or as Jeff Ashmead called it, an 'art'. Several guys in the room nodded in agreement when Jeff Ashmead talked in that homespun way about trapping being 'our right', of it being part of Montana's history andtradition. 'We've always trapped! That's what we do!'

Kit Carson, the nineteenth-century frontiersman, fur trapper, Indian agent and mythologized Western figure was mentioned. I was aware, even though I'd only been in Montana a couple of months, that a figure like Kit Carson was more complicated than the trappers nodding their approval would ever admit to. Carson became a legend for his trapping and survival skills but he is equally famous for what some people see as his role in the attempted ethnic cleansing of the Navajo people. Working for the American government, Carson was given the job of controlling the Navajo, who were considered at the time to be a threat to American expansion and domination. From 1863, Carson waged a brutal campaign against the Navajo, killing livestock and crops, most famously destroying thousands upon thousands of centuries-old peach trees in a scorched earth programme. Weakened by these attacks, many Navajo Indians surrendered. It was at this point that Carson then forced 8,000 Navajo men, women and children to walk over 485 kilometres from Arizona to a reservation in New Mexico. Hundreds died of exhaustion, disease and hunger along the way, with more perishing in the ill-equipped reservation, which had no fuel for winter, no grass for their horses and no clean water.

To the men in this room, Kit Carson was a figure to be revered. I might have been imagining it, but I felt surrounded by people who dreamt of having the freedom of those nineteenth-century mountain men to kill whatever they wanted with impunity.

It was time for lunch. Before leaving the room, I noticed a laminated piece of A4 stuck on the wall with a quote attributed to someone called Jim Posewitz: 'It is the land, as wild as we can sustain it, that both the hunter and the hunted need to survive.'

I was the only person with a paperbag lunch. The others all climbed into their pickups and drove off. I sat on a bench overlooking the empty parking lot while I ate a cheese sandwich, some carrot sticks and an apple feeling very unlike a trapper.

I looked up Jim Posewitz on my phone. He is the founder of an organization called Orion – The Hunter's Institute. According to Orion's website, Posewitz is pursuing two goals: 'improving the image of hunting with an emphasis on fair chase ethics' whilst 'putting hunters at the forefront of our nation's conservation ethic'. He's exactly the sort of person I find impossible to understand. Is it just semantics? When he extols the virtues of 'conservation' does he really mean the preservation of a way of life based on when the trapper ruled and the West was dominated by men who slept under the stars, dreaming of the dead wolves at their feet the next morning? As Rick Bass says about hunters in his book *The Ninemile Wolves*, 'There's nothing harder to stereotype than a "hunter."' I would add that this is also true of trappers: they claim to love the wilderness, they call themselves sportsmen, outdoorsmen, and yet they are happy inflicting pain on animals in return for the price of their fur. Most hunters eat their prey, whereas trappers do it for money.

After lunch I felt distinctly uneasy. The afternoon session began with Jeff and Mike talking about 'the other side', and every now and then throwing a hard stare in my direction.

'The other side's got lots of money,' Jeff shouted. 'So I encourage you to keep that in mind.'

There was much talk of how to weight the traps – at least twelve to fifteen pounds – to avoid getting all those other pesky non-wolves. You have to make sure to get the wolf 'above his wrist'. And then there was talk of the 'dispatch'. Jeff told us that he once shot an alpha male right through the heart. Communal nod of respect. And that it's imperative to check your traplines every forty-eight hours – not just because it's ethical, but because it gives the 'other side' less time to photograph squirming animals chewing off their own legs. Although, according to Jeff Ashmead, the leg-chewing thing was a myth. But still, you didn't want to risk it.

'I got picketed going wolf-trapping for a problem wolf,' Jeff paused. 'I got poked, prodded, cameras shoved in my face and people shouting "The public has a right to know: did you kill the *right* wolf?"' He looked at me. 'They try and get under your skin, these people. But God gave me two feet to run out of there. And I did.'

He went on, 'You know, bear cubs used to be an hors d'oeuvre out here. City people just don't get how it works. Animals are here for us to use, not abuse. But what I felt coming from those people was hate. Those folks just *hated* me. It was coming out of their pores. The toughest thing I had to face was those guys going through my pickup. The police could have arrested them on terrorism charges after 9/11.' But, as Jeff told it, he did the generous thing and let the protestors go free.

This was the preamble to discouraging the trappers from taking photos of themselves with their prey. 'Anyone been around Photoshop lately?' he asked to laughter. 'Just don't post any photos of yourself with dead animals, OK? Just don't.' He mentioned the recent case, in September 2014, of Toby Bridges, a Missoula man who had accelerated his car into some wolves near the Montana-Idaho border and then bragged about it on Facebook, describing his bespoke roadkill in graphic detail and posting photos. The men nodded. They'd all seen Bridges' photos, no doubt.

It was time to go outside and see how we were to lay a trap. We filed out of the meeting room into the blinding sunshine and followed Jeff to a tree, where we huddled under its shade. Knowing how animals work is a big part of laying your trapline. 'I listen to the birds,' he told us. 'Crows and magpies talk a lot.' Then we were onto bait. It is illegal in Montana and Idaho to bait your traps with lures, Jeff informed us. But apparently everyone does it. In the official handbook I was still holding there was mention of a company called The Snare Shop in Iowa, which carry lures on their website with names that sound like computer games:

CONGREGATION*
The maker took over 500 predators on this lure alone in 3 years. None better.

TOTAL CHAOS*
This age-old formula is a cat meat-based bait.
It is the last bait your predators will ever taste.
Hundreds of predators have been taken on my line with this bait. Predators can't resist – compare to any!

GREED*
Northwest Predator and Wildlife Control Lure.
A M-44 lure that works great at trap sets also.

An M-44 trap is a spring-loaded metal cylinder, baited-with scent, which fires sodium cyanide powder into the mouth of whatever tugs on it. According to a for-merWildlife Service trapper, 'It's not a painless death.' Animals who ingest the sodium cyanide 'start whining. They start haemorrhaging from their ears and nose and mouth. They get paralysis and fall over. Then they start convulsing and they're gone. They are suffering endlessly until they die. It'll make you literally want to puke.' A quick look at eBay and other online shops will point you to bottles of scrotum juice, urine and other ingredients to add to your traps.

As the day came to an end, I wasn't sure what the ritual was. People peeled off and headed to their pick-ups. No one shook hands or exchanged numbers. We were here as a formality so we could head out into the woods, lay some steel, kill some predators, harvest some pelts, make some money. I went home to my new house in the American West. That night I dreamt of wolves running as fast as they could through dark woods. That is what wolves do. They run and run. They cover ground like magic. These silver wolves looked at me with hate in their eyes. They didn't know

I was from 'the other side'. That there was nothing that would tempt me to injure any one of them. Nothing at all. From me they were safe.

Chris Justice, the executive director of Footloose Montana, the non-profit whose fundraiser I had just been to, invited me to a benefit screening of *She Wolf*, a documentary about an iconic female wolf who had led a thriving pack in Yellowstone Park before being shot dead by a hunter. I'd met up with Chris a few times and over coffee he'd given me gruesome photos of animals with bloodied feet, their leg bones exposed, their dead faces still showing signs of shock and pain. I could barely look at them. He told me about the 50,000 animals that Montana trappers report each year to Fish, Wildlife and Parks. He also told me that although there is an official 'furbearer' trapping season from September through May, there is no such thing for 'predators' and 'non-game wildlife'. Despite being trapped for their fur, wolves are classified as predators. You can kill them all year round because they are not protected as 'furbearers' under the law.

Chris was mystified as to why I wanted to speak to the pro-trapping people. He was a hunter and didn't have a problem with killing animals humanely for food, but the suffering inflicted on trapped creatures, the barbarity of their deaths, made him alternately rage with fury and fall speechless with frustration.

Before the screening of *She Wolf*, Chris got up on stage and demonstrated with a stuffed animal and a trap what can happen to 'non-target' animals – like your dog – when they're caught in a leg-hold trap. Hundreds of non-target animals, such as lynx, who are endangered, are trapped each year. While he was giving his demonstration, I noticed a few audience members laughing and exchanging glances. One of them stood out. He was clean-cut and sat very straight. He did not look like someone who would be fighting to get trapping outlawed from public lands.

After the screening, I followed him into the lobby of the cinema and asked him what he had thought of the film. I don't remember his exact words, but he made it clear he thought the whole evening was bullshit propaganda. It turned out he was Jason Lee Maxwell, the vice-president of the Montana Trappers Association. I took his number and the following day I called him up, told him I was a writer, that I was new to Montana, that I wanted to learn more about wolves and the people who trapped them. I rambled, unsure whether what I was saying was completely true. I still didn't know what I was doing in Montana. I was still feeling my way.

Jason Maxwell suggested that we meet at Great Harvest, a bakery just down the road from my house. I got there early and sipped a coffee at the counter. The sun was beating through the window and I was sweating. It was autumn but felt more like summer. I watched Maxwell step out of his pickup in the parking lot. Baseball cap, camouflage jacket and trousers. He was young, handsome and clean-cut and his reserved charm disarmed me slightly.

I asked him about his background and he took his time choosing his words. He told me he was from a family of ranchers. His mother and father had day jobs and ran the ranch in their evenings and weekends. During calving season they didn't sleep. He had been in the army and had fought twice in Iraq.

For Maxwell, however, it was all about keeping his parents' cattle safe, though he admitted he also enjoyed it, he liked being outdoors. Then he brought out that trope about it being part of his 'history'. We chatted for about an hour. He had lived in Montana all his life. The lens through which he saw the land and its animals was not a lens I had ever held up. Who was I to tell him what he should or shouldn't be doing on his own land?

The next day, we emailed each other. He sent me pictures of animals that had been gored by wolves. I had seen one of the photos before in some anti-trapping literature, which had reported that a mountain lion had killed the animal, not a wolf. I wrote back to Jason to tell him.

'Yes, that's right. I made a mistake,' he wrote. Then he invited me to go trapping with him, adding that Eve 'would love it'. I agreed to go and we set a date a few months away. But then the emails dried up. He stopped replying. I started reading in the newspaper that Maxwell had been accused of harassment and the story was getting ugly.

About a year later, I bumped into him while I was with my husband and daughter at the Montana State Fair. He was manning a booth extolling the virtues and pleasures of trapping. He was polite and smiley. I reminded him that we had been supposed to go out trapping together and he casually dismissed it.

I interrogated myself over my obsession with trapping wolves. I told a friend in London of this desire and she replied, 'Why? You know what you think. Seeing a trapped animal will not get you any more clarity.'

I carried on following the trapping debate in forums and chat rooms. I read the comments sections after articles to do with the 'sport'. Both camps were angry, vicious, full of hate. There was a sexual undercurrent to the slurs from both sides. Anti-trappers were referred to as 'bunny fuckers'. Trappers, on the other hand, were accused of compensating for their lack of virility by making animals suffer. It is a political minefield that goes on as long as you are willing to scroll. Many of the pro-trappers brought up the subject of abortion. The bunny-fuckers were fine with 'killing babies', so why the fuss over wolves? The incomprehension between the two sides seemed insurmountable.

I came to the realization that I will never understand

what makes a person want to lay a trap. Instead of hating one side over the other, my default position was total and utter incomprehension.

But somehow, mysteriously, my interest in wolves increased. My dreams were full of them running silently through trees at night. They run for reasons we don't understand, travelling huge distances. I liked knowing they were out there somewhere, maybe dodging pieces of steel buried under leaves, baited with the musk of other wild animals. I was seeing silvery forests in the night and grey and black wolves and pups in their dens. I was also seeing deer jumping over fallen trees in the forest, stopping for a moment to sniff the air, only to be pulled down in a bloody mess by an alpha wolf. I could now understood those around me who spend their lives watching wolves, studying them, thinking about them and their place in the stories that come from this land.

This whole time I had my eyes and brain trained on the wrong subject. I was no longer fascinated by the trappers, but by the trapped. I decided to start focusing not on the predators, but the prey.

Autumn was turning to winter, a glorious spectacle. Piles of leaves the colour of mulberries and gold gathered on our front lawn. The giant sun spread a deep lemon-coloured light across Mount Sentinel. Eve now had a group of very good friends at school and Jason was busy working on a self-funded film project, while I found myself delving ever deeper into what it meant to live in Missoula. My body, like everything else, was transitioning: my periods seemed to be more erratic. My moods as well. I was trying to allow these changes to move through me. I picked up a couple of books from the Missoula Public Library on menopause. One was called *Your Perfectly Pampered Menopause: Health, Beauty, and Lifestyle Advice for the Best Years of Your Life*. Like everything else on the planet, menopause has spawned an industry. Despite my extreme dislike of the word 'pampered', I opened the book at random: 'If you are at a high risk for breast cancer (particularly if you, your mother, or your sister has had this disease), then according to the American Cancer Society, even one drink a day may increase your risks further.' My mother had a lumpectomy in her sixties. My father's mother had a double mastectomy and eventually died of breast cancer. But more importantly, it was breast cancer that got my sister Mary in 2004. This was a tragedy that took me years to process. I remembered asking Mary shortly before she died if she had any advice for me. 'Just live your life *not* thinking about cancer. That's my advice.' I chucked the book back on the shelf and picked up *The Wisdom of Menopause*, a well-thumbed tome written by Dr Christiane Northrup, and again opened it randomly: 'There is still a significant number of women who experience midlife depression or an exacerbation of underlying depression when they enter midlife.... Remember that depression, sadness, or anger often accompanies the emotional growth spurt that our psyches are undergoing.' I didn't check it out. I had never read a self-help book and I didn't want the librarians to pigeonhole me so soon after moving here. I wanted to be seen as that foreigner who reads Proust, not that middle-aged crank obsessing over her menopause. While standing in the stacks poring over those books, I realized that no one had ever spoken to me about menopause. It is a strangely hidden rite of passage. I wondered if it might be because society simply cannot stomach the idea of women ageing, of sagging bodies, nipples pointing downwards. I tried bringing it up in conversation and eventually decided to keep quiet.

Meanwhile, Christmas was creeping up, and a month later Jason would be turning fifty. One of the reasons we had moved here was because Jason had announced a few years back he would rather kill himself than spend his fiftieth birthday in London, the city of his birth.

Over the years, our once rough and very cheap neighbourhood in East London had morphed into something unrecognizable. I simply didn't understand where I was living anymore, nor who my neighbours were. All those articles about Hackney and Shoreditch in *The New York Times, GQ, Esquire* and *Vogue* portrayed a place I no longer wanted to inhabit. These pieces were invariably illustrated with shots of graffiti along gritty canals with the words 'hidden', 'secret' and 'tucked away' in their headlines. These tucked-away 'curated retail experiences' were not exactly hidden from me, but they were largely out of reach due to the price of whatever they were selling. The local hardware shop would overnight become a 'pop-up', the cans of primer and stacks of paintbrushes replaced with beard trimmers and cashmere slippers. Elderly neighbours were selling up and moving away, their old houses gutted and redesigned for the modern urbanites who, these days, consisted of tech executives, bankers and advertising people. My new neighbours recently left the boxes for their his'n'hers Body Mass Indexing devices on the pavement (recycling isn't for them) – I had to look up what they were. Where we live has, in a word, become *silly*. Prams cost the same as second-hand cars and people use machines to tell them they're too fat or too thin, rather than look in a mirror.

We had thought about moving to Los Angeles (too big), San Antonio (ditto), Seattle (too wet), Austin (too hot), El Paso (ditto and too far away), and Portland (too hip and expensive), but realized we wanted a small town, a place where the fabric of our lives and rhythm of our days would be different to life in London.

Around the time of our decision-making, I was working on a writing project on addiction, leading writing exercises in three different substance abuse clinics around the UK. I didn't know much about life in rehab, so I borrowed *The Three Christs of Ypsilanti* by Milton Rokeach from Jason. Rokeach had brought together three men, each claiming to be Jesus Christ, and watched them over the course of several years. He confronted them with each other's claims and encouraged them to interact. The three men eventually beat each other up over who the 'real' Jesus was. In time each one explained away the other two Christs as being either patients with mental illness or machine-operated cadavers. Years after the book was first published in 1964, Rokeach admitted that he had caused the men undue distress by manipulating them in order to fit his thesis. In the 1984 version of the *The Three Christs*, Rokeach wrote that although he didn't 'cure' the Christs of their holy delusions, the experiment did 'cure me of my godlike delusion that I could manipulate them out of their beliefs'.

The book ended up being irrelevant to my project but as I was reading it, it sat on my desk, its cover curving up slightly to reveal the title page – the page where Jason always makes a note of where and when his books were purchased, in this case 'Shakespeare & Co, Missoula, Montana, February 2011'. He had driven through Missoula on a job for the BBC and spent a couple of hours at this bookshop. The name Missoula intrigued me. I knew the town had a university with a creative writing department. Lots of writers I admired had a connection to Missoula. People like James Lee Burke (of the Detective Robicheaux series), Norman Maclean, Richard Hugo, James Welch, Jim Harrison, Bill Kittredge, Thomas McGuane, Rick Bass, Walter Kirn and Maile Meloy. Why had I heard of so many writers with connections to Montana? That was the first sign.   I tentatively began mentioning to friends that I was thinking of leaving London for Missoula. 'Where's that?' they would ask. 'Montana,' I would say, and they would look none the wiser. Around Christmas time I told Gary and Dawn, the owners of my local pub, that we were thinking of moving to this place in Montana called Missoula. Dawn's eyes widened. Her oldest school friend lived there. She was also a writer. Dawn said I'd like her and put us in touch.

Shortly after this, Jason and I were at a wedding.

'Missoula's the best town in the world for a writer,' said the guy I was sitting next to. He turned out to be Nicholas Evans, who had written *The Horse Whisperer* in Missoula. That was it. I'd had the three signs I needed.

A few days before our first Christmas in Montana, Alex, a very old friend, showed up in Missoula with her young daughter to have the white Christmas they don't get in LA. Another friend arrived from London to head to a Forest Service cabin with Jason in the wilderness, where they would live out their Thoreauvian fantasies. A few hours after saying goodbye to Jason, I received a phone call from one of my sisters in Ottawa. Our eighty-nine-year-old mother was unwell. She'd been taken from her retirement home to a hospital.

'How unwell?' I asked.

'Unresponsive' was the word I heard.

I put the phone down and told Alex.

'Go,' she said. 'It's your mother. Go. I can look after the girls.' I Googled flights to Ottawa, feeling terribly guilty. Alex's mother had died when she was young. Her loss has been a painful one to carry all these years. I was aware of this and I hated the thought of her covering for me while I attended to my own mother's bedside. Our idyllic Christmas with our daughters was being upended by life and death.

To get from Missoula, Montana to Ottawa, Canada would take me roughly twenty-one hours, three connecting flights and cost thousands of dollars. I had many tearful Skype conversations with my sisters about whether to go or stay. My oldest sister Kate told me I should be with my daughter. 'It's what mum would have wanted,' she said. My mother, who'd had seven children, would have agreed. They held a phone up to my mother's ear so I could tell her I loved her. She died quietly in her sleep several hours later with two of her seven children at her side. One for each hand.

This was my first Christmas in Missoula.

Jason and his friend returned from their cabin on Christmas Eve. It wasn't until I said the words 'My mother has just died,' that it started to sink in.

A lot of snow fell over the next few days, reminding me starkly of my childhood: that quiet that descends on a snowy landscape like a solid presence. When you wake in the morning, you can tell if there's been fresh snowfall by the sound of the car tyres as they pass your house. Everything was strangely calm and happy and I felt somewhat guilty for all this joy. When I told people that my mother had died a few days before Christmas and I was not there to be with her, they looked stricken.

There were many reasons for me not to be devastated: my mother was 89. She was also an alcoholic. She had just been diagnosed with Lewy body dementia – a particularly nasty progressive brain disorder involving paranoia, delusions and hallucinations. We knew something was up when Usain Bolt stopped running in the 2012 Olympics and pointed to her, saying, 'Jasmine, you need to stop smoking!' She was very impressed with him for this. Then she started communicating with Paddington Bear.

These fairly benign visions began turning violent when she was moved from her house into a retirement home. Here she endured the triple whammy of going cold turkey (although she did have people bringing her contraband wine and cigarettes), being away from the house where she had raised seven children, and suffering from her encroaching dementia. In the care facility she thought she could hear babies being tortured in the basement. It became unbearable and totally destabilized her. Nothing anyone said helped. It was just as we were discussing a move to a safer facility and maybe getting her a wheelchair that she fell ill and quickly died of pneumonia. She had always called this illness 'the old person's friend'. I think she had had enough and knew it was time to go. She was a very decisive person and her death suited her.

There's another thing: we were not close. I can't say I didn't love her, but my feelings stemmed from a sense of duty, of doing the right thing. One *had* to love one's mother, didn't one? I rarely visited her in Ottawa. When I did make the trip from my home in London she would castigate me for not visiting enough. Then

she would get drunk and say things she would have regretted if she had remembered them the next day. I would lie in bed promising that I would not visit for a very long time. The following year I would soften, go back for more and promise myself the same thing all over again. I had decided in my thirties that there was no point in trying to be loved by her, and so I gave up. I had more respect for her than anything else. I respected her intelligence and her forcefulness, but love just didn't factor much between us.

My father had always said he would die before my mother, but he was proved wrong. He had been living with Alzheimer's for over a decade and was now in an assisted living centre very close to where my mother died. The house he had designed for his wife and children in Ottawa was standing empty and had been for some time. When I say 'empty', I mean of humans. It was crammed with objects. Over 40,000 books, furniture in every room, storerooms full of letters, photos, research material for the books he was writing, printouts from unsavoury websites, puzzles, nineteenth-century clothing, a collection of umbrellas and walking sticks, sewing baskets, cupboards full of childhood toys and games, a ship's steering wheel, hundreds of pieces of art, sets of crockery and silverware, an entire darkroom full of chemicals, dozens of boxes of snapshots unfiled without their negatives, my mother's jewellery, and most of their clothing. It was a gigantic mess, which we now needed to empty out.

I have one sister in Ottawa. Sheila had borne the brunt of my parents' illnesses, my father's care and my mother's death over the years with unbelievable patience and kindness. I have another sister who lives five hours from Ottawa in Toronto. Another was living in upstate New York, another in eastern Turkey and my brother had settled in Berlin.

I made it to Ottawa for my mother's funeral, as did all of my siblings. The service was held in the funeral parlour at the national military cemetery, where my mother wanted to be buried. She was proud of her work as a wireless operator in World War II. There was discussion among us about whether to have an open coffin. I am a fan of open coffins because I think it's important to look at death. To get close to it. The open coffin voters won. But we closed it part way through the day as a compromise.

I got up at the service and read the opening of Marilynne Robinson's *Gilead*:

I told you last night that I might be gone sometime, and you said, Where, and I said, To be with the Good Lord, and you said, Why, and I said, Because I'm old, and you said, I don't think you're old. And you put your hand in my hand and you said, You aren't very old, as if that settled it.

66

The point of view here is that of an elderly father speaking to his young son.

My mother was forty when she had me in 1965. When she came to pick me up from school, my classmates thought she was my grandmother. She was younger than I was when I had my daughter, by two years. There is something touching about a small child not wanting to believe their parent is old. And although Robinson's book is a stunning examination of the non-existent limits of a parent's love (among other things), the excerpt, with its complicated perspective, demanded that people know about my relationship to my mother and the age gap that had dogged me as a child. I was trying to recast it as a positive element between us, but it required too much from the listener to make this leap. It was not a good choice.

The day after the memorial, everyone left except me. I had decided to stay a little longer to help my sister Sheila. We had twenty-four hours in which to empty my mother's room in her care facility. I wanted to handle her belongings, to sort through her clothes and fold them, to run my hands over the plastic Virgin Mary she always had on her dresser, the matching white brush and comb set, the pin trays. And her sweaters – she loved her coloured cardigans. I told Sheila that I would do the smalls, deciding what could go to charity, what could not. It was therapeutic and it carried on my relationship to her: one of duty. I took solace in being able to help Sheila while also ritualizing my connection to my mother, adding to the bank of memories I had of her. This action, these two women sorting through their dead mother's belongings must be one of the oldest performative acts in the world. Sheila and I laughed about life and death and compared memories of our upbringings. We are very different people. She is twelve years older than I am, got married and had her children young and works as a chartered accountant. Sifting through my mother's things alongside her comforted me and I think she felt the same way. It brought us closer and erased the difference in years and the chasm of experiences separating us.

A month after my mother's death, Jason and I took Eve out of school for a few days to drive up to a place in northern Montana called Polebridge (population 24), roughly fifteen miles from the Canadian border. It wasn't a town exactly – it was a mercantile which baked giant bear claw pastries and had a few cabins scattered around it. The cabins had no running water but they did have electricity and wood burning stoves for cooking and heating. This was where Jason wanted to turn fifty. Friends lent us snow shoes so we could explore Glacier National Park, which you can walk to from Polebridge.

I wasn't sure if it was my mother's death or my general menopausal moodiness but I was feeling out of sorts. Something inside me was off kilter. On our first night there, I was kept awake by the sound of rain on the roof and a fly buzzing in the cabin. In the morning I woke to complete silence but for the drip-dripping of melting icicles hanging from the cabin guttering. These were sounds I associated – from deeply ingrained childhood memories – with spring. In Ottawa, roads turned into small creeks as the snow disappeared from March to May. The playground would turn to mud and everywhere would be the sound of gushing and dripping while crocuses and trilliums pushed their heads up towards the light. But we were still in January. In Northern Montana.

There was just enough snow for us to strap on our snow shoes and go for a hike into Glacier. We had also brought a sled, but the snow was too sticky for that. It was so warm that we stripped down to our T-shirts.

My feeling of being out of sorts had something to do with the weather. Bears had been spotted coming out of hibernation in Washington state and Nevada. In Juneau, Alaska, temperatures had been above freezing this past week – even at night. Meanwhile the East coast was buried in snow. It seemed too late to regain anything resembling a balanced harmony in the natural world, which was perhaps another reason my mother's death did not derail me. There was comfort in the cycle of life behaving as it should: parents are supposed to die before their offspring. My sister Mary dying before our mother was an affront to the way life was supposed to be.

Our drive to Polebridge had started with the Rattlesnake Mountains on our right just as we left Missoula on Highway 93. These mountains merged into the sharper, more jagged Mission range, whose snowy peaks are set back from the highway beyond grassy stretches of land dotted with houses, barns and ranches. This is the view most people imagine when you mention 'Montana'. It is the Montana of John Steinbeck's 1960 travelogue *Travels with Charley*, in which he wrote, 'It seems to me that Montana is a great splash of grandeur. The scale is huge but not overpowering. The land is rich with grass and color, and the mountains are the kind I would create if mountains were ever put on my agenda.'

We took a slightly meandering route passing through the upmarket ski resort of Whitefish and the nearby Columbia Falls, a town that once made its money from timber and feels like it is searching for its next resource. North of here, the towns fade out and the mountains rear up. All the clamouring in my brain was quieted when I focused on these jutting masses of stone.

However, even when I focused on the elemental, I was reminded of our human imprint. Dotted across this terrain were thousands upon thousands of burnt stumps left over from two massive forest fires: one in 1988 and an even larger one in 2003. The later one

devastated the west side of Glacier National Park and the damage is still there. The word that kept creeping into my mind was: blasted. It was a blasted, barren landscape of blackened trees. The devastation we had seen on the way up to Glacier was the result of summers too hot and dry not to burn. The 2003 fire lasted for three months and consumed 310,000 acres, including 135,000 acres in Glacier – roughly 13 per cent of the Park. No human lives were lost but old-growth forests and habitats for a variety of animals were destroyed.

With all this in mind, I was finding it difficult to really enjoy the weekend with the carefreeness I had wanted to. I had recently reread the introduction to Joan Didion's *Slouching Towards Bethlehem*. She had written this book with W.B. Yeats' 'The Second Coming' in mind. 'The widening gyre, the falcon which does not hear the falconer ... a gaze blank and pitiless as the sun', were 'points of reference' for her, the only images against which much of what she was 'seeing and hearing and thinking seemed to make any pattern'. Much of the essays in *Slouching Towards Bethlehem* deal with atomization, with things falling apart. It had been a struggle to write the book, she said, because she 'had been paralysed by the conviction that writing was an irrelevant act, that the world' as she 'had understood it no longer existed'. She went on to say that in order for her to work at all she would have to 'come to terms with disorder'. Maybe in these words lay an answer to the

conundrum of how to live with the constant reminder of a dying planet. Perhaps in order to move forward, to avoid wallowing in despair, one had to simply 'come to terms with disorder'. Forget about the patterns we are programmed to find in nature; tune into the chaos.

But I had another question: how much of this knowledge of disorder and of things falling apart does one pass on to one's child? I didn't want Eve to be fearful and anxious about her future and the future of the planet, yet she and her contemporaries will be the ones on the front line of extreme weather conditions as the planet heats up. How much should a seven-year-old know about all this?

I was trying to overcome the gloom inside me. The huge sky and these mountains calling us on long walks went some way to restoring something akin to joy. The three of us played outside, rolling down banks of wet, sticky snow for hours. On our last morning in Glacier, we watched the sun burn its way through the early morning mist to reveal jagged peaks the colour and shape of freshly dug quartz. In that moment all was good, all was how it needed to be. It was tomorrow and the day after that worried me to death. Disorder. Come to terms with it.

I was still doing battle with my novel and realized it was more of an idea than a functioning piece of fiction. I was thinking about ditching it but I didn't have a plan

for what to write next. One day while out walking, I went into a taco restaurant in downtown Missoula for lunch. I picked up a flyer from a pile they had on display about a group called the Buffalo Field Campaign. This non-profit had been set up in 1994 by Mike Mease and the Lakota elder and environmental campaigner Rosalie Little Thunder to ensure the protection of wild American buffalo (also called bison). Rosalie Little Thunder died in August of 2014, just weeks after we had arrived in Missoula. After reading about the Buffalo Field Campaign, I sought out her writing, which charged straight into the heart of the disputes over bison in Montana.

In 1855 General William Selby Harney, whose nickname among the Lakota was 'Mad Bear', was greeted by the Lakota people with a truce flag and provisions of salt pork. 'While this was going on,' wrote Little Thunder, 'there was a grandmother standing there with her ten-year-old grandson. She told him to hide where the tall grass was. They started shooting down the people then. And when she was shot, she threw herself and her shawl on top of that little boy. That way she hid him. She hid him and died.'

That boy was Rosalie Little Thunder's grandfather and he remembered the blood dripping onto him through his grandmother's shawl. Eighty-six members of his tribe were killed that day by Harney's men, five more wounded, and seventy women and children captured. A hundred and fifty years later, the Montana Department of Livestock (DOL) won the right to kill bison they think might be a threat to cattle. The threat in the eyes of ranchers is brucellosis, a virus carried by bison and elk which can spread to cattle causing spontaneous abortions, thus reducing the size of their herds. Although there are no recorded cases of brucellosis being transmitted from bison to cows, ranchers don't want to take the risk.

One March day in 1997, Little Thunder congregated with a few dozen people to pray over 147 bison which had been rounded up for slaughter by Montana's DOL. 'This was so strange,' she writes. 'I had my ten-year-old grandson standing next to me. And they started killing the buffalo, just like that, shooting them down. I covered his face with my shawl, and told him to go move.' She was repeating the story of her great-great-grandmother from a hundred years before. 'You get that sense that nothing changed from 1855 to 1997. Actually that time span is just a clap of thunder in our history. It's not that long.'

Rosalie then walked to the site of the killing and, as she went to talk to one of the sheriff's deputies, she was arrested, handcuffed and taken away in a police car for trespassing on private land. Her arrest and the echoes of her grandson and grandfather's experiences were two of the sparks that led to the creation of the Buffalo Field Campaign. In 1997, over a thousand bison were killed.

And so it goes every year, give or take a few hundred.

The same year that General Harney murdered Little Thunder's great-great-grandmother, a treaty was signed with Native Americans granting them the right to hunt buffalo on public lands. Like many treaties signed by the government, it has required patience and perseverance for Native Americans to uphold their rights to enact this treaty. This particular fight ended in 2006, when five confederated tribes – the Nez Perce, the Confederated Salish and Kootenai, the Shoshone-Bannock, the Umatilla and the Confederated Tribes of the Yakama Nation – were granted permission to hunt bison on federal lands outside Yellowstone Park, allowing them to carry on doing what they had been for 12,000 years.

The story of bison over the last two hundred years parallels, in some ways, the story of the land's first inhabitants. By 1900, the number of buffalo across the country had fallen from an estimated 60 million to 700. There were twenty-three bison left in the Yellowstone herd in 1900. Successful breeding has seen the number rise to almost 5,000. This herd is unique in that it is one of only eight in the United States defined as 'wild' – consisting of 400 or more animals that are free-ranging, experience predation, and do not share DNA with cattle.

According to the National Park Service, 600–900 bison need to be either culled or hunted every winter to keep the herd manageable. The Buffalo Field Campaign protests every year against this practice and documents every slaughtered animal. They would like to see bison roaming free like elk and deer.

With the story of bison and the history of their near extinction in the back of my mind, I picked up Missoula's free newspaper, *The Missoula Independent*, and read about a group of white twenty- and thirty-somethings who had set up camp for the second year running on the perimeter of Yellowstone National Park, just on the edge of Montana's yearly tribal bison hunt. The journalist called them 'scavengers' and I was immediately intrigued by this word – so ancient, so not of the civilized world.

The scavengers, who go under the name Buffalo Bridge, have created a space on the edge of the hunt where they hone ancestral skills such as brain-tanning hides, crafting items from bones and horns, and preserving and drying meat. They lend a hand to the tribal hunters, glean whatever parts of the buffalo they can, and in their words, 'honour the buffalo'.

I tracked down the leader of this group, Katie Russell, via her Wilderbabe website. For those who don't know what a Wilderbabe is, Russell explains:

A Wilderbabe is a strong woman who does what she wants to do. She is tough, able to take care of herself, and willing to walk across a mountain range for the ones she loves. With confidence, she knows she is just as beautiful crawling out of a tipi in the morning as she is dressed up for a night on the town. A Wilderbabe™ embraces the wilderness within . . . She feels herself as a part of the great circle of life around her, and honors the seasons of her own life.

In June, Katie sent me a very warm email. When I suggested going to their encampment, she replied that they'd had a very unfortunate experience with a journalist the previous winter and it had made them wary. I assured her that I was more of a 'writer' than a 'journalist' and I wouldn't be there to take sides. I had no idea whether I would write about them – my whole relationship to writing was so fragile at this point. I simply wanted to see what they did. I didn't tell her that I was feeling lost and needed to know that people like her existed. A lull in our correspondence made me wonder if I had said something to offend or had been perhaps too pushy.

Meanwhile the weather had started to turn, the sky's blazing pinks and purples morphing into silvers and greys. Winter was approaching and Katie Russell had put me in touch with Lee Whiteplume, the Nez Perce tribal conservation officer from Idaho who had become Katie's friend and an informal member of Buffalo Bridge. He had his finger on the pulse of the bison and when they might be leaving Yellowstone Park. I needed to plan my visit to coincide with the bison if I wanted to see the hunt.

I kept in touch with Lee in the hopes he could let me know when the bison might be migrating although exact dates would be impossible to pin down, as their movements were so weather-dependent. Bison only leave the higher ground of Yellowstone – where it is illegal to hunt – when the grass they feed on gets low. Their search for food leads them outside the Park to the lower, warmer and less snowy forty-acres of federal land called Beattie Gulch. This strip of land lies across the Old Yellowstone Trail from the Buffalo Bridge encampment.

In the meantime, I carried on being the good student. I regularly visited the Missoula Public Library, where I would sit and read Frederick Jackson Turner, John Muir, Edward Abbey, Winona LaDuke, Rick Bass, Wallace Stegner, John Zerzan and whatever I could get my hands on in their 'Western' section. Naively, or perhaps selfishly, I was beginning to see Buffalo Bridge as a short-cut to the 'real' American West. I was telling myself that they would give me insight into my new home and perhaps even into how I could live on the planet with sanity, if not joy.

Katie Russell eventually resurfaced, apologizing for her silence. It had been deer-skinning season and she'd been 'up to her ears in hides'. She signed off her email with 'hugs, Katie'. Eventually she invited me to stay in their encampment during the tribal buffalo hunt. Our correspondence was something I had interpreted as the beginning of a serious dialogue.

Katie's devotion to scavenging and ancestral technology seemed to be part of a larger conversation going on around me in the ether to do with a return to ancient ways, a belief that tribal life – particularly that of stone-age humans – had something to teach us about our future on the planet. Attachment parenting, the Paleo Diet, keeping your money under your mattress, investing in gold, a mistrust of Big Government, growing your own food, it was all static in the background of my new life in Montana. I sensed a movement that was gaining momentum – a movement that brought together the Left with their back-to-the-land philosophy and the Right with their emphasis on self-reliance. In the West, I was beginning to see, the Right and the Left were constantly overlapping in unexpected ways, to the point where political positions were often blurred.

For decades I had been tuned into another frequency that hummed at me from social media and news reports – one that seemed to be the basis for much of this desire to return to ancient ways. The news on this frequency was not good. There was that *New Yorker* article from July 2015 about the Cascadia fault, which everyone around me seemed to be reading. If the Cascadia subduction zone should shift – and the writer Kathryn

Schultz seemed to think it was a matter of *when* not *if* – California, Oregon, and Washington state would be hurled under the ocean and a tsunami dozens of feet high would finish off whatever was left of the West Coast from Vancouver, British Columbia, to northern California. FEMA's director of Region X, which encompasses Oregon, Washington, Idaho, and Alaska, put it succinctly, 'Our operating assumption is that everything west of Interstate 5 will be toast.'

I recently met a guy in Montana's Bitterroot Valley who had 500 gallons of gasoline stored in an old fire truck for the day when the banks collapse. He also had a bunker with enough food for his wife and four kids to survive the first wave of the apocalypse, which according to him would be the worst part of the end times. 'Imagine all those addicts storming the streets once the drug stores have been cleaned out?' he asked me. Nope, I had never imagined this. Should I?

Storing dried beef, freeze-dried mac and cheese and powdered milk for the apocalypse was something I had always associated with those whose deep mistrust of government was aligned with a desire to have their own armed militias and their community of friends who can build houses, dig wells, and defend their families. Many of the people I had been meeting at gun shows or in bars here in Montana had a fabricated 'Golden Age' as their template for how they wanted to live. And the apocalypse was their doorway into this utopia. Their golden age was located in a small window of time in the late nineteenth century when the US government was busy wiping out the Native American population but had yet to fully win over the West. Ranchers could graze their cattle to their heart's content, miners could blast gold and copper from the mountains, and trappers could harvest as much fur as they wanted with their strychnine-injecting techniques. No one told them what to do. That was the life. The conversation always seemed to loop back to the idea of freedom.

Katie Russell and the scavengers were different. They had their own golden age, which happened to be about 10,000 years earlier, when we were living as hunter-gatherers. Instead of hoarding food in their bunkers, the ancestral skills practitioners tend towards honing the skills that would allow them to survive from the land once the ATM machines have dried up. Both camps seemed to believe that in order to have a future, we must craft it along the lines of an idealized past. Otherwise we're toast.

My life in the West was interrupted by another summons back to Ottawa. The object of this trip was to help my sister Sheila carry on clearing out the house we had grown up in. 'Get a skip,' people said. 'Throw it all away!' But this was not so easy. There was the ecological side of just chucking everything into landfill, and there was the emotional side. When objects have been collected by people who once loved these objects, and these people are people you love, a chain is created that is hard to break.

The house we grew up in was still full of beautiful objects, gifts, heirlooms, love tokens, letters and art and books – lots of books, still tens of thousands of them. Here were a few things we found while going through my father's things:

Letters from Eliott Erwitt to my father about
a night of drinking they survived in New York
City in the 1950s

Love letters written to my mother from my father, which were truly heartbreaking

Slide rulers from my father's years studying engineering at MIT

Plastic shapes used for making aeronautical drawings: seven triangles, thirteen wing shapes, one circle in a very worn case and one smaller Italian triangle inscribed with F.LLI D'Amico Roma

A cardboard binder stuffed with some of my father's early attempts at drawing. Some good, others not so good

Over 120 silk ties

Printouts from adult websites along with print-outs of emails to and from his children. There are photos of my baby daughter he has photo-copied and written on to help him remember her name

Twelve pocket calculators

An ashtray with the diamond-shaped Agfa Film
logo on it and one that says 'A Meal without
Wine is like a Day Without Sunshine'

A hand-blown, spherical, clear glass paper-
weight from Italy, fired with streaks of copper

The most arresting objects, however, are in boxes.
Dozens of them. My father spent years in the early
stages of his Alzheimer's taking photos around his
house. He would place favourite objects – in his case
a tangerine, a banana and a rock – onto newspaper
headlines, or onto photos he had taken of politicians on
the television. He would photocopy these photographs
and sometimes write on them and rephotograph them
and then photocopy them again, sometimes with the
same banana, tangerine or rock. So you might find a
photo of Pierre Trudeau on TV, his mouth mid-sen-
tence, looking furious, with a rock next to his head. A
speech bubble about 'revolution' might be drawn over
Trudeau's face. This would then be rephotographed and
annotated. Or you might find a photocopy of a photograph of a banana next to a *National Enquirer* headline
about a grandmother who was found with an 89-year-
old foetus inside her. Then this would be photographed
with a rock. He created layers from his meagre surroundings. There are thousands of photocopies of these
photos, sometimes positioned with a rock, a banana,

a tangerine. An echo chamber, a hall of mirrors. His loneliness and his frustration at being incarcerated in the suburbs is visible in these photos of his TV screen, of the newspapers that landed every morning on the mat at his front door and the objects he had at hand.

In the 1950s and 1960s my father photographed artists in Paris, New York, Ireland and London. He created the photo exhibit at the 1967 Montreal World's Fair, *Man and his World*. He was devoted to the medium. The tangerine, the banana and the rock really moved me because what they represented was his shrinking world. He went from photographing Europe to taking snap-shots of Ottawa, then fire hydrants, lawn ornaments and stop signs in his suburban neighbourhood. His world closed in on him further as he photographed his meals, his television, his slippers and finally the rock, tangerine and banana. And then nothing. Is there a name for someone who saves photocopies of photos of photocopies of their own photos? A photophiliac? There is a sort of madness inherent in much that has been left in my parents' house. But there is so much brilliance, too. These are not objects one can just chuck in a bin.

I wasn't sure if my father could be considered a hoarder. When I talked about him, I tried to use the present tense because he was still alive, although he was not the same man who had raised me. With his advancing Alzheimer's, he was in a long-term care

facility. The influence he had had on my life was enormous. So much that I liked about myself and so much that I battled with were down to my father and my total unguarded love for him. His appetite for life was enormous. Food and drink, cigars, playing the maracas, listening to Dizzy Gillespie, singing to the Clancy Brothers, belly-dancing, flamenco (in fact any kind of dancing), a love of art, theatre, design, architecture, and almost any creative act (except video art which he found interminably dull as a rule: 'It's not film and it's not photography, what the hell is it?').

In retrospect my father probably was a hoarder. But he didn't hoard mail-order can openers and pyjamas from the Sears Catalogue. He hoarded clippings. As if by piling up writing on the subjects he was interested in, the words and ideas would become part of him. He lived inside walls lined with words. He also hoarded modernist art and posters, design and photography magazines. What to do with it all? Does it count as hoarding if the things collected are beautiful objects? The worth in these things is not financial. It was difficult trying to give most of it away.

When we moved my father out of the house and into the long-term care facility, my sister Sheila counted almost 45,000 books left behind. That was after my mother had taken it upon herself over the last decade or so, when she was sure he wouldn't notice, to put out one box of books every week with the recycling.

It drove my mother crazy and she kept saying, 'What am I going to do with all this stuff?' When she died at Christmas it was no longer her problem.

We invited every bookshop and library in Ottawa to buy some books, and many in Toronto. Any institution or second-hand bookshop who could not afford to buy any was invited to take whatever they wanted for free. I called my old school, where I had spent hours of my teenage life reading, where I discovered the poetry of Sylvia Plath and Leonard Cohen. They took a few books each by Jane Austen and Elizabeth Gaskell. Do you know how hard it is to get rid of books? And I am not talking dog-eared paperbacks. I am talking a first edition G. K. Chesterton, Eric Gill's *Essay on Typography* in the typeface bearing my name, those Patrick Leigh Fermor books with their John Craxton covers and heaps of Faber books from the 1940s, 50s and 60s, many bearing that hand-lettering by Berthold Wolpe, typefaces that were so intimately tied to the books' contents. These are objects of simple beauty. Then there were piles of Swiss-designed books on architecture, Allen Lane-vintage Penguins, art books with reproductions using inks no longer made. No one wanted these books any more, I mean no one. Except the photography books, which we donated to Canada's National Gallery along with my father's archive.

The saddest thing I unearthed among the mountains of books were the empty journals. I counted them:

there were twenty-three. For the past twenty years, my father had talked of writing his 'Book'. It had a title, *The Necessary Revolution*. It was about how all the previous revolutions were based around technological or mechanical advancements or around political disillusionment, but really the one revolution that was needed above all others was a revolution of 'love'. For much of my adult life I kept telling him to sit down and write it. He would visit me in London, we'd have dinner, and I would get cross hearing about how he had worked out the cover design. 'That's not down to the author, Dad! Get some chapters written,' I would say, frustration pouring from me as I could see his ideas being undermined by his utter lack of discipline and his love of boozy nights. In the end, those journals which he wanted so badly to fill with his 'Book' were sold at a garage sale for twenty-five cents each.

On this past trip to Ottawa I visited my father with my sister Kate. He was very sleepy and didn't respond much. Kate and I were upset that our visit was not a better one. But what is not so good from our point of view is not necessarily bad from his. Perhaps a 'bad' day for an Alzheimer's patient is exactly when they want to hear the comforting words that they are loved. Just because he couldn't show us much didn't mean he wasn't taking it in. But this was the first time I hadn't heard him say my name. Normally, even with his speech being so minimal, I would get a 'Jo-jo' from him. But not this time.

With my mother gone, my father slipping away, the house being emptied, and my menopause leading me into hormonal depths and troughs, I decided it was time to tackle driving. Something practical to ground me, something that could convince me I was in charge. I told my husband that I wanted to write an essay called 'Learning to Drive' all about how life lived as a passenger is so different from life lived as someone behind the metaphorical wheel. 'Who would read something with that title?' Jason asked.

Once I was back in Missoula, I spotted it at the library: *Learning to Drive and Other Life Stories* by Katha Pollitt, a journalist whose articles I often read in the *Nation*, a magazine I happened to have just published in for the first time. Pollitt's book beautifully tackles the subject of a woman taking control of a car at the age of fifty-two, which she cleverly links to her politics, her partner's affair, and motherhood, which for her came late. This book, I decided while reading it in the stacks, had been written for me.

My driving instructor loved the fact I had just had a piece published in the *Nation*. He read it regularly.He also read the *Guardian* and *The New York Times*. Sometimes our conversations got so voluble and intense that I had to ask him to be quiet so I didn't crash his car. After two months of lessons he felt I was ready for my test. I disagreed with his assessment but deferred to his better judgement. He knew the person who would be testing me. 'She's really nice. She'll pass you,' he told me. I took the test and despite speeding twice, swerving into a bike lane, and not being able to locate my hazard lights or my windshield wipers, I passed. Welcome to Montana.

As I was planning my trip to Buffalo Bridge, an email landed in my inbox. It was my father this time. I had had an argument with Eve about whether she could trick-or-treat by herself with friends and no adults. The streets in Missoula, unlike those in London, are very dark and I didn't trust her ability to navigate them at night without getting lost. She was getting bolder, more independent. She was eight now and more capable than I had been at her age. We compromised. I trailed her several houses behind while chatting with other parents. We ended up at a Halloween party where there was lots of booze and parents from my daughter's school were dressed as 'cereal' killers covered in Shreddies boxes, and as the character Sadness from *Inside Out* – all blue face paint like an actor from the Blue Man Group. They took their costumes seriously in Missoula. I lost track of how many glasses of wine I had. I met Evel Knievel's relatives at this party. They had travelled from Butte and in my slightly drunken state I told them how much I had loved Evel as a child and how much I loved Butte. They were very sweet and polite. I was able to momentarily forget all about my dead and dying parents and my ageing body and my flailing novel.

A few weeks later I was back on a plane heading for Ottawa. I arrived on 4 November to find my father lying in bed, still breathing but with his eyes closed. Once again I was with my sisters Kate and Sheila – my other siblings were too far away, too busy. The three of us sat with him night and day. The staff where he was living were so attentive, patient, kind, absolutely committed to giving their time to elderly dementia sufferers and stewarding them through illness into death. The oddest thing about being at my father's bedside was that this dying process felt so much like giving birth. It was a passage from this life into the next – or into oblivion or whatever it is one believes in – just as pushing a baby out of your body is a passage from one realm into another for both: the baby becomes a child, the woman becomes a mother. Both are unknown territories.

My sisters and I took turns being up by his head and down by his feet. We swapped places and laughed a lot. Black humour is essential when you are in a room with a dying person. We decided that we would not move him to a hospital where he would be force-fed and hooked up to invasive equipment. What we were witnessing was nature doing what it does best when it is left to do it. One of my sisters was appalled that we were not doing more. She made it clear to us, the loved ones 'do everything to keep a person alive'. Over the phone she railed against my sister Sheila for not doing more. We were keen, however, to allow our father the smoothest, safest and most loving transition possible.

I had never helped a person die. Staff members mentioned to us over and over that the aural sense is the last one to go, so we played music, we talked and we included him in our conversations. No one knows exactly how it works, but research has shown that even when people are unresponsive, they can still hear. One afternoon, my sister Kate was up by his head and holding his hand and I was across from her holding his other hand. Sheila was by his feet. Kate spontaneously began telling my father that it was OK for him to go on this journey, to do it alone, to leave us behind. All through his life, my father had suffered from wander- lust. He travelled whenever he could. When we were young, he would take us everywhere with him. Kate began a soliloquy. She told him that this was the one trip we couldn't accompany him on. But we would be fine, we didn't need to go with him this time. Sheila and I were in tears and my father's body let out an almost indiscernible sigh. He had been assured of safe passage by his eldest child and it seemed to calm him. We decided to go home that night to get some sleep. It had been three days of near constant vigil and we were exhausted. At 6.45 the following morning, the phone rang. It was the nursing home. 'Come,' they said.

We threw on our winter boots and coats and ran to

the home, which was just down the street from Sheila's house. We arrived at 7 a.m.; he had died seven minutes earlier. One of the nurses told us that she sees this all the time. Her theory was that people don't like dying in front of the people they love most. They don't want to distress them or they feel it is an intensely private rite that they must do on their own. I took my father's hand and it was still warm. This act was so intimate and natural. He looked completely at peace. We could sense his presence in the room. Sheila, who is a practising Roman Catholic, believed this to be his soul. My eldest sister Kate believed this to be his spirit. I had no word for it. But he was there in the room, ghostly but vibrant – a sort of energy. We opened the window and felt him leave – everything really did go cold.

I thanked my father for allowing me to witness his death, for giving me the chance to shepherd him to wherever he was heading. He was a devout Catholic so in respect of that I pictured him going to heaven, which was where he wanted to go. He always said there was a special place there for musicians, especially his beloved jazz players. I pictured him with Dizzy, Duke, Stan Getz and Stéphane Grappelli, biting the tip off his cigar and tapping his toes with a large glass of whiskey by his side.

Grief has a way of making one's normal landscape appear unrecognizable. After my sister Mary died it was as if I'd had to learn to walk all over again, how to breathe and speak. Living in Missoula was making it easier for me to grieve my father. I was in a new city, a new landscape with different air, different people, different light, so this new landscape without my parents was not one I felt had been altered. I didn't know it well enough to feel it had gone awry.

My second Christmas in Missoula felt so normal it unnerved me. We tobogganed, we went for walks in the snow. My daughter was perfectly at home here. She made skis out of cardboard cereal boxes (didn't I do that in Ottawa?) and slid down the street. The snow, the glinting light, the huge skies. I didn't ever want to leave this town. I got a bit of teaching at a small independent creative writing school. I was editing books remotely for a publisher in New York and writing the odd piece of journalism. It didn't add up to a living but perhaps it could have, given a bit of time. Jason was working on a script which he was preparing to make into a film. But Missoula was an expensive town and we were coasting on our savings and the small amount of rental from our house in London.

In September we'd moved into a smaller, cheaper bungalow in a slightly less affluent neighbourhood. One day just after we'd moved into our pink stucco bungalow, I heard a dog barking aggressively from across the road. I looked out my kitchen window to see a man standing on his concrete porch. He was leaning over the railing, looking at the barking dog. In a flash, the large animal leapt at the man's chest. He collapsed down the stairs and the dog carried on going for his head and his torso while a woman stood next to him screaming. I called the police. The dog eventually stopped. The woman grabbed him by the collar and the man lay bleeding and immobile on the grass while a police car pulled up. This was our new neighbourhood.

Our house didn't have a basement so we shared our ground floor living space with hobo spiders. I laid spider traps next to the little colonies of mushrooms that grew along the edges of our musty carpets. I would check them obsessively. Every few days there'd be a new casualty and I would be thankful that none of us had been bitten.

Despite the lower outgoings in our new house, we were finding it difficult to stay afloat. I had started applying for more permanent jobs but those were hard to come by. I felt sick thinking about leaving this place, but I simultaneously experienced a sinking sensation, a vertigo, when I thought of leaving London behind for good. And then there was the giant elephant in every room in the United States: healthcare. I had started getting links to 'Go Fund Me' pages to help friends and their family members raise money for medical bills. The reality of a system which excludes people without savings or highly paid jobs from accessing medical help unnerved me. Jason didn't share this worry. He is a believer in things just 'working out'. I don't share his faith. Despite wanting to stay in Missoula forever, the thought of leaving London behind churned my gut. I had spent twenty-five years building a community of friends there. It was where I gave birth to my one and only child, where I had worked all my adult life, where I had sat in neighbours' houses crying from fatigue and worry about motherhood, the death of my sister, and wept over the loss of lovers. I had a past there, full of stories. When we moved to Montana, I never really considered the future and the question that was now hanging between Jason and myself – the question of whether we should stay or go.

The fraught subject of where I belonged in the world seemed to make itself present late at night. I would lie awake in the dark weighing up whether to uproot ourselves from here or from London. Either decision would require strength and commitment. The daytimes were full of writing and parenting and the day-to-day diversions that can keep one busy and distracted. I began driving a small truck given to us by a friend. This was a new me. I had never pictured myself being a 'mom' and driving my kid to ballet classes and soccer games in small town America. I blasted the radio and rolled down the window, laughing at this new version of myself. We were still living out of suitcases and I felt so light and unencumbered, my movement through space unhindered. With my parents gone, I felt freer than I ever had. A friend told me I was now an orphan. I liked that. I decided not to think about London while I was in Missoula. This forced me to do that thing New Agers write books about and Buddhists actually do: live in the moment. I was a mum and so I did mum things and I was a partner and did partner things. And I wrote. I wrote a lot. And I tried not to think about those twenty-three empty journals. Or maybe those were what I was trying to compensate for with all this writing.

And then I heard from Lee Whiteplume. The bison were moving out of Yellowstone Park.

I called Katie Russell who told me they were setting up camp. They needed a week or two to settle, and then I would be welcome to join them. They would have room for me and my sleeping bag if I needed it. I began questioning my intentions. Why was I so drawn to them? What did I want? What did I intend to learn? I didn't really know, except that everything in my life felt transitional and fragile, and that I was seeking a path that aligned with my desire to live on this planet with a purpose, with joy. The cycle of consumption everywhere around me was not one I wanted to be part of.

When I was a waitress in Toronto in my teens, there was a customer who came in almost every day. She would order a Diet Coke, a Caesar salad and a chocolate brownie covered in vanilla ice-cream, chocolate sauce and whipped cream (otherwise known as Death By Chocolate). Her food choices told me everything I needed to know about my culture. We balance out our empty calories as if this culinary arithmetic were sane. People of my generation were the first to be simultaneously obese and malnourished. We poison the rivers

and then try to clean them by pouring more poison into them. I wanted to live where things made sense. In my mind, the scavengers knew what they were doing. I needed some of their certainty.

On a grey January day, I pulled up to a small parcel of land on a dirt track in Montana's Paradise Valley. The tall, jagged, snow-covered Absaroka and Gallatin mountain ranges were visible in the distance and the entrance to Yellowstone National Park was less than eight kilometres away. There hadn't been a lot of snow that year and the ground was muddy. The encampment consisted of a one-room cabin, a wooden barn, the bare ribs of a tipi, a horse corral, a couple of Porta Potties and several small square canvas tents shaped like little houses, known as wall tents. Smoke from the chimneys of wood-burning stoves wafted up from the tents while two men scraped at stretched buffalo hides. Someone had arranged a circle of bison heads and hooves mandala-like on the ground between the tents. But what really struck me were the animal parts scattered everywhere. Bison heads and hooves, horns and bones lay around the place. Three dogs sniffed at some rib cages. Across the dirt road from the Buffalo Bridge camp was Beattie Gulch, where I had just watched a herd of antelope disappear into the foothills of the Gallatins. This forty-acre stretch of land, essentially a grassy dip under a thin crust of snow, was where the bison would be coming to graze once their food source in Yellowstone Park started to run low.

When I arrived, Katie wasn't there. She was in Bozeman, the nearest town, getting supplies. I was greeted instead by Josh and Gerry, who stopped their hide-scraping to say hello. Josh, a cap-wearing, bearded forty-year-old in earth-coloured Carhartt trousers and handmade leather boots reminded Gerry that it was time to focus on their meat processing and take a break from their personal projects. Josh explained that they had to prioritize certain activities in order to keep the community going. The meat would spoil if it weren't tended to, whereas the hides could wait. Gerry kept scraping.

Josh then led me into the small wooden barn where cuts of meat and organs were being stewed, boiled and prepared for canning, drying, freezing and preserving. I watched as he pulled strands of cooked meat from a bison's neck the length of an oar. Josh offered me some and, although I am not a meat-eater, I politely took a sliver. It tasted how it looked, strong and musky, with the consistency of what I imagine pulled pork to be like – the bison flesh melted in my mouth, leaving a fatty residue.

On the floor sat a large, shallow pan the size of a baby's bath. Straddling this was a giant ribcage which was so enormous it looked more like the cartoon version of a dead animal in *Roadrunner* than anything I'd ever seen. This had been a gift from a hunter. In return for helping with field dressing, skinning and quartering bison out on the hunting grounds, members of Buffalo Bridge are sometimes given meat or hides. It was an informal arrangement and they certainly hadn't expected it. Josh summed up one of the many roles of Buffalo Bridge, 'We are doing the work of the Native women. The whole tribe would have been active in processing a bison. Now we're part of this process.'

Five bison hearts varying in size from that of a grapefruit to a small watermelon were arranged on a counter in the barn. Livers were waiting to be cooked, some a bit too old and shrivelled for anything to be done with them, others plump, shiny and red, the colour of new lipstick. A metal crock-pot bubbled with a stew made of bison, carrots and potatoes. Breathing in here was like licking wet fur.

Josh told me about his old job in a hair salon in LA, another installing pool tables, and then a spell working on an urban farm in Portland, which became a 'dead end'. The city bureaucracy made it impossible to make a real go if it. He then worked on a farm in Oregon but 'couldn't relate to living in the world in that sedentary way'. This was when he mentioned the hoop, or the sacred hoop: the seasonal migratory way of living by following one's food source. This lifeway was practised for thousands of years by Indigenous Americans in the Great Basin, the area that is now Nevada, Utah, and portions of Oregon, Idaho, Wyoming, Colorado and Montana. It was a lifeway that worked with the seasons, leaving plenty of the Earth's resources untouched for future generations. He explained how the traditional hoop that the Shoshone walked was huge. They deliberately planted wild gardens from southern Nevada to central Idaho. In the early spring, they would start at the southern end of the hoop, digging up edible roots such as kouse, or what the Europeans called 'biscuit-root'. When this root was dried and pounded, the flour was used to make bread and biscuits, which could last for months. Onions, garlic and other wild foods grow in the arid ground of what looks to most people like inhospitable territory.

By early summer the Shoshone would be in southern Idaho, still digging their food, but here they would find camas lilies whose roots, when roasted, tasted like sweet potato. They would hunt buffalo here and then head north, where they would find vast bushes of huckleberries and other fruits. The lakes up in Idaho's mountains would be teeming with salmon, which they would eat fresh and smoke for the winter. As the fruit began to wane in August or early September, the Shoshone would head south back to Nevada to harvest the nutrient-rich piñon or pine nuts. By November, they would travel further south to the geothermal country of central and southern Nevada, with its healing hot springs. As they travelled the hoop, they deliberately put the seeds of the plants that they harvested back into the ground in order to keep the cycle intact.

'If you want to know more about this, you need to meet Fin,' Josh told me.

Fin had been following this path for thirty-five years and was trying to establish camps for each season – winter camp, root camp, berry camp and piñon camp – so that the fabric of this ancient lifeway would not unravel with the barbed wire, the parcelling up of land for cattle, the roads and the damming of rivers.

I asked for her full name.

'It's Finisia Medrano.' He spelled it out so I could write it down. 'She was born a man in 1956, downwind from the nuclear testing in Nevada. Everyone calls her the Tranny Granny,' Josh said, alluding to her nickname, which combines her deep knowledge of land with her trademark irreverence.

I watched Josh delicately slice neck meat from a buffalo's bones before throwing it into a big pot to be cooked and then pressed into sterilized Mason jars. Every now and then a piece went into his mouth.

In came Barnes, a new Buffalo Bridge member, who was on fat-rendering duty. Barnes was a Montana transplant from North Carolina with a degree in experiential education. When he wasn't foraging for food in the Bitterroot Mountains, where he lived as a 'nomadic homesteader', he worked as a volunteer fire fighter and practised new techniques learnt at ancestral skills gatherings. Like many of the scavengers, he was cagey about giving me his surname or any information about where he lived. As a result of some bad publicity in the past and also a general sense that they want to remain under the radar, there was an implicit mistrust of journalists and outsiders and a desire for me to respect their anonymity as much as possible. As Barnes poured the buttery, yellow fat into Mason jars to be used for candle-making, leather priming, salves and cooking, another member joined us.

I introduced myself to Alex, who was holding his three-month-old son. I reached my hand out to touch the baby's plump fist. Alex reeled back in alarm and told me I was not to touch his baby. At first I thought he was joking, and I reached out again. But this was no joke: the baby was not for touching. I was 'from the city', and Alex, who was not going to inoculate his child, was worried that I might be carrying germs. I was a new parent once, and I understood this aggressive need to protect one's child at all costs. But the effect of this no-touching policy made me feel that I was an impure agent capable of contaminating this lifestyle. Once again, I was from 'the other side'.

Another member from the community showed up. Ania's job this afternoon was to cut the flesh from the giant cartoon ribs. Donning a hat and long skirt, she focused on the meat while the winter light fell through the window, giving her the look of a Vermeer painting. Ania began telling me about her two children who were nine and eleven.

I asked if they were at Buffalo Bridge.

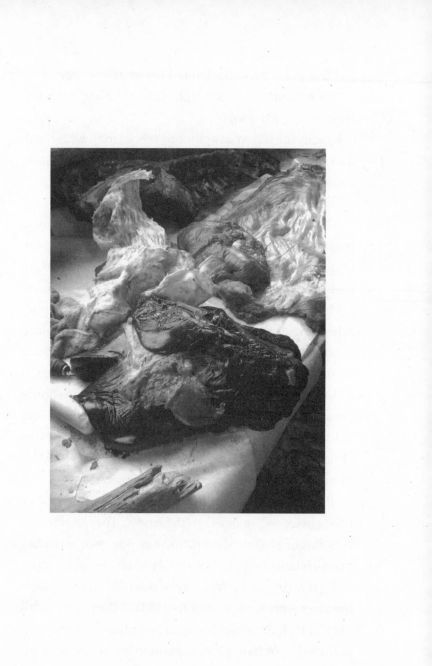

'They're with their dad in Portland,' she replied.

I mentioned that my eight-year-old daughter went to school in Missoula.

'I sent my oldest daughter to school for a while,' she told me. 'And she played with Polly Pockets, you know those plastic dolls?'

I nodded.

'Up until that time, my kids had only ever played with toys made of wood or cloth, but here they were playing with plastic! I didn't like the fact that they had these outside influences that had nothing to do with me. So I took her out of school. I've been home-schooling and unschooling ever since.' Unschooling was a new one for me. Similar to home-schooling, but somewhat freer, unschooling is a child-led approach to teaching that relies on play and exploration. Some people call it 'delight-directed learning' because its aim is to keep the spark of curiosity and delight alive in children which, the theory goes, can be extinguished in more traditional educational settings.

I asked Josh, Barnes, Alex and Ania about whether their choice to live closer to the land had been informed by a larger philosophy around rewilding or anarcho-primitivism, or perhaps simply a vision of hunting and gathering as a purer way of existing on the planet, but they were keen to emphasize that they were 'non-political'. They simply would not be drawn into the politically hot issues around land ownership, hunting and who had the right to it and who didn't. Members of Buffalo Bridge made it clear that they were here to learn, to share and to respect the buffalo – not to get involved in the politics around land issues.

In Montana the culling, hunting, and managing of bison is a very hot topic. On one side you have the Buffalo Field Campaign (BFC), whose mission is to stop the killing of any bison from the Yellowstone herd. Their ultimate goal is for these animals to roam free, like elk and deer. These animals are related to the herds that roamed here before Europeans arrived. Through the combination of hunting and culling, the number of bison in the Yellowstone area is kept around the 3,000 mark – an arbitrary figure dreamed up by the Interagency Bison Management Plan (IBMP). The IBMP was created in 2000 to 'manage' these animals – a ridiculous word for wild animals. It is made up of members of disparate organizations like the National Park Service, the Animal and Plant Health Inspection Service and the Montana Department of Livestock, among others. It also includes three tribal entities: the Confederated Salish and Kootenai tribe, the InterTribal Buffalo Council and the Nez Perce.

The Department of Livestock and the ranchers behind them are the loudest voices in this mêlée. They see bison as a threat to their livelihood. When this group thinks of buffalo roaming free, they envision trampled fences, grass grazed to a buzz cut, and their cattle infected with brucellosis. Somewhere in the middle of all this hot potato tossing is the Buffalo Bridge collective. They were not here to get political and yet I felt their presence transcended 'recreation' and allowed them to inhabit a way of living in this part of the world which included its history, culture and land. Despite their repeated assertions of non-partisanship, I sensed their allegiances would be more in line with those of the Native hunters than the more traditional ranchers.

Josh continued filling a Mason jar with meat pulled from the enormous length of slow-cooked bison vertebra. More fat was being rendered in another part of the hut. Between every process, surfaces and instruments were cleaned and scoured. 'It's seen as bad form to give your dinner party guests botulism,' Josh joked. Much of this food would be shared at ancestral skills gatherings and with friends. 'We bring it back to our communities and to people who need it,' he explained.

With the light fading, I left the scavengers to their work. My boots crunched on the cold ground as I walked the few hundred metres across the Old Yellowstone Trail road to see whether any bison had shown up in search of some grass to graze.

It was nearing four o'clock when I approached a truck parked on the Old Yellowstone Trail, the gravel dividing line between the Buffalo Bridge encampment and the hunting grounds of Beattie Gulch. The guy in the driver's seat of the pickup was twenty-two-year-old Stormy Bacon, a registered member of the Salish and Kootenai tribe from Arlee, Montana. In the passenger seat was his friend Chase. In the bed of a truck parked parallel to Stormy was a dead bison they had shot the day before, and driving that pickup were two non-Native friends, Abraham and Logan. Their trucks were wedged into a pullout off the road, facing Beattie Gulch, where they could keep a close watch for bison. If you walked about eight kilometres from their truck, down the Old Yellowstone Trail, you'd get to the Gardiner entrance of Yellowstone Park. There hadn't been any fresh snow today so the landscape had the forlorn look of a worn patchwork quilt made up of frozen brown earth and motley scabs of hardened snow. In the background, the Gallatins towered cold and unmoving as if to say, 'We've seen it all before.'

Stormy told me he was studying highway construction at Salish Kootenai College. 'I don't have a dad,' he said, 'but my uncle taught me to hunt.' He felt proud to be keeping the tradition of bison hunting alive, and he liked the feeling of bringing meat back to his family. His friends had come to help as they knew it required at least two people to skin, dress, and quarter a bison, which can weigh anything from 360 to 990 kilograms.

As I talked with Stormy and his buddies, we could just make out, through the dusky light, some fuzzy brown smudges coming from the direction of the Park.

The animals trudged slowly and deliberately, like giant, prehistoric somnambulists heading towards Beattie Gulch. There were maybe fifty animals and as they moved, a light snow began to fall. As it was January, there were no young bison, but some of the females would be pregnant at this time of year.

Archie Fuqua, the Game Warden for the Salish and Kootenai and Lee Whiteplume, the Conservation Officer for the Nez Perce, gathered the hunters together to discuss tactics. Around twenty men and a couple of women stood in a circle on the dirt track talking quietly, working out the logistics of how best to tackle the bison. The snow had gone from a light dusting to falling in large clumpy flakes that muted the sun. A tangible silence had descended on the valley. The landscape suddenly went from colour to monochrome.

The hunters dispersed, walking in twos and threes towards the line of bison who were still marching slowly through Beattie Gulch. After about a quarter of an hour, one shot was fired. With this, some bison galloped into the foothills of the mountains and others scattered back in the direction of the Park. Another shot was fired, then at least a dozen more. I found myself rooting for the animals. I wanted them all to run away. In a matter of minutes fifteen bison were down.

I had come to Buffalo Bridge to meet the scavengers but I hadn't thought about how I would feel seeing these animals killed. I stayed behind the hunters, out of their firing line, watching and listening to the soft thuds of bison falling to the ground. *We are all prey*, I thought. My heart was pounding crazily with the adrenaline coursing through me. I felt some of the same sensations here that I did when watching the Junction Butte wolves. There I had witnessed life, and here I was witnessing death. However, in all this silence, I felt a humility that surfaced in this exchange of the animal's life for sustenance and for the enactment of an important cultural ritual. Unlike other big game hunting that goes on all over the West, there would be no photos on Facebook with smiling hunters showing off their kill. This hunt was not for fun – it went so much deeper than that.

Despite the respect with which these animals were killed, what I had just witnessed was more of a firing squad than a hunt, the result of compromises over the past two hundred years, compromises that are the direct result of the deracination of the Indigenous people from their land. Not only did the tribes in the Great Basin traditionally rely on this meat for food, but every part of these animals would have been used: hides for clothing and shelter; bones for instruments, tools and jewellery; horns and hooves for use as vessels; the fat could be rendered for use in cooking, candle-making and salves; stomachs were used as cooking pots; and sinew for twine.

Just as importantly, the presence of bison on these

tribes' land has always held a spiritual dimension and the animals feature in their stories and myths. Writing in *Sierra* magazine, the author and environmentalist Winona LaDuke quotes the Lakota Chief Arvol Looking Horse, 'The First People were the Buffalo People, our ancestors which came from the sacred Black Hills, the heart of everything that is. I humbly ask all nations to respect our way of life, because in our prophecies, if there is no buffalo, then life as we know it will cease to exist.' The last great communal Native American hunt in Montana took place in 1864.

I wandered around the carcasses feeling I should not have been there. There was a palpable sacred connection between these hunters and their prey – you could see it in their movements – and it was beyond my reach. I considered leaving but I couldn't quite tear myself away from the steaming carcasses lying in the snow.

The 1855 Treaty between the Nez Perce (and other 'friendly tribes' as the treaty specifies) and the US Government states that the

> exclusive right of taking fish in all the streams running through or bordering said reservation is further secured to said Indians; as also the right of taking fish at all usual and accustomed places, in common with citizens of the Territory, and of erecting temporary buildings for curing; together with the privilege of hunting, gathering roots and

berries, and pasturing their horses and cattle upon open and unclaimed land.

The Nez Perce and other tribes have only been allowed to enact their 1855 treaty rights since 2006. One of the conservation officers told me that the area used for the hunt – forty acres – was too small. When a lot of people showed up, it got chaotic and there was a chance someone could get hurt. The distances travelled by tribal members forced the hunting to happen too fast. Most of the people here would have driven up on a Friday after work for five to ten hours to get to Beattie Gulch. And most of them had to be home by Sunday night to start work or school on Monday morning. Although this hunt is important for both subsistence, ceremony and ritual, the history of taking land from the tribes was still evident.

Once the animals were confirmed dead, the hunters identified the carcasses they had shot by sticking a glove or a piece of gaffer tape onto a horn, before walking to their trucks to get knives, chainsaws and the sleds they needed to lug the animal parts back to their pickups.

Bison carcasses are like giant furnaces and if they're not opened up quickly, the meat will spoil. Hunters have to work fast. The two game wardens walked around checking whether people needed help. There were two unclaimed bison. The wardens decided one would go to the Nez Perce and the other to the Salish and Kootenai. Some hunters, like one woman I spoke to – let's call her Jane – had no idea how to field-dress the animal. She found the dead body lying before her, which weighed probably ten times what she did, difficult to handle.

'It's just so sad,' she repeated, 'so sad.'

'Do you feel sadder trying to open up its body than you do when you pull the trigger?' I asked.

She thought for a moment. 'The same,' she replied. 'I just don't like it.' She sounded like she might cry.

I stood next to her, holding one of the animal's hind legs up, as she tried to slice it along its belly with a shaky hand. She kept stopping, barely able to get the blade through the thick, furry skin. She had a friend with her who had gone to the truck to get the instruments they needed.

Bob, a Salish hunter, was with his son and grandson, and they worked with incredible speed and efficiency. This was the first time the three men had hunted together. It was as much a symbolic act as a practical necessity for Bob to be here with his grandson. He told me that he thanked the Creator for putting the animal in his path. But once the animal was dead it was about getting the meat home. I sensed among the hunters who didn't want to speak to me that this taking of life had a large spiritual dimension to it – something far too important to discuss with a stranger. I wondered if perhaps my curiosity should be tempered by my respect for cultural practices. Was witnessing this hunt another example of the colonial mindset at work, a sense that I would wander this land unhindered even if it meant going where I shouldn't? This thought bothered me but I couldn't shake my desire to try to understand what I was seeing.

The soundscape after the silent stalking of bison and the cracking of gunshots was that of knives being sharpened. There was little talking as hunters hunkered over the animals to take them apart. It is difficult, dirty and very bloody work. As innards were removed, a smell of methane and sulphur drifted through the cold, still evening. As heads were being sawn off, air gushed through windpipes. Bison are the largest land mammals on the continent and this fact hits you as you watch these giants slowly bleed out onto the snow.

Just before the light started dimming, Barnes showed up in his handmade narrow-brimmed hat, wielding his favourite knife and a headlamp. He was thrilled to take over from Jane. Despite the cold, he stripped down to his T-shirt and got busy slitting open her first bison. Once the cut was made, he launched himself head first into the stomach cavity to cut the remaining fibres that were holding the stomach and organs in place. He got in so deep I could no longer see his head. It took him about forty-five minutes to field-dress the first bison. He seemed to revel in the animal's blood, making red handprints on his overalls like a child finger painting. His relationship to this animal appeared to tap into something ecstatic and ritualistic deep inside him. After he finished with the first one, he sauntered over to Jane's second kill and started the whole process again.

Extraordinary crane-like mechanisms were being set up with which to winch the tons of meat into the beds of waiting pickups. Lights, the kind you see on film sets, were being hoisted onto the field, with some hunters predicting they would be out there all night. Knives were continuously being sharpened as the thick fur, fat and bone dulled their blades. I headed back to camp.

I got back to the Buffalo Bridge encampment to find Katie unloading supplies of Mason jars, groceries and a family-sized bag of M&Ms. I was struck by how much she resembled the photos on her Wilderbabe™ website, where she models her handmade 'buckskin fashion' and accessories, as well as listing her primitive skills classes. She is fresh-faced, maybe thirty years old. She greeted me warmly with a hug.

I followed her into the communal tent with its sofa, picnic table and wood stove. Here she pulled a couple of cashmere sweaters from a goodwill bag along with a fake leopard print maternity dress. She was in her second trimester and held the dress up to herself. 'I've got a housewarming to go to and now that I'm pregnant, I still want to look good,' she exclaimed.

Alex and a few others watched her while they tucked into bowls of bison stew by the fire. Then Josh and his partner Ania showed up. They had heard the shots and were bundling up to go out and offer the tribal hunters what knowledge and manpower they could. Alex offered me the sofa in the communal tent as a sleeping option. Katie reminded me that people would be coming in late, that I might get disturbed. It might be better to make the eight-kilometre trip into Gardiner to get a motel.

'They have a Best Western,' she told me.

I said goodnight and headed into Gardiner where I found a Super 8 Motel for thirty-four bucks. While I was checking in, a middle-aged woman in a grey bob told me there was a bluegrass festival in the motel. 'Right in that wing over there,' she said, dragging me to the window to see where the music was coming from. People were clapping and swaying.

'There's lots of food and dessert and beer. You should come!'

I would have loved an evening of bluegrass. Something simple and life-affirming. But once I got to my room and flopped onto the bed, I knew I would be going nowhere tonight. I was trying to process what I had just seen: the ancestral skills practitioners with the 'unschooling' of their children and their passion for ancestral skills. Their desire to return to a time when cities had not yet been imagined and books had not been printed. The hunters who wanted to demonstrate their love for their families through the timeless and significant act of hunting and bringing back meat. The bison bleeding from their faces into the snow. Katie and her goodwill bag of cashmere sweaters. And my own questionable intentions, my desire to be here prying, searching, digging where perhaps I should not be.

I opened a beer and drank it in bed. The death by firing squad approach to the bison hunt was not what I had expected. After having watched my father die recently and seeing my mother in her casket just over a year ago, I had been thinking a lot about death, what constitutes a good death, and how we in the 'civilized' world are so afraid of it, cut off from it, and so reluctant to see it as simply the other side of birth. How we forget to be prey.

No one in the Buffalo Bridge encampment batted an eyelid at all those animal parts lying on the slushy ground. It is probably hardwired into us to be comfortable living among dead animals, but I was disturbed by them. There seemed to be a moral dimension at play among those who practised ancestral skills: living off the land, foraging and hunting are seen as morally superior among those who adhere to this Palaeolithic Renaissance. In this worldview, living in a city is a sign of weakness, of being unable to fend for oneself, of relying on hospitals and public transport, conventional medicine, inoculations and being under the thumb of a corrupt government. I couldn't work out where I fit among what I had just seen.

It was still dark when I woke up and drove to Beattie Gulch for one last look before heading home to Missoula. The sun was rising as I left Gardiner. I stopped to watch a herd of elk and mule deer skip across fields of snow in the dawn light. The tip of Electric Peak – the highest mountain in the Gallatin range – was pink against the lightening pale blue sky. More snow had fallen overnight and some of the gut piles on the hunting grounds wore little white capes. Other mounds of stomachs, organs, entrails and embryos bigger than human newborns were bulging and red, removed from their hosts after the snow had done its dusting in the middle of the night.

A scattering of crows cawed from the high tops of the few spindly trees. But the innards had been left alone. Where were the coyotes, the wolves, the non-human scavengers?

When I went to say goodbye to the Buffalo Bridge community, Lee Whiteplume was visiting. Tall, with broad shoulders and a square face, he had a direct gaze which he trained on me not unkindly, but with intensity. He had been out with the hunters until late the previous night.

'Someone called us their guardian angels,' Ania announced. She brandished the knife given to her as

proof of the hunter's gratitude. She and Josh had also been out on the field giving what assistance they could until the wee hours.

Barnes showed up brushing his teeth. He hadn't returned to camp until after three in the morning. Alex was busy sanding a bison horn. It was as smooth as a baby's fingernail. His partner bounced their child on her lap next to him. Josh and Ania were on breakfast duty, cooking up bacon, eggs and potatoes supplemented with the giant bag of M&Ms and Kettle Creek potato chips. Katie was organizing her purse on the floor. I watched transfixed as she laid out its contents: strips of elastic, a handmade leather needle holder, thread, scissors, pieces of buckskin – one of which was used as an impromptu teether for Alex's baby. I had brought my own coffee and sat and watched them eat their breakfast. After they'd eaten, Katie called a meeting to talk about how they saw Buffalo Bridge moving forward. I asked if I could stay and listen but was told, very firmly, that it was private.

I wandered back to Beattie Gulch. A few hunters were starting to gather although there were no bison to be seen on the horizon. Clouds passed across the sun. Shadows on the snow came and went. Despite the sense of community and camaraderie among the hunters and the scavengers, a profound melancholy had risen inside me.

I had become obsessed with Finisia Medrano. I would stay up late Googling her at the kitchen table in our small, damp, rented bungalow in Missoula. The mushrooms growing on our carpets were thriving. The hobos continued to walk into my spider traps and I would examine their fat, striped bodies before chucking them in the bin. The infestation of wasps in the kitchen ceiling had come out of their hibernation with the beginning of summer and buzzed loudly above my head, sounding like an electric razor.

While I typed away at my MacBook Pro, I was keenly aware of the arsenic and copper inside it, both of which were probably mined in Chile. I knew that the process of pulling these elements out of the ground was killing whole villages and poisoning rivers. In the Republic of Congo, children as young as seven are digging cobalt out of the earth with their bare hands. Their lives were being cut short so my battery could have a long one. It was the same story for the bismuth from Mexico, the gallium from Guinea, the cadmium, chromium, manganese and platinum from South Africa, the lithium from Zimbabwe, the mercury from the only mercury mine in the world in Kyrgyzstan, the vanadium from Kazakhstan, the antimony from Tajikistan, and so on. But every morning I powered up my computer, made a cup of coffee, and scrolled through the petitions in my inbox: dozens of them every morning, asking for money to combat child labour, to save the orangutan, to clean up rivers running orange from the mining of copper used in the making of my computer. Every morning I put on the mask of schizophrenia I needed in order to get through the day, a mask I imagined someone like Finisia did not need. I assumed her reliance on modern technology and the extraction industries needed to power any devices she might have would be minimal, perhaps even non-existent.

It was becoming even more impossible for me to live in the West without keying into the stories of rivers, land, wildlife, and the fragility of it all. In his book *Desert Solitaire* the writer and gonzo environmentalist Edward Abbey saw wilderness not simply as an escape from the contraptions and distractions of the modern world or as a means for us to commune with the wildness inside us, but for him it was a 'base of resistance to centralized domination...a refuge from excessive industrialism...from authoritarian government, from political oppression'. For Abbey the West, with its vast untrammelled space, had a political dimension, albeit one that he was often in conflict with. He excoriated human beings for contributing to overpopulation and yet went on to father five children. He loved nature and yet took pleasure in throwing beer cans from his car as he drove along the highway – allegedly to measure distance. He was open-minded, and yet there are streaks of racism in his writing, particularly when it comes to Mexican immigrants. His 1975 novel *The Monkey Wrench Gang* was one of the main inspirations behind the founding in 1979 of Earth First!, the activist group dedicated to defending 'Mother Earth'. Whatever one thinks about Abbey's writings and legacy, one thing is clear: he believed in the primacy of wilderness and its place in combating the onslaught of a 'Brave New World'.

The West is one of the last places on Earth where thoughts around wilderness as inoculation against the darker forces of modernity are still in the ether, in the discourse, in people's decisions to live off the grid, on the land, in the hoop. For the first time in my life, I was beginning to understand the West and its promise, real *and* imagined, of freedom, escape, transcendence, and its promise to turn us from predator to prey.

I gathered the courage to add Finisia as a 'friend' on Facebook. My need to meet her was gaining in urgency. I got an almost immediate response posted publicly onto my timeline which began: 'Why would any stranger want to be my friend when I have a public profile and not even the cops have to spy on it?' The irrational aggression and paranoia in her response made me anxious. Why would the cops be spying on a 61-year-old transgender rewilder? She was not the sweet middle-aged woman with dangly turquoise earrings and a penchant for reading tea leaves that I had been expecting, but an angry, quarrelsome rewilder who travelled on horseback, harvesting roots while replanting the wild gardens of the West – and she was looking for a fight. After a short volley of private Facebook messages, she softened and finally agreed to meet me near the town of Frenchglen, Oregon (population 12).

The irony of being on Facebook was not lost on Finisia. It was her one concession to modernity and technology, the only way for her to keep in touch with people. She was eager for others to join her and if she went offline completely, no one would be able to find her. In *Growing Up in Occupied America*, the book she self-published in 2010, she writes, 'I look at my industrial addictions, from horseshoe to shoe goo. I'm not saying I'm guiltless. I am saying my participation with it breaks my heart to shivers. So, I am looking for a way of life I don't have to be ashamed of.'

I was convinced I would crash on the ten-hour trip from Missoula to Frenchglen. I'd only been on a highway once and it was a terrible experience. I felt myself losing control when I went over 45 miles an hour, which meant I ended up being tailgated by angry motorists. The image I'd always had of myself as an absolutely terrible driver had been borne out. Then Jason agreed to drive me and so of course Eve had to come along. Her idea of hell was ten hours in a car under a burning sun. Jason tried to sweeten it with the fact that he had arranged for us to go to a picnic in Idaho half way through the drive.

'A picnic?' Eve perked up.

'Yes, in Kamiah, Idaho. There'll be other kids there, too.'

I looked at him, confused. Who were these friends of ours with kids in Idaho he had been keeping secret? 'I've been invited to a "Three Percenters" picnic,' he told me. I knew he'd been in touch with them and was thinking of making a film about the Patriot movement, the groups of people who, like the Bundys, were anti-government and followed the Constitution to the letter.

The Three Percenters (otherwise spelled '3%ers', 'III%ers' or 'Threepers') believe in the sacredness of the American Constitution. On their official website – and it is important to distinguish the 'original' Three Percenters from imitation groups who they say are violent and do not represent them – they describe themselves as 'a national organization made up of patriotic citizens who love their country, their freedoms, and their liberty'. They are 'committed to standing against and exposing corruption and injustice'. The history behind their name stems from their belief that during the British colonization of North America, in the 1700s, only three per cent of Americans actually fought against the British Empire. According to the Three Percenters, many of these Americans who were against colonial rule from Britain

> banded together to push an ideology they all shared. This ideology identified and acknowledged that every person has from birth certain rights. These are not granted by any authority other than their Creator. The limitation or denial of these rights is defined as tyranny and oppression.

The people who were on call to fight this tyranny – the group making up roughly three per cent of the population – were called Minutemen. They would 'meet, train, and prepare to defend themselves, their family, and their townships from an ever encroaching empire'. Today, the Threepers see themselves as the descendants of the Minutemen, 'the last defense to protect the citizens of the United States if there ever comes a day when our government takes up arms against the American people'.

It would be facile – and dangerous – to dismiss this organization and its complex background for being ridiculous. Movements like these are growing. Although seemingly at the opposite end of the political spectrum from the 'Liberal snowflakes' they dismiss in chat rooms, the Three Percenters bizarrely intersect in some places with the Left. They are against Big Agriculture and the Monsanto-made pesticides. Like many on the Left, they do not trust Big Pharma and its 'sinister' vaccination programmes. They are sympathetic to homeopathy, organic farming and generally making do and mending. The overlaps between them and those on the Left who run off into the woods to build their own houses and churn their own butter are plentiful. But the overlaps stop when it comes to guns and tolerance and, for some of them, religion. The Three Percenters claim not to be racist, but many patriotic organizations hide a deep-seated anti-Muslim, anti-Semitic and white supremacist agenda behind this claim. The Three Percenters of Idaho sent people to the Malheur Wildlife Refuge in support of the Bundys. On their website, whenever Barack Obama got a mention (and he did fairly often), his middle name 'Hussein' was always included.

Anyone can join the Three Percenters. There is no fee, no induction ceremony. All you have to do is take the Three Percenter Oath:

1. I will NOT obey orders to disarm the American people

2. I will NOT obey orders to conduct warrant-less searches of the American people

3. I will NOT obey orders to detain American citizens as 'unlawful enemy combatants' or to subject them to military tribunal

4. I will NOT obey orders to impose martial law or a 'state of emergency' on a state.

5. I will NOT obey orders to invade and subjugate any state that asserts its sovereignty

6. I will NOT obey any order to blockade American cities, thus turning them into giant concentration camps

7. I will NOT obey any order to force American citizens into any form of detention camps under any pretext

8. I will NOT obey orders to assist or support the use of any foreign troops on U.S. soil against the American people to 'keep the peace' or to 'maintain control'

9. I will NOT obey any orders to confiscate the property of the American people, including food and other essential supplies

10. I will NOT obey any orders which infringe on the right of the people to free speech, to peaceably assemble, and to petition their government for a redress of grievances

Remember, we do not seek after violence, but if violence is ever called for, WE are the III% of the population that will stand and fight against a tyranny.

What was with the camps? This is where I started to worry. There appeared to be a vivid streak of paranoia around the government taking away their rights – particularly the right to own, buy and trade firearms. After Barack Obama was elected in 2008, their paranoia skyrocketed. With the Trump administration in power, they seem more vocal, more confident.

On the morning of our trip, the temperature was hovering around 30 degrees, and the Montana sky was that expansive, cloudless, deep blue. Eve had spent the day running the children's portion of the Missoula marathon. We met her at the finish line and bundled her into the car as if we were kidnapping her. She was red-faced and hot. Poor kid was miserable as she would have liked to hang out with her friends after the run. We placated her with an ice-cream from the Big Dipper on Missoula's 'Hip Strip'.

'Are you filming at this picnic?' she asked Jason.

'No, just meeting the people who run this militia group. They want me to introduce myself and tell them all about why I am there.'

'You didn't tell me that!' I said.

He laughed.

From the back seat we heard, 'What if they don't like your speech and they kill you?'

Jason explained that although the Threepers would be armed, they weren't going to kill anyone. As he was talking, we passed a sign reading 'Antlers Galore!' and another saying, 'Talk to me, God'. Now we were in Idaho, driving through thick forests and craggy, chaotic mountains, past turnoffs for hot springs and gushing rivers. We didn't stop because .we wanted to get to Kamiah (population 1,300) in time to find a motel and a bit of food before it got late. We rolled up to the Clearwater 12 motel, which had a room for 59 bucks, and we found a restaurant that would make me a bean burger.

The meeting the next day wasn't until one o'clock so we spent the morning wandering around town. Kamiah had a wide main street lined with low buildings. With their false fronts, their balconies and fussy gables, they gave off that outpost vibe – like something from a western. There was a cuteness to the town. Many of the signs were written in that Playbill font reminiscent of 'WANTED' posters and ads for Rodeos. The sign for the pizza restaurant exclaimed, 'We toss'em, they're awesome!' There was one dentist in town and twenty churches. In the background you could see the edge of the four-million-acre Nez Perce-Clearwater National Forest – a reminder that this had once been a very different place.

We found the picnic under a gazebo in a park right in the centre of Kamiah. There were maybe forty people of all ages standing around, chatting. Most of the adults were armed and wearing T-shirts with the Three Percenters logo. Almost everybody had a copy of the Constitution sticking out of their back pockets, next to their holsters. A table under a canopy was laden with burgers, bowls of potato chips, condiments and a pile of store-bought desserts. Eve and I tentatively grazed while Jason said hello to the two organizers, Brandon Curtiss and his partner Brooke Agresta.

Brooke was the first to stand up and speak to the crowd. She was smart and quick. I wouldn't want to be in an argument with her. Much of what she said made sense but I had read enough about the Three Percenters of Idaho to know that what we were seeing here was not the whole story. There were speeches about how they saw themselves moving into the future and how they could improve their image, and also about the volunteering and social work they do. They are keen to let people know they are ready to help with relief efforts when natural disasters strike.

Eve was bored. She headed to a nearby playground but didn't want to be on her own. While watching her climb a large metal train in the playground, I missed Jason's speech. I had wanted to see the Three Percenters' reaction, which Jason later told me was polite and friendly. I had returned to the meeting by the time the formalities were over and found myself talking to a Native American member of the group. I asked him a question no one had ever been able to answer for me.

'All these people I meet who are filling their bunkers for the Apocalypse, what will happen when they run out of oil?'

'Aha,' he said as if he had been waiting for someone to ask him this for years. 'I'm working on that one!' He told me he was growing crops of soy so he could make his own bio-fuel. His main concern, like mine, was the environment. I had not been expecting this. He also refuted the claim that the Three Percenters were racist. His membership was a case in point. He found them tolerant and very accepting. Just like everything in the American West, it was more complicated than it seemed.

I had found it difficult speaking to the picnickers with their visible firearms not because I was worried they would use them, but because the dialogue felt so loaded. And with a bored eight-year-old hanging off my arm, it was hard to concentrate. Eve was getting

fidgety so I took her for a stroll through Kamiah and left Jason to mingle. As we passed the Hub Bar and Grill on Main Street with its metallic Harley Davidson sign, my thoughts turned to Finisia. She would give me answers. Eve and I were still walking the streets under a very hot sun, looking in shop windows, when Jason found us. We got in the car and within four hours we were driving through the scrubby, barren deserts of eastern Oregon.

I found it impossible to drive through this landscape without thinking about Abbey's *Desert Solitaire*: 'Where is the heart of the desert?' he asks, only to conclude that deserts have none. The desert for Abbey was 'completely passive, acted upon but never acting, the desert lies there like the bare skeleton of Being, spare, sparse, austere'. The desert 'says nothing', he wrote. But I felt this desolation we were driving through was shouting at me. I could see it mouthing the words, but I simply couldn't make them out. I didn't speak the language of the desert. It was not silent; I was deaf.

We were driving down route 205 south of Burns, Oregon. The dry ochre ground was dotted with minty-green sagebrush. Mirage-like buttes were rising and falling in the distance. We were a stone's throw from the Malheur Wildlife Refuge, where the Bundy clan and their anti-government friends (some from the Idaho Three Percenters) had only just been expelled from their forty-one-day occupation.

Resistance to a central government, often in the form of violence, is the essence of the myth of the Western Frontier. Things have changed very little in the 120 years since Frederick Jackson Turner penned his essay about the closing of this Frontier and the mindset that went with it.

Eve noticed the horses first, and then the lean-to along the side of the road, next to a wooden fence and a collapsing outhouse. Frenchglen sits in a lush, grassy valley irrigated by small, meandering canals. It was an oasis in the eastern Oregon desert. A dark green tarp was stretched across six poles at waist height. Eight horses stood in a home-made paddock with a single electric wire wrapped around the makeshift corral to keep them from running away. Jason parked up as Finisia emerged from under her tarp to greet us.

She was dressed in her trademark wide buckskin skirt, large-brimmed leather hat, and – despite the June heat – a thin wool sweater. Her long uncombed hair spread across her shoulders, giving her the air of a nineteenth-century gunslinger from a travelling Wild West roadshow – she could have been the sharpshooting, travelling-show markswoman Annie Oakley's wilder older sister. The lines on her weatherworn face had the detail of a Dorothea Lange photo. She stuck her roll-up in her mouth to shake my hand.

As soon as I said 'Hello,' she started immediately, in

a deep-voiced and very fast delivery, to tell me about my domestication.

'The problem with you is that even your internal flora have been domesticated! It takes forty to fifty days to acclimatize to a wild food diet and some people begin to starve in that time.'

She was not interested in the social niceties of small talk. This could have been the result of thirty years of solitude on the hoop, or simply because Finisia wanted, above all else, to get her message across: the Earth is dying and those of us who do not throw off our domestication are responsible for its death.

The type of slow, painful starvation I would experience if I were to live Finisia's hunter-gatherer life could be prevented by the administration of 'warm, spring bear poop' as a high colonic enema.

'How do you administer it?' I asked.

'You know, with one of those rubber whoopedy-doo things,' she said, drawing a roller-coaster shape in the air with her finger. Those of us who are domesticated may suffer a fever from such an enema, but once that has passed and we have survived, our insides would be 'rewilded' and we would achieve 'food freedom'. Until then, I remained an 'ecocidal whore of Babylon' – 'Babylon' being her name for civilization.

A soft-spoken figure clad in buckskin appeared. This was Michael Ridge, who had been travelling with Finisia for many months. Handsome, in his early

twenties, Michael had the limpid blue eyes, the long hair and the slender features of a prophet. His jaw wore a fresh, red gash. We shook hands and he wandered off with the horseshoes I had brought at Finisia's request to start shoeing up their smallest packhorse. He and Finisia were curt with each other and she told me he had royally pissed her off. Something to do with a horse, his ex-girlfriend who had been with them until recently, and some expensive chains they had lost. The story had too many detours for me to follow.

The afternoon sun was coming down hard. Finisia invited me into the shade of her tarp. Jason and Eve headed off into Burns to give me some time alone with her. I took a seat on her thin sleeping mat while she sat cross-legged across from me. In the distance a few bald, mustard-coloured dollops of earth rose from the foothills of the Steen Mountains. Scattered around us were the necessities of a migratory life in the American West: a large pouch of tobacco, rolling papers, lighter, bug spray, knife, spade, eight small potatoes, a bag of coffee, a Mason jar of preserved buffalo meat (from Buffalo Bridge, she told me), a jar of jalapeños, a cook-stove, a finger piano, some blankets and a drum made of animal skin, wood and feathers.

Finisia pointed out that one of the poles holding up the tarp is a titanium rod. 'I can lift all kinds of rocks out here with that and chase my roots,' she said, meaning the biscuitroot or lomatium, the staple food that

Native Americans have been living on for thousands of years, which was also her mainstay. 'If it gets hit with lightning out here, it explodes and I turn into a pink mist,' she said with an unexpected Irish-sounding lilt. At times her voice goes all cigarette-tinged Bette Davis. Her cackle lasts several seconds. She identifies as Irish-American but was partly raised by Native Americans. It was at her stepmother's place on an Indian reservation near Coeur d'Alene, Idaho that her real education began at the knee of Native elders, whom she referred to as her 'other Grandmothers'.

In *Growing Up in Occupied America*, she writes

> They taught me how to beat the rice of Benewah Lake...they taught me how to pick the seed pods of the yellow pond lilies, they taught me how to dig biscuitroot...My brown skinned Grandfathers talked of Sacred Hoops that "the people used to live on until the whites came and killed us and forced us onto reservations to be assimilated or die." They took us Salmon fishing, they mourned for the old days and old ways. My brown skinned Grandmothers and Grandfathers taught me we are living in Occupied America.

The sun disappeared behind the Steens, throwing a grey-blue light onto the vast landscape. The mosquitoes started buzzing, and every now and then I heard the stomp of a horse's foot and the swish of a tail swatting the bugs away. Our conversation turned to the Bundys and the occupiers of the Malheur Wildlife Refuge, only a few miles from where we were sitting.

'When I pick the piñon nuts in Nevada, I'm the felon! But the forests up here are dying and they're busy trying to kill it as fast as it can grow because it's interfering with the goddam grazing of a cow!' Finisia started to cry and wiped her eyes with the back of her hands before going on. 'So climate change has got the ponderosa forests dying and burning, the lodgepole forests are dying and burning, and ninety per cent of those forests will be dead and completely gone in ten years. That's a fact. They're never coming back. But I'm hauling the piñon seeds from Nevada and I'm the criminal. I'm the outlaw. I'm under indictment with Homeland Security as an extremist.'

She reached over and pulled a piece of paper from a beaded buckskin bag. It was the manifesto she wrote in jail, handed to the courthouse and sent to a friend to disseminate after she was locked up in Idaho in 2008 for planting seeds on public lands. I could just about read it in the fading light:

I would like it to be known that the reasoning in my violations is a deliberate act of civil disobedience....
I have been violating US Government treaties...
by engaging in that Indigenous life way that was

disallowed to force the Native onto reservations and to complete the genocide of that life way.

I find life in this civilized way unconscionable and immoral! I find myself without freedom of conscience in it. For twenty-five years I have been planting back the native food flowers of lomatium, cymopterus, bitterroot, yampa, lilies, and berries without permit on public lands . . . This is my duty to God and to Earth. I have been doing this secretly, knowing that I am a violator of statute, code and treaty . . .

This hoop in the west is the last place on Earth where it is even possible to live in that symbiotic way. All over the Earth this aboriginal planting has been done away with. The Earth has been made to be like a girdled tree and here in my home in the west is the last small ribbon of bark . . .

I am sick at heart to have sneaked around like a criminal for 25 years doing this.

There is much of the nineteenth-century, mountainman outlaw in Finisia with her buckskin, her jail time, her horses, rifles and foul mouth, but the model she most identifies with is the hunter-gatherer, the original inhabitants and stewards of this land.

For Finisia, like many rewilders, the rot of civilization began with agriculture. Once we became sedentary and started storing our food rather than going out to find it, we became landowners. Our gaze shifted from seeing land as belonging to all people to seeing it as something to be owned and exploited. Once grain was stored, it could be taxed. It became a commodity. The West is full of people trying to escape dependence on Big Agriculture, Big Oil and Big Government. For some, living sustainably consists of incremental urban rewilding; for others it is living off-grid, by the light of home-made candles in tiny solar-powered homes. Finisia's radical rewilding approach is the most extreme, the most severe, the most committed. For her, the life of the hunter-gatherer is the only climate-change-proof one.

'I'll be watching the superstorms from my cave while the rest of you are blown to pieces,' she laughed.

Finisia, of course, shuns the whole Paleo movement as a fad and an example of the hypocrisy practised by the hipster hunter-gatherer types who buy their pre-packaged Paleo Diet snacks from Whole Foods in Portland, Austin and Seattle. Finisia also sees many ancestral skills gatherings as 'mere fashion'. At such gatherings you can learn to braintan hides, make your own shoes, create fire with friction, do some gourd crafting or join 'gratitude centered mead circles'. Finisia would like more people to join her on the hoop, replanting the wild gardens rather than play make-believe caveman at festivals.

Life on the hoop was a way for Finisia to live according to her conscience – not as a way to lose weight or brighten her smile or expand her ancestral skill set. When I asked her about groups such as the Rewild Portland non-profit set up around fifteen years ago by Peter Michael Bauer as a way of bringing ancestral skills to city-dwellers, Finisia threw her hands in the air. 'Everything they have, they got from me!' she exclaimed. 'I have not found people to live on the hoop with me. But I'm a fashion designer for terracidals who want to look like beautiful motherfuckers while maintaining a life in terracide. And I have had success in that in the thousands!'

Bauer's incremental approach is at odds with Finisia's. A few years ago, he spent three days on the hoop with her and described it to me as like being next to a volcano: 'You just never knew when she might blow.' He also told me a story which shed light on the difference between Finisia's all-or-nothing way of doing things and his slower, gentler manner of moving society towards sustainability. On one of the chat rooms he managed as part of his Rewild Portland online community, a father had posted a note about taking an afternoon off work so he could go foraging for the first time for dandelion greens with his young son. Finisia commented on his post to say that an afternoon was bullshit. The guy needed to quit his job and devote himself to rewilding or face the fact that he was a worthless ecocidal. Peter blocked Finisia from the group after that outburst. It's not that he totally disagrees with her, but he feels the best way to get people engaged is to allow them to find their way into rewilding in their own time. Her aggression, he thought, was turning people off from doing what little they could for the planet.

Finisia became livid when she recounted to me how a couple had recently come to her to bless their baby. 'Why would I want to bless another terracidal?' she asked. Like Edward Abbey, Finisia believes overpopulation to be one of the biggest environmental problems we face, yet one we won't confront. However, unlike Abbey, Finisia has not produced five little 'terracidals' of her own. When I put to her that there must be lots of people seeking a true path, looking for meaning, and willing to travel the hoop with her apart from the odd visitor like me, Finisia whirled her arms through the empty air around us.

'Where are they?' she asked, tears welling up again.

'There's Michael,' I said.

There had been others with her recently, too. Friends of Michael's who according to Finisia 'fucked up' and almost got her horses killed. From what she told me, I sensed that of the people who have spent time on the hoop with her, some go back to 'civ' and carry on replanting as much as their lives will allow, while others are lost souls. They aren't particularly dedicated to the hoop but don't have anywhere else they need to be.

Michael was sitting quietly on a folding canvas chair. He had a terrible headache. I asked him if he ever got hungry out there in the wild and he replied that yes, he was often hungry. It was hard work living this way, and dangerous. You had to look after your horses because you relied on them, you needed water and you needed to know how to cross difficult terrain. There are fences, there is barbed wire, there are roads you have to take sometimes when you can't cross certain ground because of barriers. Drivers are not used to seeing a pack string – animals tied together – and the horses can get spooked. In fact, just knowing how to tie a pack string is an art. Very few people have the strength to live like this anymore. It is a criminal offence to plant or harvest on federal lands or stay in one place for more than fourteen days, which makes this way of life illegal as well. Stewarding the Earth in a sustainable way means breaking the law. You cannot afford to be ill or get hurt on the hoop as your physical strength and your wits are indispensable. And then of course there is the solitude, the big empty space, where, as Wallace Stegner wrote,

People are few and distant, under a great sky that is alternately serene and furious, exposed to sun from four in the morning till nine at night, and to a wind that never seems to rest—there is something about exposure to that big country that not only tells an individual how small he is, but steadily tells him who he is.

Few of us would survive both the physical and the existential challenges.

I asked about winter camp because Finisia was trying to find a spot from 'Samhain to Beltane' (translated from the Pagan as: from 'Halloween to Easter') for her horses and for herself. The people behind Burning Man had just bought more land in Nevada, and Finisia was going to offer them some creative planting – painting the Mona Lisa in the desert in biscuitroot – in return for a place to live over the winter. But it wasn't looking hopeful. Now that they'd gone corporate and were catering to the Tech Bros flying in by helicopter, and providing wealthy festival-goers with air-conditioned trailers and waiting staff, she wasn't optimistic that her brand of grassroots rewilding would be of interest to them. When I asked Finisia about how she had been getting through winters, she did admit to getting food stamps from the government, and I could see from her face that it pained her to the core. She felt that if there were enough people doing the hoop and planting and gathering, she wouldn't have to rely on the government.

Jason and Eve returned. They were hungry and asked if there was anything we wanted from Burns, the town nearest to Fin's camp. Finisia and Michael asked for burgers. 'But won't that undo your wild digestions?' I asked. Apparently it was OK once in a while to stray. Burgers were not their only concession to the modern world. They posted memes about environmentalism on Facebook regularly. The only way Finisia could keep in touch with people was when she got within reach of WiFi, which wasn't too often. She had rigged up a way to charge her old slider phone with a portable solar panel.

Once Jason and Eve headed back into Burns, Finisia told me how our ecocidal ways would often send her spiralling into some very dark places.

'Do you ever think about ending it all?' I tentatively asked.

'I'd sooner kill you than kill myself,' she shot back. 'You're the problem. Not me!'

We talked until the black sky had stretched from east to west, dotted with pulsing white stars. Jason and Eve returned with supper. Michael looked tired. Finisia ate her burger and then sang some songs in Shoshone. I didn't want to overstay my visit so I picked up my notebook and started gathering my things. But before leaving, I asked Michael how he'd got the gash on his chin: 'Finisia got mad at me. We had a fist fight,' he said. Neither of them would go into detail.

We left Finisia under her tarp and Michael sitting on a chair in the dark smoking a roll-up. It was late when we got to what had been described online as a 'cabin' in the 'Steens Mountain Resort'. It turned out to be a mobile home smelling of plastic and bedbug spray. I spent the next couple of hours killing the mosquitoes that had rushed in when we opened the flimsy door.

When we arrived at Fin's camp the following morning, she was up and ready for the day. I spotted my copy of her book *Growing Up in Occupied America*, which I had accidentally left with her. She caught my eye line and said, 'There are some things I want to talk to you about.' My copy of *Growing Up* was full of marginalia. My mind scrolled through some of my comments. None were unkind, but I felt sick nevertheless. She then zeroed in on a passage I had circled and underlined:

> I had two choices, suicide or wolfman. . . . I tried and failed suicide. . . . Sexual mutilation seemed a compromise. I knew if to keep the innocence of children safe, I chose this route, I would be outcast forever. . . . I chose it anyhow. For my own reasons I chose it.

'It's not a "fear of my manhood"!' she told me, pointing to where I had scrawled this in the margins. 'You don't understand.'

She patted the mat under her tarp. I hunched under

the low roof and we took our places across from each other. A spliff was wedged between her ring and middle fingers. She alternated drags on her joint with drags on a roll-up while she squinted out at the mountains, golden brown under the bright sun. The only sound was the swoosh of the horses' tails in the long grass and their intermittent stomping.

Finally Finisia took a deep breath. 'Every transition requires more than one cause. I could always see that no child would ever be mine. That dick was just waitin' for a trap. Like a mouse waitin' for a trap, my dick would put me in slavery forever. And for what? For not even having a family. For nothing. Remember, I was growing up at a time where I could see males being culled in war, they had a draft system and they were just waiting to kill me. Even as a child I said, "Fucking women aren't dying that way. I wish I was a goddam woman."'

Finisia paused and waited for a few tears to fall. She took a deep drag from her cigarette and her joint before speaking again. 'I grew up watching the body count,' she said wiping her eyes. 'The reality at nine years old is that you're already fucked. And I'm waitin' my turn to go to Vietnam but they quit that shit just before I got eligible.'

I was watching her handsome, broad face, following the smoke curl up and disappear. Her cheeks were wet with tears.

'And then you know I'm out there sexualized the way I was,' she paused, and I knew she was referring to the section in her book in which she outlined her sexual initiation when she was twelve years old at the hands of an abuser, whom she called Roy D' Raper. Roy worked with her brother baling hay and lived with her family. 'When he came home after dinner,' Finisia wrote,

> he would throw me a quarter and ask me to rub his back in my bed. I was glad to do it. . . . This had become a comfortable ritual, when one night Roy D' Raper rolled over and exposed me to the largest penis I had ever seen. It was really the first time I'd seen an erection on anyone. He looked at me with such longing; it almost looked like love. He said I did that to him. I sure didn't know quite what he meant. Well, he jacked off while I watched; I sure couldn't keep my eyes away. I never saw anything like this in all my days.

Finisia was confused by this 'mysterious power' she seemed to wield over Roy – a power which until then she had not been aware of. This carried on with Finisia rubbing his back, Roy rolling over, masturbating, and then falling asleep next to her.

> This became our new ritual, until one night he asked me to touch it, he asked me if I wanted to. Well yes

I wanted to. . . . He told me what to do and did the same for me . . . I asked him why I didn't make a mess like him. He said I was too young to, that's all, and I would grow up.

Roy went off to Vietnam leaving her with a 'new toy' in exchange for her 'innocence'. She also started feeling guilty and wondering if she might be gay. Then 'news came back from Germany. Roy was coming home. A thing called a "Bouncing Betty" came up, and among other damage, separated Roy from his manhood in a permanent way.' She admitted to feeling confused, maybe a bit avenged but what really stayed with her were the feelings of being both 'sexualized and feminized'. She thought her insides and outside should match up and now they didn't. 'I didn't know anything about sex until Roy, and after him, what I knew was all wrong for what I was plumbed for, so I started praying to God.'

Finisia's internal and sexual confusion carried on after that. She started getting into trouble, stealing, doing drugs. She tried to blow up her high school, got locked up, got fostered out, started an underground newspaper. She hitchhiked around the country and as her hair grew, 'catching a ride got easier'. I've seen photos of Finisia from when she was a young man. She looked like a surfer dude, all wispy hair, toned chest and a big, broad smile. While hitchhiking she got raped and this, she said, tore out what was left of her 'man soul and replaced it with a woman one'. She hated her penis and the compulsion it wanted to exercise over her. This was when she moved to Point Dume, just off the Pacific Coast Highway, and dug herself a cave six metres straight up a rock face with her bare hands and feet. Bob Dylan was building his house in nearby Malibu at the time. They met once, she told me, when he showed up at her cave to make sure his son wasn't hanging out with her. She laughed telling the story. Here she lived on seaweed, ate raw mussels right off the rocks. When she got her cave 'upholstered like a giant pussy', she told everyone she had been born from it, 'the child of the Earth and Sea'. People started to visit. 'I became famous on that beach,' she wrote. 'I had fourteen-year-old virgins naked, selling Lucky beer in a bottle to the lecherous crowd. We smoked pot and did L.S.D.... I got real acquainted with my unconscious mind.'

Finisia looked straight at me fixing me in the eye. 'You gotta understand the person I was at that time. I'm being passed around by everyone who wants a diddle, all over Hollywood.' She paused, taking a moment to stare out into the distance. 'So, this beautiful French woman kept coming down and visiting. Gorgeous thing. She came down with her three kids. Her daughter, the oldest, was fifteen, all the way down to a nine-year-old son. And they'd come out and visit. One day she invites me to her house. I go to her house and of course we're diddling away and as soon as she leaves off, her fifteen-year-old daughter comes in, and then the other kids...' Her voice dropped. I thought she might start crying again, but she carried on, 'Crazy stuff was going on all weekend. You know, when I left there I felt like I had a monster between my legs that I needed to kill. I am a *fucking white man*.' She half-whispered this last sentence as if it were the most improbable truth, still shocking to her. She paused again and rolled a cigarette while more tears fell. 'There were myriad things all adding up to just one small venue for my escape. That's what it was. It was all cumulative and yet everybody wants just one reason. Transitions require many reasons. Believe me. Just because you know you are killing the Earth is no reason for you to quit. None. That kind of transition would require many reasons. It's not simple.'

We sat in silence, which was the only response to such an outpouring. A difficult story, but one that further revealed her complex humanity to me, the sacrifices she has made to save her soul. She carried on smoking. I watched. I had no words, no questions. I felt strangely close to her.

Eventually she said, 'So, wanna do some digging?'

We crawled out from under the tarp and looked for Jason and Eve who were chatting to Michael as he checked his horse's new shoes. Eve was transfixed.

The story of Finisia's physical transition, her migratory life, her need to be out here in the wilderness – these were all the necessities to her survival, her conscience, her psyche. We drove off in search of biscuitroot. Finisia knew this land and the roads that stretched out before us better than anyone. She knew it in that way some people know their child's sleeping face or their lover's body. She knew what it needed, she knew how to tend it, how to derive joy from it, and she wanted to share it.

When Finisia was still living in her cave she met a man called Max Miller and they started dating. 'Max was an atheist Jew. Max was a social engineer. Max had interesting pictures of himself with Presidents. He had done advertising. He had done public relations,' she wrote in *Growing Up in Occupied America*. He was also born in 1911 – forty-five years before Finisia. He 'paved her way into womanhood', she told me, adding that she really loved him. Still did. He had saved her life by paying for her operation. After her transition, Max felt responsible for her welfare. His favourite film at the time was *My Fair Lady*, which Finisia found equally funny and telling. They were married by someone who turned her house into a chapel for the day. A white bedspread draped over the TV acted as the pulpit. Max hated her smoking and so months after their wedding, Finisia went out into the woods to cure her addiction to cigarettes. She went cold turkey. It worked, but she also had a religious experience which convinced her that she could no longer ignore her Christian faith. She cried as she walked home. When she got there, she told Max that she no longer smoked.

He said, 'Right.'

She also told Max, 'I think I'm a Christian.'

He said, 'Bullshit.'

'No,' she said, 'I think I am.'

Max's response was to immediately divorce her. After signing the papers, Finisia walked out of their house and out of Los Angeles with a sleeping bag, the clothes she was wearing and a change of underwear and socks. It was August 1984 and she was twenty-seven years old. She walked for a year. When her pack got to weighing thirty-five kilos, she decided she needed a horse. She worked so she could buy two. Her shift from a sedentary life to a nomadic one wasn't instantaneous. She was spending more time on reservations and in the backcountry where she was drying fruit, digging roots, learning to live 'outside of Babylon'. It got so she and her horses were more comfortable in the wild than in cities. She had tragedies on her travels. Lovers were killed. She was shot in the foot. But she carried on. Eventually she got a wagon which she painted with 'PULLING FOR CHRIST ACROSS AMERICA'. On the road in Florida, her dog Tank got eaten by an alligator. She carried on. This was the beginning of her life on the hoop.

After driving for maybe forty minutes, we stopped. The whole way, Finisia had been screwing her eyes up at the scrubby tufts of sagebrush, looking for the pale green lacy tops of the biscuitroot plant. She could see what most of us could not. This land was certainly not passive, nor silent. The invisible heartbeat – the one that Edward Abbey found difficult to hear – kept Finisia company, drove her on, kept her alive. We stopped and walked into the desert a few times, but found nothing. We drove some more and then got out of the car again and walked for maybe a quarter of an hour until the hot sun had us sweating. We nibbled on wild garlic and onions as we went. Finisia was becoming anxious as she wasn't finding any lomatium. Their roots are traditionally dried and pounded into flour and made into cakes that can last for months, which is perfect for hoop life, but Finisia preferred to sauté them fresh in oil with wild garlic.

We made our way to a tree in the distance and sat in its shade for several minutes. Finisia rolled a joint and began singing a mournful Shoshone song called 'Hone Jon'. It was about a peaceable spirit that moves with us. As soon as we got up and began walking again, Finisia found some biscuitroot. We were elated. The atmosphere lifted. I could see so much life around us. So many roots diving into the darkness under the ground. Finisia showed Jason and me how to dig one up, gently, without harming it. She took extra care with Eve. She was sweet and patient with her. As you dig the root, its seeds fall, ready to be replanted – a perfect symbiotic

circle. The roots looked like thin, pale carrots. I put a few in my pocket to cook later.

'There's another song in Shoshone about yampa,' she said when we got back to her camp. 'When its seed is ready to plant, the root has already shrivelled. Very tricky for food that way. So, if you really want it around, you have to leave a whole bunch of it undug and gather its seed and plant it deliberately. It acts like a domesticate. It is our pet, the song says. You have to give it extra attention.' Her voice was low and focused, as if she were talking about a favourite child.

We were standing next to her tarp preparing to say goodbye. Michael was packing up to leave. I wasn't sure if this was to do with their fight, but I sensed he wanted to branch out on his own.

'Write your piece as a grand narrative,' she instructed me. 'Forget your fucking essays, write my story as fiction, baby.'

Finisia and I hugged. I felt bereft at leaving her alone to plant these wild gardens. She was so very alone in this vast landscape.

When I got home to my bungalow and started unpacking, I opened her book. Inside the front cover she had written: 'With understanding comes brevity; with wisdom comes sorrow. Sure ya wanna step? Sounds like a slippery slope to me.'

When I was visiting Buffalo Bridge, I asked Josh if he knew Peter Michael Bauer from his years in Portland. 'You'll find nothing there,' he replied. As someone who has lived in cities my entire life, I wanted to see whether there might be a path towards a more sustainable future for us 'civilized' folk who like to walk to art house cinemas and bookshops. I found a phone number for Peter online and left a rambling message. I was somewhat in awe of him: he'd been writing and teaching about rewilding for over ten years. His 2008 collection of essays *Rewild or Die*, written under the name Urban Scout, had been recently updated and republished. As part of his non-profit organization Rewild Portland, he and others taught earth-based skills ranging from friction fire and carving tools out of bone to felt-making and pottery. His online presence was dizzying: there were essays, forums, classes and podcasts.

He returned my call the same day and I was surprised at the levity in his voice. Despite being someone who worried about melting ice caps, species decimation and the degradation of soil and water, Peter didn't exhibit the earnestness of the typical eco-warrior. In an interview I found online, he was asked why he chose to live in a large city when he cared so much about planting native seeds and living a life that incorporated the qualities of the hunter-gatherer. His response was simple, 'Because I *like* people.'

On his website he was advertising a day of Himalayan blackberry basket-weaving. 'Over the period of European colonization of North America,' he wrote,

> this plant has become a serious invasive. Its rigorous growth and thorny vines makes it a pain to remove. Its sweet and delicious berries are eaten by many animals, thus spreading its seed quickly and efficiently. We are happy to say that we have found a use for this plant (other than eating the berries) that will encourage more of its removal: its strong and durable bark provides a great material for weaving!

Before clicking the 'buy' button, I noted the things I was supposed to bring to the course: gardening gloves, shears, an awl, an axe and 'Paleo snacks to share'.

I chose the 'coil basket' option rather than the 'sun visor'. A woven Himalayan blackberry sun visor might send me tumbling into the world of *Portlandia*.

★ ★ ★

On my way to Portland from Missoula, I changed planes at Salt Lake City, a large airport which jolted me out of my quiet Montana life. So many people, so many *loud* people. I was no longer used to crowds. A mother and daughter combo in matching pink pork pie hats sat across from me in the waiting area. The mother was pregnant and wore a one-shouldered T-shirt that read: WILD ONE. The girl, who was maybe five, wore heart-shaped Lolita sunglasses. There was a lot of aggressive gum chewing.

Once I landed in Portland I took a train and then a bus to my Airbnb. Two guys walked past me as I rolled my suitcase along the sidewalk. They were going for that late nineteenth-century saloon-owner look: the slicked back hair, the bushy beards, the highly polished brogues, the sleeve garters. One guy said to the other: 'Who knows where the nose hair stops and the moustache begins?'

The next morning, I took a bus to the park where the basket-weaving class was being held. I tried to ignore the nugget of guilt in the pit of my stomach stemming from the non-Paleo hummus and bread sticks I was bringing with me for lunch. But I had remembered gardening gloves and a wide-brimmed hat to keep the sun off my face. Although it was early June, the temperature as I set out that morning was in the low thirties centigrade. Portland was expecting to hit thirty-eight degrees by midday. Was weaving baskets with invasive species fiddling while Portland burns?

Peter was sitting in the shade of a tree. An older gentleman had arrived early and chatted away while Peter set up. A friendly young woman from Quebec joined us. A couple rolled up on their bikes. It turned out they had gifted each other this class. We all introduced ourselves and I found myself riveted by the tall, thin, female half of this couple. She had a timeless look about her and reminded me of those sepia photos of Isadora Duncan dancing with scarves on lawns. She was a eurythmy therapist, an occupation I had never heard of. It is a Rudolf Steiner technique in which every sound is ascribed a corresponding physical movement. 'P', for instance, is a hard sound, so your hands go to your mouth and then move firmly outwards like an airline hostess pointing out the exits. She demonstrated a few more letters while her partner remained silent.

Peter patiently showed us how to start making our baskets with a small circular piece of wood into which he had pre-drilled holes. This would form the base. We coiled some hardy Scotch broom around it, and then wove strands of the Himalayan blackberry through the Scotch broom. It was one of those boring and repetitive tasks that I am simply not very good at. My mind wanders, my focus shifts, just as it does when I try anything crafty. I don't know if it is the second wave feminist in me, but whenever I am asked to do any kind of job that puts images in my head of women barefoot with babies strapped to their backs, I baulk. I rebel.

After a break for lunch, we returned to our places and formed a circle in the shade. The monotony of the weaving was beginning to have a therapeutic effect. I told myself how good it was to *slow down*. I felt myself giving in to it. A concentrated silence descended as we pulled our strands of blackberry stalks from barrels of water, ran them through our fingers, removing the softened thorns with our thumb nails and then wove them in and out of our coils of Scotch broom. As we worked and the shadows lengthened, I began to appreciate the skill involved. As with knitting, I was hopeless at getting the tension even. My basket was by far the messiest. It was not even remotely pretty. It was the wonky handiwork of a neurotic, domesticated city-dweller. I was reminded of those upsetting photos that were popular when I was a kid which showed the results of webs spun by spiders which had been fed mescaline, caffeine, amphetamines and LSD. The drug-induced webs were a mess and hopeless at catching flies – they were both ugly and non-functional. We admired each other's baskets and swapped tips as we coiled and wove, coiled and wove. Peter quietly made a basket while he recounted why basketry was one of his passions. His very first attempt had become a gift for his mother. Weaving, he told us, was his favourite form of crafting.

★ ★ ★

According to the Mesopotamians, our world started as one big basket when a wicker raft was placed on the oceans by the gods. Dusted with soil, it became our landmass. Ancient Egyptians made special baskets to hold their freshly baked manna or bread. And then there was baby Moses, who bobbed along in a basket through the bulrushes towards his rescue. Every ancient civilization seems to have baskets as a common denominator. For Native Americans – and Peter reminded us we were sitting on land stolen from them – weaving is an art form. Basketry is used to make ceremonial costumes, fishing nets, animal snares and cooking utensils, which are woven so tightly and with such fine reeds that they are waterproof. But Peter taught us something that had never occurred to me: no one has ever been able to mechanize the production of baskets. They are one of the last commodities on Earth to resist the machine in favour of the human hand. I began to see baskets in a completely different light. The process of making them is the same the world over: reeds, which start off as wet, malleable strands, are shaped by human hands and left to dry whether in the Philippines, Bangladesh, India, China, Japan or the United States. You can feel the thrum of fingers even in the baskets on sale in Walmart.

Our group was coalescing. The conversation was flowing, though the male half of the couple remained silent. He was making disturbingly good progress with his basket and I complimented him. He looked sheepish and didn't reply. His partner, the eurythmy specialist, smiled at me, 'He's not very good with compliments,' she said.

It is easy to be cynical about the efforts of a few people on a patch of grass in Portland as they add a few non-essential baskets to the pile of stuff in the world. To some of the rewilders out there, Peter, with his non-profit and his life in the city and his 'urban hunter-gatherer' website, is all talk and no action. And yet, as long as there are cities, there will be people living in them. Peter's is an incremental approach, one that doesn't demand that we give up everything and return to our caves – although I think he is perhaps working towards something along those lines for himself. He is deeply humane and I sense he can't quite bring himself to give up on people.

As five o'clock approached we finished up our weaving. The sun was strong and the air was heavy, almost tropical. I headed back to my Airbnb via a cheap Mexican diner. My stomach felt out of sorts and I was sweating. My landlady had put her air conditioning on for which I was shamefully grateful.

Once in bed under a blanket, I pulled out *Sightlines* by Kathleen Jamie. The John Berger quote on the front had impelled me to pick it up: 'A sorceress of the essay form,' he had called her. Jamie's essay 'La Cueva' described her visit to a cave in Spain:

There was a time – until very recently in the scheme of things – when there were no wild animals, because every animal was wild; and humans were few. Animals, and animal presence over us and around us. Over every horizon, animals. Their skins clothing our skins, their fats in our lamps, their bladders to carry water, meat when we could get it.

Jamie compared Palaeolithic paintings to later ones made by our Neolithic ancestors. The earlier painting of a horse was 'fresh . . . with a single red line the artist has caught the droop of the jaw; another line its neck. . . . Why the animals should appear in deep caves, we don't know. Hallucinations, maybe. Shaman work.' We do know this horse appeared when humans were still nomads, but the later paintings, which are a mere 5,000 years old, were done when we were sedentary farmers. These consist of a 'panel of crazed black hatchings and scores, like combs or rakes'. The tour guide who was shining a light on these paintings said, 'Everyone tries to interpret these marks. Many people say they are calendars but no one knows.' Jamie added: 'Whatever they were, compared to the Palaeolithic animals, these black hatches seem anxious and nervy, as though they addressed new human concerns. To what problems were such markings the solution?'

My lopsided, barely functional basket sat next to my bed. It was the woven equivalent of the anxious, nervy scratchings on the back wall of a cave. Peter and the others, with their evenly woven baskets, bore the calm, even rhythm of the Palaeolithic. But what problems was my basket trying to solve?

I was running late to meet Peter at a café called Anna Bannanas in North Portland. He was patiently waiting for me, wearing a bright green Rewild Portland T-shirt emblazoned with his raccoon logo, a pair of dark trousers, and a wool REI hat he had bought with his dividends years ago. He greeted me warmly, with a hug. His long, dark brown hair escaped in strands along his shoulders. He could have been a pixie or a holy man. An impish Huck Finn dying to go build a raft or a lean-to.

'I always cared for the environment as a child and I always wondered why people couldn't just collectively *not* destroy the environment,' he told me. 'When I was sixteen, I started having philosophical thoughts.' This was when he dropped out of high school and ran away from home in Portland to Tom Brown Junior's Nature Observation, Tracking and Wilderness Survival School in New Jersey to learn ancestral technology. 'I had this urgency,' he said. 'I had this sense that civilization is going to collapse tomorrow and I needed to learn the skills of our ancestors to *live with the Earth*.' He spoke these last four words slowly as if there were a full stop between each one.

'Back then there was the greenhouse effect. But climate change wasn't on the forefront of people's minds and I think that with the hottest days now on record, well, it's pretty obvious to most people who are paying attention that we need to change the way we are living or something bad is going to happen. Something bad has *already* happened all over the world for the last 10,000 years. So the apocalypse has been happening in stages.' He laughed. His sandwich arrived and he thanked the server.

'Climate change is just another symptom of everything that we're doing. The oceans are going to acidify way faster than climate change is going to burn up the planet. There are a lot of things that are happening, you know. Climate change is just one of those things. And it makes me feel terrible.' Again, there was that laugh.

We were getting onto a question that had been an obsession of mine for some time. I was trying to work out how to feel the intense grief at the dying planet and the rapid extinction of species while simultaneously carrying on with a productive life. I had been in mourning for decades. My urge to inhabit and enjoy life was at odds with the story running on a loop in the background: the story that is affecting us all, the one where the planet dies at the end. I asked Peter about this. How he could be upbeat and yet be so aware of the myriad environmental crises?

'There are a lot of different things that help me.

One thing is to just let yourself cry about that stuff and to actually feel the enormity of the problems we are facing. So part of my inspiration behind building a rewilding community in Portland is to be able to share that grief collectively and not have to feel it by myself.'

He went on to tell me of last year's summer camp for kids he ran on the shores of the Willamette River. 'All summer there were salmon dying in droves everywhere. They aren't able to return to spawn because they are dying from the heat.' He paused for several seconds. 'That was the worst experience I have had yet and I imagine that things will just continue to get worse. So, at the end of last summer I got friends together and we went out into the middle of nowhere and we had our own grieving ceremony, I guess you could call it. I didn't feel I could carry the weight of it all by myself, I needed to share it in a collective, safe space.' He looked away from me to the boiling hot pavement and laughed from what sounded like frustration. 'Things are heating up this spring and we'll probably have that as a regular thing. It will have to happen more than once a year. Just to keep the grief flowing and not dwelling. Because the more I dwell on those things, the more I feel paralysed, and then I cease to do anything. Whereas if I can feel the acceptance of those things and allow the grief to be continuously flowing, and not try to stop it then I think that's sort of what we can do collectively to continue to move forward and for us all to try and have a positive impact any way we can before we die.' It was this kind of attitude that got him the name Mr Doom and Bloom. He was seeing the hope in these dark times.

What does hope look like I wondered as I set off back to Missoula, basket in hand?

Hope is keeping the traditions alive, the act of rewilding at our fingertips, the weft shuttling through the warp. It is a group of strangers in a park removing invasive weeds and turning them into baskets. It is, perhaps, fiddling while Portland burns, because sometimes fiddling is all we can do. It is putting our hands to work, hands that could be doing so many other things but instead are moving, weaving one strand through another. It is humans being human and creating the things that machines can't.

Spring was slowly coming to Montana. My daughter was happy at school. My husband had inexplicably given up drinking and had started wearing his shirts tucked into his jeans. It was a 'look' here. My body was still changing and I was silently inhabiting the strangeness of this transformation. It is probably the only significant bodily change in one's life signalled by a lack: a lack of blood, a lack of desire, a lack of fertility. My bleeding was getting lighter and less frequent. I felt intensely alert to everything. My mild depression had lifted and Missoula was now home. Although I was feeling settled, it was more to do with the fact I was inhabiting space and time in a way that felt transitory. The question of whether to stay or go had been absorbed into the day-to-day fluidity of life. I was dipping in and out of people's lives; I was becoming infertile; I was watching my child grow up; I had witnessed a lot of death. The scavengers and the nomadic rewilders were all leading lives I was not brave enough to live. I continued to hover while trying to work out where I might land.

My life in Missoula was a life in permanent flux. The city held few memories for me and was being filled with new experiences. The metaphor I kept coming back to was the idea of seismic resistant architecture. In the past, the heaviest and most solid buildings were the ones people thought could withstand earthquakes. But we now know that the buildings that can withstand earthquakes are the ones designed to sway and move. I felt like a ductile building. The quake of my parents' deaths made me sway and bend, but I remained standing.

With so many of my thoughts swirling around fluidity, I began looking closely at rivers. The map of Montana is criss-crossed by blue ribbons of water. Probably the most famous book to come out of that state was Norman Maclean's 1976 autobiographical novel *A River Runs Through It*. The 'It' of the title is Missoula, and the river is the Blackfoot. Robert Redford directed the film version of Maclean's novel in 1992 with Craig Sheffer playing the central character, a lightly disguised Norman Maclean, and a young Brad Pitt as his brother. The most famous quote from the book was one that Missoulians will proudly recite when they're drunk or homesick, 'The world is full of bastards, the number increasing rapidly the further one gets from Missoula, Montana.' But the quote I liked to remember was this:

Eventually, all things merge into one, and a river runs through it. The river was cut by the world's great flood and runs over rocks from the basement of time. On some of the rocks are timeless raindrops. Under the rocks are the words, and some of the words are theirs. I am haunted by waters.

The Blackfoot river is a fast, cold streak of fresh water that enters the Clark Fork about five miles east of Missoula. Its journey begins just outside Lincoln, Montana, a town we had visited out of curiosity when we first arrived in Montana. It was where Ted Kaczynski had hidden away in his cabin to write his manifesto, and where he was eventually arrested in 1996 after his bombing campaign killed three people and injured a further twenty-three. Also known as the Unabomber, for his targeting of universities, Kaczynski's manifesto *Industrial Society and its Future* can be read either as a work of flawed genius or a screed of dangerous ramblings. His writing alternates between florid, opaque prose and disarmingly direct instructions in which he advocates a nature-centred anarchism. He had probably wandered the banks of the Blackfoot while searching for hares to shoot and mushrooms to collect.

The Nez Perce called the Blackfoot watershed Cokahlah-ishkit, meaning 'The Road to the Buffalo'. Today when you hike this part of Montana, with its lush forests and gushing river, you can easily imagine

how it would have provided a wealth of animals, fish and plants, an abundance of food and medicine. Fed from melting ice high in the surrounding mountains and underground springs, it is a cold river. Meriwether Lewis crossed the Blackfoot Valley en route to join his travelling companion William Clark during their epic 1804–06 journey to map the West and to find a water route to the Pacific Ocean. They never found the Northwest Passage, but their journals paint a vivid portrait of the West in the early nineteenth century. Lewis believed this part of Montana to be one of the most beautiful landscapes of his trip.

While reading about rivers in Montana, I came across an alarming report about this waterway written by the Frontier Group, the non-profit environmental think tank. In the early nineties, when Redford was preparing to shoot *A River Runs Through It*, they had had to use the nearby Gallatin river because the Blackfoot was too polluted. I had been swimming with Jason and Eve in the Blackfoot many times. I caught a second kidney infection after one of these trips, which led to another whopping great medical bill. The river looked stunning, but like so many places in Montana, when you scrutinized its beauty, another story emerged.

One could begin the story of the Blackfoot River thousands of years back, when it was created by a glacial lake outburst known as the Missoula flood, during the last ice age. I will start in 1975, when a dam burst, dumping thousands of tons of toxic mining waste into its pristine waters. According to the Frontier Group, this release of toxic material along with 'decades of other mining activity, grazing, logging, irrigation and road runoff' led to plummeting trout populations and a river deemed 'unhealthy'. Local groups banded together to raise funds to clean it up. Restoration work began to reconnect stream channels, to replant vegetation along the river, to build fences and to prevent livestock from wading into the water. Much of this work was funded by a $1.2 million injection from the Environmental Protection Agency to the Montana Department of Environmental Quality. Some good news came of these efforts. The Frontier Group reported in 2017 that the Blackfoot was now a healthy river, home to wild and native trout.

> Nearly 3,000 acres of wetlands have been restored, and the removal of barriers has opened up an additional 600 miles of streams to fish. Fish populations have begun to rebound. For instance, cutthroat trout in the middle Blackfoot River have increased from less than one pound of trout per 1,000 feet of river in 1989 to 26 pounds per 1,000 feet in 2016.

Despite the good news, the story wasn't over. The area around the Blackfoot River, known as Milltown, was

still a Superfund site, because it lay downstream from the mining runoff of Butte's heyday, when this part of the United States was the most mined place on the planet. The rivers here were thick with poison. The EPA's most recent report explained:

> The Milltown Dam and Reservoir were located at the confluence of the Clark Fork and Blackfoot Rivers, a few miles upstream of Missoula. From the 1860s until well into the 20th century, mineral- and arsenic-laden waste from mining activities in the region flowed into the headwaters of the Clark Fork River, contaminating the river and its beds and banks.... As contaminated sediments and mine-mill wastes moved downstream, about 6.6 million cubic yards of these sediments accumulated behind the Milltown Dam over time. These mining activities and the downstream transport of mining-related wastes contaminated floodplains, sediment, surface water and groundwater with heavy metals.

The preliminary assessment of this site began in 1982 and has yet to be completed. I could no longer look at the Blackfoot river with the same awe I once had. I knew its complicated history. I also knew that there were seventeen other such Superfund clean-ups ongoing in rivers in Montana.

★ ★ ★

One cold winter weekend, Jason, Eve and I decided to take a trip to a small town we'd been hearing about which had a motel set around some hot springs. We got up early and drove through Missoula's starlit, pinky dawn to White Sulphur Springs (population 1,000). Gripping our mugs of coffee, Jason and I looked out onto the lightening sky while Eve dozed on and off in the back seat for several hours. At the outpost of Garrison we zoomed past the snow-capped conifers of the Helena National Forest.

'My ears just popped,' I heard Eve say from under a blanket in the back seat as we crossed the Continental Divide at MacDonald Pass. Then it was all downhill to White Sulphur Springs. The light had crested above the distant mountains, its hues of pale pink and purple fading as we rolled down a very grey Main Street. The town was a mixture of boarded-up shops and a few new, thriving businesses like the women's wear store Red Ants Pants and the soon-to-open Two Bassett Brewery. There was a real estate office, a cinema, a pizza place, a few gas stations, a couple of bars and, off the Main Street, a small library bursting with books and fliers advertising zumba classes and meetings for the over 55s. The town also had what it called a 'Castle', which was a thick-stoned Victorian manor house built in 1892 by Byron Robert Sherman with money made from ranching, stage coach operations and silver mining. Like so many settlements in the West, White

Sulphur Springs has had its share of booms and busts.

At the end of Main Street, as the town merged into farmland, there was the unfussy White Sulphur Springs Spa Motel with its pools of hot, sulphurous, health-enhancing spring water. We soaked in the hot water while the snow fell on our faces. It was in one of these hot pools that I overheard a man with an Australian accent talking about 'the mine'. My ears immediately pricked up. I bumped into him later that day in a bar down the street. He told me he was there to work on a copper mine, run by Tintina Resources, which would be dug a few kilometres from town.

As soon as I got home from our hot spring weekend, I looked into Tintina. It's a Canadian company based in Vancouver with funding from Australian interests. The man I had been chatting to was the Australian Bruce Hooper, the business development officer of Sandfire Resources and the President and CEO of Tintina. The company was still working on getting clearance to start digging what would be an open pit copper mine twenty kilometres from Sheep Creek, at the headwaters to the Smith River, which in turn feeds into the Missouri River. If anything were to leach into the water, it would be catastrophic. A group set up to fight the mine, Save Our Smith, explained this succinctly:

The mine would drop below the water table, and Tintina would have to pump water out of the mine to keep it from flooding. The pumped wastewater would contain arsenic and other toxics. Tintina's proposed copper mine is particularly concerning because it will mine through sulfide minerals, which when exposed to air and water can react to form sulfuric acid in a process known as acid mine drainage. Tintina is also planning a major expansion beyond their original permit application, and has purchased several mineral leases and claimed several forest service tracts.

The Smith River is precious spawning ground for rainbow and brown trout. This proposed mine, now officially called the Black Butte Project, was being sold to Montanans as a 'local' concern. Mr Hooper, an Australian, was listed on Tintina's website as 'living in Helena, Montana with his wife and two children'. Montanans respond well to locals.

Hooper has been in the mining industry for thirty years and it was easy to find a list of the companies he has worked for. Two jumped out at me: BP and Rio Tinto, companies responsible for some of the worst ecological disasters of the past few years. Who can forget BP's *Deepwater Horizon* oil spill in 2010 in the Gulf of Mexico, the largest marine oil spill in history which killed eleven people and injured a further seventeen? I remember watching this black stain expand over the Gulf like a giant, fatal bruise: almost 5 million barrels of crude oil gushed for five months while the world witnessed BP's ineffective and bungled attempts to stem the flow until they were eventually able to cap the hole. It wasn't just the oil that was poisoning the water: the two oil dispersants used by BP – Corexit EC9500A and Corexit EC9527A – were considered by the EPA to be highly toxic and not particularly effective, and further poisoned the Gulf and its banks. BP had chosen to use them because they were the only ones available during the week of the explosion. Three years after the night-marish disaster, infant mortality of dolphins was six times what it was before the spill and the effects on marine life are still being tallied. Tuna, sea turtles and other animals are washing up on beaches dead and deformed, while oily deposits embedded in sand will probably remain forever. In 2014, BP was found guilty of gross negligence and reckless conduct and in 2015 they finally agreed to pay a fine of 20.8 billion US dollars – the largest corporate settlement in US history.

Rio Tinto has such a long and storied history of human and labour rights abuses and ecological destruction that it's difficult to know where to start. In a headline in August 2016, the *Sydney Morning Herald* called the company 'unprincipled, shameful and evil' for their behaviour at the Panguna copper mine on the island of Bougainville. The island had been an Australian colony until 1975 when it was politically absorbed into Papua New Guinea. Rio Tinto began operating the Panguna mine in 1972 and it rapidly became the largest open cut copper mine in the world. As with so many mines in 'far away' places the company were fairly blasé with their working methods. Rivers were poisoned with toxic sludge, people were dying because they could not eat the fish, and very little of the money the company was making from the sale of copper was finding its way back to the island. In 1988 a group of angry workers broke into the mine to protest against environmental destruction, poor wages and what they saw as the unfair distribution of profits. They stole some explosives and sparked a separatist rebellion that turned into a civil war lasting from 1988 to 1998. Rio Tinto walked away from the mine and never returned. Acid-laced mine tailings have essentially killed two large rivers: the Jaba and Kawerong. Rusty and abandoned trucks and machinery sit motionless while locals refer to the area around the mine as a 'no go' zone. Aerial photos of the mine echo the toxic turquoise lake of the Berkeley Pit, but there is no EPA here to help clean up the site. Rio Tinto, despite being asked by the government of Papua New Guinea to help, have absolved themselves of any kind of clean-up operation.

Having read about mining in Montana and around the world, I called Tintina Resources, the company behind the Black Butte Project, and spoke to a chirpy woman who said she'd be very happy to book me in for a tour of the proposed mining operations. We settled on a date and she thanked me for my interest.

Tintina's headquarters are housed at number 17 Main Street in a shopfront in White Sulphur Springs. It looked like it may have been a department store at one time. Billboards were propped up in the large casement windows extolling the virtues of Tintina: the jobs they would create, the safety record they hold for being a company that cares, the money they would bring to the town.

I parked up outside their office. The place had the feel of a church basement from my suburban childhood: linoleum floors and plasterboard partitions thumbtacked with laminated information sheets, although in this case they were diagrams of rock formations and water flows. Chairs had been lined up in several rows facing the partitions. At the back of this room wooden shelves were piled with rock and mineral samples. Whiteboards sported banal messages about taking the garbage out and fixing the smoke alarm. The other participants consisted of two clean-shaven young men. One of them was from Salt Lake City and the other was from Billings, Montana. They were both hydro equipment salesmen.

Cal Moore, a friendly middle-aged man in cream workpants and a dark green fleece introduced himself as our

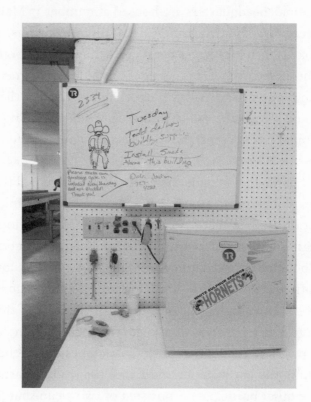

tour guide for the morning. He had a homespun way of talking which made the content of his speech all the more unnerving. He ushered us to take a seat and stood in front of the laminated charts, lists and graphics to begin his talk.

Meagher County, in which White Sulphur Springs sits, got its name from Montana's first acting governor, the fiery Irish nationalist Thomas Francis Meagher (pronounced 'Marr'). But Cal didn't go into the history of this larger-than-life historical character – he talked instead about Jerry Zieg, who had grown up on a ranch on the Smith River, had been home-schooled there, and was now vice-president of exploration for the mine. Despite being a local boy, his experience in mining took him to Alaska in 2005, where he managed NovaGold's exploration projects.

The Vancouver-based NovaGold and the Toronto-based Canadian mining conglomerate Barrick had been trying for years to get the rights to dig for gold in Alaska. They found a huge deposit in a very remote area between the Yukon and the Kuskokwim rivers, an area that for over a century had lured gold prospectors. The closest city to the proposed mine site is Anchorage, Alaska, 365 kilometres away. Because this proposed gold mine, the Donlin, is so far away, there hasn't been the same level of resistance to it that we have seen with other more visible mines in Alaska, such as the Pebble. That does not mean it is not worrisome. NovaGold's dream is to produce an average of 1.1 million ounces of gold each year for roughly twenty-seven years. They have stated, however, that digging could continue well beyond that date because they believe there is more gold in the ground than they'd originally thought. Because of the remoteness of the mine, they will need to build a 1,500-metre airstrip and a base of operations that would cover more than forty square kilometres of ground with concrete. They would also be digging half a kilometre into the earth to reach the gold. The tailings ponds would cover 2,350 acres of land, the waste rock another 2,240 acres. The company estimates it would be processing 59,000 tons of ore each day. To power the mining camp, they plan on building a 157-megawatt gas power plant. To pump gas into the plant, they will use a 312-mile-long pipeline which would cross the Alaska Range mountains. And so it goes, an entire city built in the wilderness to extract gold from the Earth, mostly to make jewellery.

There have been small, quiet protests by Alaskan Natives who have been worried about toxins in the ground and water as well as the rerouting of rivers and what that might mean for salmon, their major food source. This area is home to very small Native communities that rely on subsistence hunting and fishing for their food, but also for their cultural practices. They are concerned that the mine would not only pollute their water, air and land but could destroy their way of life and eradicate their history.

In March 2018, *E+E News*, an independently owned news organization focusing on energy and the environment, published a piece about the Donlin mine in which they interviewed Pam Miller, the executive director of the Alaska Community Action on Toxics, who said, 'The ore body in which the gold is located has a high naturally occurring level of mercury. So when the blasting and processing of the ore is done, it will release substantial amounts of mercury into the air and into the waters downwind and downstream from the mine.' The article went on to explain that although NovaGold promised to capture most of its mercury emissions, some of it is expected to precipitate over the Kuskokwim area. There are wetlands near the proposed mine site and once mercury gets in there, it's there to stay. The entire system, including the people who rely on it, will be poisoned. Even the Bureau of Land Management, who are not known for hysteria or hyperbole, have said that Donlin mine's gold operations 'may result in significant restrictions to subsistence uses' in Crooked Creek and almost a dozen other villages in the region. Barrick-NovaGold pumped money into promoting the mine and the current administration under Donald Trump has allowed drilling to begin. A pristine area supporting some of the last Native villages in Alaska will be destroyed so the world can have wedding bands and the super-rich can sit on gold-plated toilets.

Cal's narrative of how Tintina got started did not go into this – it simply painted Jerry Zieg as a local boy who earned his Masters in Geology at the University of Montana. Jerry had leased some land from two families near the Smith River and after a bit of digging around, Cal told us, he had found 'some amazingly pure copper' known as the 'Johnny Lee deposit', named after a homesteader and prospector who lived there in the early 1900s. This lode contains the second highest grade of copper currently under permit anywhere in the world. It is estimated that the Johnny Lee deposit holds 415 million kilogrammes of high-grade copper. The mine will produce 30,000 tons of the stuff every year, bringing in an annual revenue of 200 million dollars. The folk who get it out of the ground will become very rich indeed.

I asked Cal about his claim that this was the only deposit they would be drilling as part of the Black Butte Project and he answered that he's 'not a geologist or a scientist' – he was just 'sayin' what they tell me!' I found out later that Tintina are hoping to dig up another deposit called the Lowry, named after another homesteader who lived above the deposit in the 1900s. When you add the Lowry deposit into the equation, you're looking at over 446,000 tons of copper in the Black Butte Project. Cal did say that the proposed mine would have the lowest acidity of any kind of mine anywhere in the world, so the damage to surrounding land would be negligible, the equivalent of 'taking a Tums when you have acid indigestion'.

I asked about the tailings – the toxic water that is the result of blasting the copper-laden rock from deep inside the earth and flushing it out with a mixture of water and chemicals – and was told that they've got a great idea for that. The rocks left over from the excavations will be pulverized to the consistency of – he paused dramatically, looking for a metaphor – 'powdered sugar'. This icing sugar will go into a tank with some detergent (Sunlight soap is the picture we all have in our heads, although the reality is probably way off) and it is then skimmed off in cheesecloth. The water drained from this would then go to a treatment plant or to a filter press and the leftover sludge would be poured into containers and sent by rail to a ship where it would be taken 'somewhere'. Cal wasn't sure where the toxic sludge would go to be buried. My guess was China or the ocean. The filtered water would be blended with concrete and shoved back into the holes in the ground. But there was nothing to worry about, he said, because it would be put into double-lined plastic the thickness of linoleum and this has never leaked, apparently. No one would ever know the land had ever been mined once they'd finished with it. Cal got quite animated when he described the burying of the chemical waste. He seemed so pleased with this happy ending.

When I pressed him about any potential leaching from the toxic waste into ground water or tried to ascertain what would happen to the chemical waste taken off in railroad cars, Cal got a little heated. 'We want to work with environmental groups and really *work* with them. This area has to last beyond the period of the mining.'

Then he was onto all the jobs the mine would create. It would transform the town from one that had been struggling since the last logging business closed its doors in 1983 into a thriving town. If all went to plan, the construction of the mine was expected to begin late in 2018 or perhaps in 2019 depending on whether the Environmental Impact Statement got its approval from the Montana Department of Environmental Quality and if the public gave their go-ahead during the comment period. They were still waiting for feedback. Construction would take two years. The life of the actual mine would be between eleven and fourteen years. In that time they would hire up to 200 extra Tintina employees. I asked Cal what kind of jobs the mine would offer the locals. He listed truck drivers (twice), accountants, electricians, welders and mechanics. The mine would be in operation roughly from 2020 until 2032. After that, who knows what would happen to those jobs.

Once Cal had finished talking we were shepherded into a people carrier and driven thirty-two kilometres north of town to look at the ground where the digging would begin if the Environmental Protection Agency accept Tintina's proposal. During the drive to the Black Butte there was talk of baseball with the hydro equipment guys. Cal would be turning seventy soon and was into golf. I asked him about his family. He was proud of his five grandkids. If he hadn't been driving, I bet he would have shown us some pictures. White Sulphur Springs was eager to expand, he said. They were hoping for twenty to thirty new kids in their elementary school.

We parked up in front of an unmarked, metal shed. It housed fifty-eight kilometres of core samples taken during the preparatory drilling. Each one was labelled and filed in brown archival boxes on shelves that stretched from floor to ceiling.

'It's like a giant rock library,' I said.

'Hey I like that,' Cal replied.

'You can have it.'

'Thanks.'

The five of us stood on a slab of paved ground next to the giant rock library and looked out onto the cone-shaped butte, which silently guarded the very desirable high-grade copper inside its belly. It was midday and warm and muggy for December. The sky was like a sheet of zinc: grey and impenetrable. A hawk dipped its wings as it soared in a circle above us. Soon, this land would be rumbling under the weight of trucks – ten trucks a day hauling forty tons of rock. Particulates would be choking the air and the trees would be cloaked in brown dust.

Cal pointed to a spot on the horizon where the tailings would be buried when the time came. 'They'll be covered in grass when we're done. All you'll see are some grassy knolls,' he reassured us, adding that the maximum area of affected ground will add up to 160 acres. 'You won't even know we were here,' he repeated.

I headed to a bar on Main Street. I ordered nachos to fill the hole gnawing at my stomach. They were out of guacamole. I ordered them anyway. The waitress told me that nearby Belt Creek was so polluted already that no-one she knew let their dogs drink from it. The run-off from old coal mines had in some years turned parts of the creek bright orange.

'There's loads of fish in that creek,' she said when she brought my water, 'but there's no way you can eat them.'

My waitress was all for the mine as long as it didn't pollute the Smith and the nearby creeks and rivers. The fact that it was twelve miles from Sheep Creek, which drains into the Smith, worried her but not enough to oppose the mine. She, like many people I spoke to, thought it would bring businesses and people to town.

After lunch I grabbed a coffee from a woman who ran a mobile coffee truck. She had floated the Smith with her family dozens of times. She loved the river and believed wholeheartedly that the mine would not damage it. The hundreds of cracked pipes and tailings ponds that had destroyed rivers and ground water, communities, oceans, rivers, air, mountains, humans and non-humans all over the country were not a warning to her, but a mere inconvenience to the narrative she wanted to believe.

'You know who the real polluters are around here?' she asked while stopping mid-pour to give me a hard look.

'Who?' I asked.

'Those floaters! Do you know how many beer cans and Styrofoam cups I see every summer along the river?' she shook her head. 'And everyone's getting in a huff about a mine. It's crazy.'

Crazy indeed. I paid for my coffee and walked away.

A woman I knew vaguely through the Montana grapevine worked at the Spa Motel. I told her that I was having trouble finding people willing to talk about the mine. She wasn't surprised. A guy overheard me and said he'd tell me what he thought. We sat on a little bench inside the lobby of the motel. He was a tall, well-built guy, maybe in his thirties, wearing a baseball cap on top of a nest of blond curls. He used to work in North Dakota's Bakken oil fields and was passing through here, sizing up White Sulphur Springs for its suitability as a potential location for his next job.

'That mine won't just bring jobs,' he told me. 'It will bring all kinds of other stuff. They have no idea. Guys with pay cheques will want to spend that money. And they're not going to like what these guys want to spend their money on. Girls, alcohol and drugs. It'll change this town for sure, but not in the way they think.' He shook his head. I took his name and we talked on the phone a few days later. 'They have no idea,' he repeated, and those four words still ring in my ears.

I was drowning in news of poisoned rivers, melting glaciers and confused bears. Headlines like 'Grizzly Bears Are Waking Up Early This Year, and Climate Change Could Make That a Bad Habit' were filling my news feed. The planet was dying, but I needed hope. I was talking about this with a friend whose daughter is around the same age as Eve. We were discussing the challenge of feeling apocalyptic about the environment while simultaneously raising a child to believe in a future. It was a tough line to walk. She introduced me to a good friend of hers, a guy called Paul Parson who was the Middle Clark Fork Restoration Coordinator for the non-profit organization Montana Trout Unlimited. He invited me to go out in the field with him. Much of his work involved checking out land once the mining companies had left and then doing the impossible: repairing that land.

In 1872, when miners were flocking to Montana to stake their claims, a law was passed which allowed them to dig up whatever they wanted, inject any chemicals they needed to separate mineral from rock, gold from stone and copper from its vein, and walk away without cleaning up the waste. There are thousands of abandoned mines all over the state. Exactly a hundred years later, the Clean Water Act was created to regulate and control the amount of pollutants businesses and individuals are permitted to discharge into the 'waters of the United States'. For example, under the Clean Water Act, the Environmental Protection Agency can set wastewater standards for industry. When these are breached, the companies can be fined or held responsible for the clean-up.

The 1872 act is old, yet its vestiges can still be seen, and mining companies still rely on it. One case in point is the Carlin Trend mine in Nevada. Gold had been discovered there in the 1870s, but production was relatively small. In 1961, the Newmont Mining Corporation found a large deposit of gold and started mining in 1965. However, it wasn't until the late seventies, when the price of gold jumped from 35 dollars an ounce to 459, that the mine went into serious production. In his 1998 book *Montana Ghost Dance: Essays on Land and Life*, John B. Wright writes,

In Nevada's Carlin Trend, an unprecedented gold rush has ripped open huge expanses in the Tuscarora Mountains region. Over 4,000 mining jobs have been created in the last ten years. Mines with names like Goldstrike, Bullion-Monarch, Bootstrap, and Genesis are now producing 60 percent of all U.S. gold. It's a bizarre sight – cyanide mist in the aridity of the Great Basin Desert.

The mines in the Carlin Trend complex in Nevada – the driest state in the US – are sucking the underground ice age aquifers dry. By 2005, the Goldstrike mine had pumped over 383 billion gallons of water from one aquifer, and it's estimated that 10 million gallons of fresh water are being drained away every day. Many ranchers fear that the creeks, springs, and seeps needed for cattle will go dry. It's actually worse than that. It's not just that mining takes water out of the ground, it also poisons it and mining operations often leave large lakes of toxic water behind. In places like Nevada, most of which is geographically a desert, the evaporation is such that the water in these lakes disappears, leaving toxic dust behind which is picked up by the wind and carried wherever it is that the Nevada desert winds might go.

Wright goes on,

Nearly all of the Carlin Trend's cyanide gold comes from public land. In conformance with the General

Mining Law of 1872, this land costs the companies $2.50-$5.00 per acre and no royalties are paid to the taxpayers. Zero. When the minerals are used up, the companies just leave. The Environmental Protection Agency guesses that there are 557,650 inactive metal mines across the country. These abandoned hard rock holes and active mines have contaminated over 10,000 miles of America's creeks and rivers. The Mineral Policy Center estimates that cleanup would cost between $32 and $71 billion. Trouble is, most of the companies no longer exist or have gone bankrupt. If EPA Superfund cleanup ever actually occurs, it will be paid for mostly with taxpayers' money.

The Clean Water Act was expanded under Barack Obama's administration to include not just large bodies of water like the Mississippi and Puget Sound but smaller bodies that feed into them like estuaries, wetlands and swamps, in order for the agency to monitor pollution across a wider range of habitats and to protect a wider variety of animals such as reptiles and amphibians along with birds and mammals. This was one of the many pieces of legislation being overturned and revoked by Scott Pruitt, the erstwhile climate-change-denying head of the EPA at the beginning of Donald Trump's administration. It was one of twenty-six Obama-era regulations being challenged in court by an administration keen to see more public lands opened up for fracking, drilling and mining. Another one of the laws imposed by Barack Obama and currently being overturned is one that makes mining companies responsible for cleaning up after themselves. So, we're back to 1872. The added irony here is that the very people who want less government in their lives, less over-reach in terms of rules and regulations, will be the ones paying for the removal of poisons in their land and water through their taxes.

A few months after my visit to the Black Butte mine project in White Sulphur Springs, I found myself driving to Twin Creek, thirty-two kilometres west of Missoula, with Paul Parson. Paul was in his late thirties with an easy, relaxed manner. Tall, good-looking and rangy, he spoke softly, choosing his words carefully, something I had come to associate with this part of the world.

Steering his truck with his knees, he looked over at me and asked if his driving made me nervous. 'Not at all,' I said, trying to be nonchalant.

We turned off the I-90 onto Nine Mile Road. This landscape was the stuff of screensavers and photo calendars: mountains in the distance, wooden fences and photogenic barns slanting at attractive angles. It had once been ranching land but was no longer.

Paul was talking to me about mining. He came at the whole process from the other side, from the perspective of the rivers that have had just about everything poured and leached into them and left for dead. 'Private mining claims often follow rivers as you need a lot of water to mine. And mines decimate them. Rivers can heal themselves if you give them a leg up and plant the right things near them and get their meanders right, but . . .' he shrugged, leaving me to finish that thought.

Paul reclaims, remakes, and designs rivers, although he dislikes the term 'designing' when it comes to what he does – too pretentious.

We parked up a short walk from Twin Creek and met with two of his co-workers. Paul suggested we kill two birds with one stone by planting some seeds while checking out how Twin Creek, one of Trout Unlimited's latest reclamation projects, was coming along. To an outsider, the stream looked perfect – too perfect. Small waterfalls consisting of rocks piled aesthetically appeared at intervals. Each stone, dip, and curve of the creek did look 'designed'. It was alarming how this near-perfection in nature looked so unnatural. I watched the three men walk along the stream. If you had come upon them by accident, it would have been clear that they were not out for a hike. They ran their fingers through the grasses and shrubs they had planted from seed: willow and hawthorn and rose. They touched the trunks of the three cottonwoods they had left in place which had naturally seeded others nearby. They admired the conifers they had planted as saplings. They poked at the mushrooms and squatted to examine some scat: elk and bear and goose, full of seeds. They nodded to each other every now and then.

'We know what a healthy stream looks like,' Paul said. 'It's in our mind's eye.' They stopped and listened to the sound of the water and talked of the meander. Like artists or physicians, they called upon all their senses to review their work. Certain plants were thriving more than others. For the first time in a long while the creek met up with the Nine Mile River and will soon be able to support trout. This was a success story.

'Native trout are really sensitive to climate change,' Paul said. 'They can't survive in warm water. They are an ice age fish. Ex-mining water is the worst for them. It's often standing water, doesn't flow, gets warm as a result, and the flows that were created from the digging go in straight lines and this causes a lot of sediment. Trout are very sensitive to sediment.' Paul wanted to show me what a creek looked like before he and his team had got their hands on it, so I had something to compare Twin Creek with.

We drove a few miles to the Mattie V Creek, which has been sitting stagnant and polluted for decades. Paul had taken Mattie's great-grandsons fishing to show them what a good stream looked like and said, 'This could be on your property.' He was hopeful that they would come round and back the clean-up on their property.

It was a horribly ugly spot. Water the colour of split

peas buried slanting trees half way up their trunks. Hills of sludge had been piled into grassless tors around the site. It was unnervingly still and claustrophobic. We didn't stay long.

Back home in Missoula I couldn't stop thinking about rivers. We are lulled into thinking that because these waterways are constantly flowing, they possess what we desire more than anything: a sense of permanence and immortality along with a fluid ever-changing nature. But even rivers can die.

In sixth grade, we memorized that our hearts and brains were 73 per cent water, our lungs 83 per cent. I had always seen fresh water as precious, magical. I used to believe that water could think. If my brain was mainly water, why couldn't it? Every single living and non-living, visible and non-visible object around us – our food, our phones, the retinas in our eyeballs, the dust in the air – all of these rely on fresh water at some point in their creation. Our body is a walking river. Water flows from us. The liquid inside us will out eventually. In middle school I was taught about the water cycle: river to rain to snow to mountain glacier to melting ice, and back to river. But we were not told that this cycle was one of the many ways the Earth breathes in and out.

Water's ability to seemingly clean itself, to rejuvenate, to flow and keep flowing no matter what we throw at it is a strange sort of illusion. If you fell a forest, the trail of destruction is there for people to see. But water is different, it keeps the secret for you. Many rivers – despite their dams, their drying out, their dead fish, their pollution – are still flowing. Sometimes they run yellow or orange or green. Some may look crystal clear but are carrying thousands, if not millions of particles of arsenic, cadmium, phosphorus, nitrogen, mercury and lead. Around a million kilogrammes of toxic chemicals are dumped in American rivers every year. Of this, 680,000 kilos are carcinogens, 284,000 kilos are chemicals linked to developmental disorders and 16,000 kilos are associated with reproductive problems. Some rivers, such as the 3,058-kilometre-long Rio Grande, are drying up and disappearing altogether, but many, in a heartbreaking display of trying to do the right thing, just keep flowing.

Montana is lucky: 40 per cent of its rivers are deemed 'good' by the Environmental Protection Agency as compared with, for instance, 21 per cent in the coastal plains around the Gulf of Mexico. You know things are bad when the best bill of health is one in which you are more sick than healthy.

The first known use of the word 'reclaim' can be found in the fourteenth-century anonymously penned poem 'Cursor Mundi', whose title in English means 'Runner of the World'. Its 30,000 verses were written by a cleric in the North of England as a way of tracking history and religion up to his lifetime. In the 'Cursor Mundi', to 'reclaim' is to 'call back a hawk'. In the fourteenth century, the word was also used to mean 'to reduce to obedience'. And today the word retains that sense of control in its definition, 'to bring land under cultivation'. Now, among ecologists, rewilders, and environmentalists, to 'reclaim' land is to return it to a pristine Eden-like state. But just how far back do we go in reclaiming a river or a tract of land? Does one go back to 1492 when Columbus set foot on American soil, which is what some American environmentalists used to think? Others believe that 1778 is a more desirable marker – the year Captain Cook landed in Hawaii. Whereas for some, the foundation of Yellowstone Park in 1872 is the ecological baseline to which we should be aiming in our reclamation projects. And for the more dedicated contemporary nomadic rewilders like Finisia, whose life revolves around ancestral skills and giving back to the land more than she takes, we should be looking to the Palaeolithic period as the most ecologically healthy baseline. The debates are ongoing. But many of us seem to think we need to look back in order to move forward.

In 1963, the National Park Service published the Leopold Report, named after the zoologist and conservationist A. Starker Leopold. Starker was the son of Aldo Leopold, one of the founders of the land conservation movement in the United States. Aldo Leopold's

1949 book *A Sand Country Almanac* contains a chapter on Ecological Conscience in which he put forth the idea that 'conservation is a state of harmony between men and land'. The authors of the Leopold Report were already aware of the problems and the conflicts in reclamation. 'Restoring the primitive scene is not done easily nor can it be done completely,' they wrote. 'A reasonable illusion of primitive America could be recreated, using the utmost in skill, judgment, and ecologic sensitivity.' Even in 1963 there was the awareness that wilderness could now only exist in America as a 'reasonable illusion'.

It was beginning to dawn on me that we would not be able to stay in Missoula. Neither Jason nor I had full-time employment. Our healthcare, which had taken us a year to secure, was expensive. Even for the smallest of issues, like a grazed hand or an ear infection, it was a time-consuming and labyrinthine bureaucratic nightmare. We hadn't been back to London once in the time we'd been in Missoula and we had started getting cryptic reports from the company we had entrusted our house to that it was being 'trashed' by our tenants. Eve, however, was in her stride, running half-marathons, performing in *The Nutcracker* (as a sheep), cycling to the park with her friends. She was blossoming with the freedom she had in Missoula and her proximity to nature. Her shyness was dropping away. It became very clear to me that in London she had been a consumer before she was even a child. I had flashbacks of standing with Eve as a toddler at the Old Street roundabout in London waiting for a bus. I remember so vividly both of us on a drizzly night, exhausted, breathing in car fumes, staring at an advert for underwear that was plastered on the bus shelter. The photo of a pubescent girl posing sultrily was larger than Eve. In the photo, the model's hand was perhaps the size of Eve's head. I watched Eve gazing at this girl, at the lace trim, at the shadow of her cleavage and at the pouting lips and wondered what it was telling her about women, about sex, about objectification, about her future. In Missoula we didn't have to confront giant photos of half-dressed, sexualized children. Girls were asked about their capabilities, whether they could hike, climb a mountain, draw a picture, write a letter; they were not judged on what their bodies looked like. It was this distinction that allowed Eve to overcome what had been a serious self-consciousness. In Montana she didn't feel observed; she felt free. She was seven when we came to Missoula. She was nine now and much more aware of her surroundings. London was almost a distant dream to her, but one that held a sort of exotic, perhaps even forbidden, promise.

Despite the pull to stay, I was beginning to feel that part of the allure of my life in Missoula was its temporariness. I needed time to think about where I wanted to live, to settle. But this was one thing we did not have: we needed to apply to schools and terminate leases and navigate the bureaucracy of moving across borders and continents.

When I interrogated myself, I realized that living in Missoula had always, in the back of my mind, been a temporary state. The Russian language has different forms of the verb 'to leave' depending on whether one intends to return. The one-directional 'идти' means 'to go', whereas the multi-directional 'ходить' means to leave with the intention of returning. This distinction makes perfect sense. Did I really think we would stay forever? And yet leaving seemed all wrong. I didn't want to plan our exit. I felt sick at the thought of packing up, turning our backs on these landscapes, this sky, these people. I wanted to stay but I couldn't see how to do it – this was a lack of imagination I would come to regret.

I was again floating between two states – one of leaving and arriving, one of being in the moment and thinking about the future. It was difficult. Jason was gutted at the idea of ripping up the tender roots we'd put in the ground here. The thought of being back in London, the place of his birth, a place that held few secrets for him, drove him to a very low mental state. This was the kind of thing that ended relationships. It was not enough to live in a place for the sake of a person. One had to want to be there.

Saying our goodbyes was hard. Worse than hard. It was horrible. But we'd set the cogs moving for our return and now it felt impossible to stop them. There were too many places we wanted to see one last time, places we never managed to get to, conversations still ongoing and plans not yet fulfilled. We went on our

final camping trip with friends. We made 250 bucks selling everything at a giant garage sale, which Jason couldn't bring himself to attend. We gave back the cars we had borrowed. A friend showed up unexpectedly as we were sending our boxes off to be shipped back to London. She brought a Missoula tea towel and the dog-eared copy of the Lewis and Clark diaries that we had taken with us when we canoed down the upper portion of the Missouri River together. Before I knew her well, she had knocked on our door late one Sunday night. She had heard there was going to be a snow storm and handed me a bag with her daughter's old snowsuit and winter boots. Eve's London clothing would not have got her to school and back without getting frostbite. We hugged and cried and now it felt final: Jason, Eve and I were leaving this place. I gave my friend a plant as a way of keeping some of my roots in Montana.

I sat down with a cup of tea one afternoon during our final manic packing session and a thought hit me: I hadn't seen Eve's passport for a while. My heart raced as I realized I had packed it into one of the boxes we had just loaded onto a truck to be shipped to the UK. There was no way of getting it back now. I paced the peeling linoleum of our kitchen trying to think straight but only being able to think in metaphors: was this a Freudian message signalling my desire to stay? Jason called the British embassy and we were told we could get Eve a temporary passport in San Francisco. Our flight was leaving in three days from Seattle. More phone calls to British Airways. I changed our flights. Instead of an eight-hour drive to Seattle, we had a seventeen-hour road trip to San Francisco – more fluidity as our final drive became our last adventure.

Our trip started, as so many of them had, in Idaho. We stayed a night in Grangeville (population 3,140), a small, pretty town which prided itself on hosting the state's oldest rodeo and the world's largest egg toss. The following day, we hugged highway 95 along the border between Idaho and Oregon, eventually dipping down into Nevada. We came upon the outpost of McDermitt (population 500), which straddles Humboldt County, Nevada and Malheur County, Oregon. This is mining country – mainly mercury. The last mercury mine closed here in 1990 and since then the population of this incorporated community (it's too small to be a town) has been falling.

Just as we got to the Nevada border, I spotted the bright red 'Say When' casino and restaurant. On my right, I noticed a squat white building over whose forecourt dangled an old-fashioned sign written in that Wild West typeface: Borderline Treasures. Another one read: Antiques. The side of the building announced: GAS, SUNDRIES, GROCERIES, BEER, POP. It was closed. But just beyond this was a chain link fence running alongside the road. Jason slowed. Attached to the fence were cast-off bits of wood painted with:

FOSSILS, ROCK STUFF, ROCK SHOP, TURQUOISE. Animal skulls and bones topped the fence like a Mad Max-style crenellation. What lay beyond that fence was a sprawling outsider environment built of rocks, crystals, minerals, bones, glass bottles and scraps of metal. Somewhere among the piles of shimmering objects was a bright pink house and a large empty Victorian hotel also covered with signage. A guy appeared from the darkened doorway of a wooden hut. He looked to be in his sixties. A long ponytail snaked down his bright green undershirt.

This was Joe White Buffalo, who called himself a 'shaman'. He told us that the rocks he collected were 'storytellers', reminders of geological time and of our impermanence. Tables laden with fossils, some the size of my head, others as small as a pin, chunks of turquoise, chalcedony, carnelian, fulgerite and petrified rocks were scattered around the place. He invited us into his shed where we handled stones that were millions of years old. He told us about his life, his time in Vietnam and the twenty-seven ghosts living in the empty hotel where he sometimes slept. He was sure they were kind ghosts. His house was on the border of Oregon and Nevada: 'We eat in Oregon but we go to the bathroom in Nevada,' he told us – more for Eve's enjoyment, I think. As we were leaving, he gave Eve some very beautiful seashells, telling her she was a 'child of the sea'. Her job, he told her, was to watch over the animals in the oceans. She gave me a worried look. She knew about the gyre of plastic, the turtles with intestines full of rubber bands and party balloons, the sea lions whose necks were tangled in shopping bags, the marine birds full of cigarette lighters, toothbrushes and flip-flops. I could tell she was thinking, 'How the heck can I do that!' But she gave him a tentative smile and thanked him. There was something of Finisia's impassioned way of speaking in Joe. But where hers is a life dedicated solely to feeding the planet, Joe's was focused on his rocks. Like them, he was sedentary.

We stopped for a night in Winnemucca (population 7,400), a somewhat melancholy place. The road into town was lined with casinos and fast food joints. Their parking lots were full of shiny jacked-up pickups. There were few people out on the street and those who were walked slowly, as if slightly dazed. We found a room in the Scott Shady Motel, whose glorious neon letters beckoned us from the highway. Built in 1928 by Swiss immigrants as a summer camp, the place has a faint utopian 1930s vibe – think Butlins designed by Le Corbusier. I could imagine group calisthenics on the lawn followed by a healthy swim. The architecture seemed all out of place here and slightly disoriented me. All three of us were quiet. I didn't sleep well.

The next day we made it to Reno, Nevada – 'the biggest little city in the world' as the sign says. It seemed to be on a more human scale than Vegas, although it

had its fair share of people pushing shopping trolleys piled with TVs, shopping bags, clothing, furniture, bicycles and dogs. The typography and signage were stuck in the 1950s, with lots of flashing swooshes, vectors and arrows. Our casino-hotel had two conferences on simultaneously: the Mini Miss America pageant and a therapy dog gathering. We shared elevators with six-year-olds dressed like American Girl dolls, hair in perfect ringlets, little bodies zipped into pristine tulle dresses and feet in shiny patent leather shoes, while Dachshunds sported knitted coats announcing, 'I am a working dog, please respect me'.

A bellhop insisted on carrying our loaded suitcases to our room while warning us of the Mini Miss America Pageant: 'These kids are all from the south. It's all big hair. Reminds me of Cormac McCarthy or Faulkner. It's like something from *The Sound and the Fury*.' He paused. 'If you go to the pool, bring extra sunscreen, there's a huge hole in the ozone layer from all their hairspray.'

The next day we arrived in San Francisco just in time for our appointment at the Consulate. True to their word, they prepared a visa for Eve in about forty minutes. It was my first time in the city and I didn't immediately warm to it. The streets were claustrophobic and the gulf between the haves and have-nots screamingly apparent. I couldn't help but think about that open letter which had gone viral a few months ago, written by the San Francisco tech entrepreneur

Justin Keller. In his letter addressed to the city's mayor, Keller complained that homeless 'riff raff' were turning the city into an 'unsafe' and filthy 'shanty town'. His Presidents Day weekend had been ruined by homeless people, he said, whose 'pain, struggle, and despair' were things he felt he should not have to see on his way to and from work every day. I could feel the presence of wealthy tech bros all over town.

We drove to City Lights bookstore and the Museum of Modern Art. They were great – of course they were great – but I had lost my appetite for culture. I don't know whether it was from two years in Montana, or from reading Keller's letter, or not being allowed to use a bathroom downtown without buying a coffee, but the city seemed cold and aloof.

We had two days until our flight back to London. Jason and I were in denial. Eve was just her usual going-along-with-it-all self. An hour north of San Francisco was Point Reyes – a vast coastline of dunes, beaches, cliffs, dramatic headlands, marshes and grasslands which are home to elephant seals, elk, pelicans, herons, raptors and shorebirds. We drove out along a narrow road dotted with posh cafés and headed towards the ocean, where we could look out onto infinity. The diminutive scale, the shingle houses, the tourists – it all reminded me of Cape Cod. After two years in Montana, we were used to having the wilderness to ourselves. We'd become greedy for space and silence.

But we did get to see an arrangement of elephant seals aptly named for their strange, antediluvian trunks and the trumpeting noise they make.

It was a cold day, and we stood on Limantour beach leaning into the wind, watching the breakers crash against rocky headlands. We ran after the waves, happy to let the water freeze our toes until they went numb. The horizon was lost in a fog giving the day an aptly melancholic tone. This was the last day of our two years in America.

B ack in London I found the journal entry I had written on our final road trip to San Francisco. There was very little in it:

> Driving from Grangeville, Idaho to Winnemucca, Nevada – sign:
>
> Adopt a Highway
> Llama Joy
>
> Eve tired & sad. Lots of goodbyes yesterday.
>
> Idea: edible board games for long car journeys: Tic Tac Toe with Tic Tacs.

We had left Missoula exactly a month ago and we were still living out of our suitcases. The couch-surfing continued.

'Mum, where are my swimming goggles?'

'Where is my bicycle lock key?'

I had become the keeper of the suitcases, as if by

some kind of magic I could see everything inside them.

London continued to overwhelm. I went to Morning Lane in Hackney, which used to be where illegal raves thrashed through the night in burnt-out buildings when I first moved to East London in the early nineties. It was now the site of a Gieves and Hawkes, a Nike superstore, a Burberry outlet and an Aquascutum retail space. I lost all sense of where I was. I had been hit with urban vertigo, with the version of London I had known slipping away. It made me feel old. I could hear myself saying to Eve as we walked through Hackney, 'Oh, this is where I went to a book launch where a guy dressed like an ape almost jumped off the roof,' or 'Your dad and I used to DJ at parties in this building.' I told myself to stop this narration. It bored us both. But every bit of land, every bit of space was now monetized, and profits were being turned over at an enormous rate. There was very little space just for the sake of space. It was dizzying. On my high street, I could still just about buy cans of paint, toilet scrubbers, spools of thread, sewing needles, stationery, old lady slippers and Tupperware. But when I delved further into Hackney there were fewer and fewer of these shops selling the necessities of life – well, the necessities of *my* life.

The 'simple life' had been turned into a desirable lifestyle with its own low-key industry. Books like Marie Kondo's *The Life-Changing Magic of Tidying Up: The Japanese Art of Decluttering and Organizing* is only one example. Kondo famously used to rip the pages out of books in order to keep only the words she liked so she could save space. According to her, one should only own thirty books at a time, or fewer. The books Kondo instructs us to keep are the ones containing 'necessary information' – it all comes back to data and information. Despite the fact that the hard, cold facts of *War and Peace* would be useless to most of us, I am still upset that my old copy, which fell apart long ago, to the point where I called it *War in Pieces*, was lost during one of my many moves. How have we got to a place where our books are valued simply as vessels of information?

While thinking about this, I was assessing our belongings. We had a storage container full of things we hadn't brought with us to Montana. None of it was necessary. Jason and I thought about leaving it there forever. I fantasized about the whole container being consumed in a fire so I never had to deal with my stuff again. Living out of a suitcase for two years had been liberating. Meeting Finisia and seeing her belongings scattered around her had changed me forever.

I lay in our friend's flat, where the streetlights slanted into our temporary bedrooms, and thought about my other life, the one I had just left. And I thought about a rewilder I never got to meet: Lynx Vilden. Like Finisia, Lynx was well known in the American West for her dedication to the Earth. I was still emailing friends there and being told of gatherings and films and camping trips and goings on that I was missing. I was still tracking stories from my life there. I found out that Brandon Curtiss, the president of the Idaho Three Percenters, had been skimming money from rent he had been collecting in his job as a property manager. He had also used funds that had been raised by the Three Percenters for his own benefit. Thirty-six members of the Three Percenters of Idaho, many in high positions, left the group in protest of Curtiss's alleged misuse of funds. In November 2016, Curtiss was charged with 'felony aggravated assault' when he partially pulled his gun out of its holster on the woman serving him legal papers on behalf of the home owners who were suing him. 'Get the fuck off my property,' he told the woman. 'I have a gun and I'm going to use it. I'm going to fucking shoot you if you don't get off my fucking property.' After telling Curtiss she would leave, the woman placed the summons on his porch.

Part of being middle-aged in my case seemed to involve not being terribly interested in city life anymore. I once thrived on the dark, dirty streets of London, finding excitement in bars, clubs, in the general mayhem. My energy was chaotic and I was up for whatever was going on. Not so anymore. In Rebecca Solnit's *A Book of Migrations*, the author captures a trajectory which felt so familiar to me: 'When I was younger, I used to envy Europe for having culture and long lines of history and tradition streaming back from every person and place.

Now when I visit, theirs seems a place that poses too narrow, too domesticated a definition of what it means to be human.'

Growing up in Canada, I also dreamed of living in Europe. I landed in London where I have been for almost a quarter of a century. I am done with it. I understand the narrowness Solnit mentions. The streets, with their garbage swirling around my feet, look dystopian to me, futuristic, like a nightmare. Our local park is home to people living in tents, shitting in the bushes. They have nowhere else to go. I must have been blind to it all before. Or I had simply hardened myself so I could move through my days.

I feel physically hemmed in here knowing that beyond the borders of this metropolis lies not wilderness but suburbs and then countryside. Land without wild plants or animals is pastoral and quaint. Coming from Canada to Britain as a twenty-five-year-old, I enjoyed the fact that I felt less insignificant in the landscape, less out of control, less in danger, less like prey. But now that I have seen how a desert can be 'home', how with knowledge and practice you can live an entire life on the back of a horse, eating roots, nuts, berries and the odd animal, I no longer enjoy feeling like I am at the top of the food chain. *I want to be prey.* I was struggling to intellectualize these feelings or make sense of them without resorting to a romanticized notion of wilderness. Jason was faring much worse than I was. He was moving through his days with anger and sadness. 'Why did we ever leave?' was his mantra. I thought I knew, but I wasn't so sure anymore. Eve was happy to be back. Her return had been seamless.

My dreams were becoming apocalyptic. Everything was burning and there was no water to extinguish the flames. In the meantime, I had discovered a new movement pulling me back to the West. It was called ecosexuality. I sensed there might be overlaps between ecosexuals, who put their love for the planet on equal footing with their love for humans, and rewilders, like Finisia and Michael, who put their love of the Earth *above* their love of humans. There had been an ecosex symposium in London in 2013, the year before we left for Montana, in which the organizers had hoped to createan event that would present opportunities to 'explore how we can utilize ecosex strategies to protect our planet and create the kind of world that we want to see'. They believed that ecosexuality was 'a viable environmental activist strategy' and they promised it was 'gonna be fun'.

Then I heard there was going to be an Ecosex Convergence in the woods of Washington state in June – our first summer in London since our return. It was to 'bring together wild souls who express a love for Life by stewarding and merging with the Earth through the whole of their bodies, minds and spirits'. The gathering was to be called 'Surrender' and was described as 'a cauldron for deep connection, healing, and collective creation where life is sacred, our bodies are sovereign, and the Earth is our beloved partner with whom we collaborate to create abundance'.

A quote on the Ecosex Convergence website, by the writer Terry Tempest Williams, whose book *Refuge* had been an important one in my life, persuaded me to buy a ticket:

> It is time for us to take off our masks . . . and admit we are lovers, engaged in an erotics of place. Loving the land. Honoring its mysteries. Acknowledging, embracing the spirit of place – there is nothing more legitimate and there is nothing more true. That is why we are here. That is why we do what we do. There is nothing intellectual about it. We love the land. It is a primal affair.

Their website showed people dancing, group hugs, lots of floaty, Indian fabric. The organizers made it clear this was not an orgy in the woods. Magic was spelled with a 'k' and we were invited to commune with mycelium.

Apart from Peter Michael Bauer, most of the hunter-gatherers and rewilders I'd met had been a fairly misanthropic bunch. The ecosex subculture was the only one I had found that linked ecology with sexuality and social justice. What did ecology look like when it celebrated humans? Ecosexuality would tell me. And I would get out of London for a while and perhaps work out a more sustainable way for us to move back West.

As I was packing, I said to Jason, 'I wonder if I should bring some condoms?'

He looked at me with a strange expression.

'I don't think you should be asking me that.'

Chuck picked me up on the dot of 10 a.m. from a house in Northeast Portland, where I had been staying with friends. What you first notice about Chuck are her long unshaven legs, huge blue eyes, easy smile and unfaltering politeness. She has an open, yet somewhat reserved air about her. She moves with confidence, as if ready for any eventuality: rain, sun, the end of the world. It was all to be taken in her stride. This was good because Chuck and I were complete strangers and were about to drive two hours to Wahkiacus (population 91), a tiny unincorporated community in Klickitat county, Washington, where Surrender, the fourth Ecosex Convergence, would be taking place.

It hadn't been easy finding Chuck. Back home in London I had given up on getting to Surrender. Despite having my Montana driver's licence, I still wasn't comfortable behind a wheel. I had come up empty-handed after asking every person I knew in Montana if they or a friend would be able to ferry a fifty-two-year-old woman and all her camping gear to a sex festival. At the last minute Jason remembered someone we knew who had recently moved to Portland. She had a friend who had a friend and so on . . . which led me to twenty-seven-year-old Chuck, who had just quit her job and sold a house she had co-owned with her ex-fiancé. In her words, she was 'out to find freedom'. So when I suggested that in return for driving me to the Ecosex Convergence, I would spend 230 dollars on a ticket for her and cover her gas and lodging, she couldn't believe her luck.

We headed east from Portland along Highway 14 hugging the Columbia River, which cuts through high basalt cliffs strung with thin waterfalls. I was distracted from the scenery by our conversation. Chuck seemed to know a bit about ecosexuality. She was twenty-five years younger than me and identified as non-binary and there were overlaps between her social circle and that of the ecosex community in Portland. She proudly showed me how her driver's licence now had an 'x' instead of an 'm' or 'f'. Chuck also mentioned that she was into the kink scene.

I aired my insecurities about ecosex – or more specifically, my reluctance to be sexually open with strangers.

'You'll just have to get in touch with the untouchable goddess within you,' Chuck shot back.

A dirt road after the tiny town of Klickitat (population 362) took us up some steep, sharp switchbacks. We came to a patch of cleared, hard-packed land dotted with a few small wooden huts and some open-sided wall tents selling T-shirts and scarves printed with Indian patterns and the Sanskrit sign for 'om'. Beyond the cleared area was a forest of Douglas fir and oak. People were hefting coolers and backpacks out of their trunks. As we rolled up to the Surrender reception booth in Chuck's white Subaru, we were greeted by three smiling women. They told us where to park and where we could pitch our tents. I signed a bunch of paperwork giving the organizers the right to use photos of me and waiving any responsibility on their part should I get injured doing aerial silks, a form of acrobatics using long strands of fabric. A friendly middle-aged woman with close-cropped red hair asked me which 'pathwork' I had signed up for. My mind went blank. All I could remember was that mine had the word 'Magick' in it and had something to do with deities. She initiated me by sliding a bit of string around my neck from which a small shell dangled, then hugged me.

I stood slightly stunned in the drizzle. The planning that had gone into this trip had conspired to make me feel extremely tired. Crossing the ocean with my camping gear and finding someone who would agree to drive me were only two of the many logistical issues. But here I stood in a pair of jeans and a heavy fleece to ward off the cold, surrounded by people in gauzy 'I Dream of Genie' numbers, in bikinis, circus pants, flowing dresses, bare chests, leather straps criss-crossing torsos, hats, tattoos and tribal piercings. I was a schoolmistress among mermaids and sprites.

I first came across the term ecosexuality while reading about Annie Sprinkle, a former sex worker, feminist stripper, artist, writer and activist, reputedly the only porn star with a PhD. I had seen her perform at London's Institute of Contemporary Arts in the mid-1990s, when she was keen to show us all her cervix. I was struck by her vibrancy – she is a tall, curvaceous red-head who favours bright red lipstick. She came across as engaging and intelligent but, most of all, I remember that she combined intellectual ideas around women's bodies with a playful sense of the absurd. She surfaced for me at a point when I was weighing up Catharine MacKinnon and Andrea Dworkin's anti-porn stance with the more sex-positive attitudes in Sallie Tisdale's 1995 book *Talk Dirty to Me*. Sprinkle's openness wasn't something that came naturally to me, and yet I was enticed by it. I wanted to be the kind of person who could embrace it.

The ecosex festival had grown organically out of Annie Sprinkle's mission to make sex less shameful and environmentalism more sexy. In 2004, Annie Sprinkle and her wife and collaborator, the academic, artist and activist Elizabeth Stephens, embarked on a seven-year art project they called the *Love Art Lab*. Each year, they would marry each other anew and every wedding was to have a different theme, location and audience. Their 2008 wedding to the Earth was perhaps when the idea of ecosexuality became enshrined in a movement with a name.

In their *Ecosex Manifesto*, Sprinkle and Stephens write:

> We are the Ecosexuals. The Earth is our lover. We are madly, passionately, and fiercely in love.... We treat the Earth with kindness, respect, and affection.... We are skinny dippers, sun worshippers, and stargazers. We caress rocks, are pleasured by waterfalls, and admire the Earth's curves often. We make love with the Earth through our senses. We celebrate our E-spots. We are very dirty.

By seeing the Earth as their lover, they differ from ecofeminists, who tend to frame the Earth as a mother figure.

There is a playful and provocative side to Sprinkle and Stephens' manifesto, but they are serious about raising awareness of the Earth's degradation at the hands of corporate interests. Their film *Goodbye Gauley Mountain: An Ecosexual Love Story* follows their efforts to save the Appalachian Mountains (the second most biodiverse region in the world after the Amazon) from mountain-top removal mining practices. Stephens grew up in the shadow of Gauley Mountain and has a personal connection to the place. But instead of earnest pleas for help, they reframe environmentalism in terms of love stories, tragedies and dramatic relationship upheavals and breakups. It's as if Pedro Almodóvar had directed Al Gore's *An Inconvenient Truth*.

Although some might see the ecosex endeavour through the lens of the 1960s counter-culture, I traced it back further to the ideas of the scientist, psychoanalyst and student of Freud, Wilhelm Reich. In the 1930s, Reich tried to marry Marxist concepts, such as the rejection of private ownership, with sexuality. He saw marriage as a form of ownership, with women as property. In his view, many of society's ills could be alleviated if humans could free themselves from constraints around sexual desire and its fulfilment. The family and the gendered role of women were particular bugbears of his and he advocated for a more tribal approach to social units. The premise of his work is in some ways no different from the free love gospel preached in the 1960s, though for Reich sexuality was a serious tool with which to reject fascism.

Reich had narrowly escaped the Nazis during the 1930s and settled in the United States, where he came up with his Orgone Energy Accumulator (OEA), a phone-booth-sized structure lined with metal and insulated with steel wool. He was convinced that this device improved the 'orgastic potency' of its users by harnessing energy. By extension it also aided their general mental and physical health. The FBI, however, saw things differently and counted Reich as subversive. By the mid-twentieth century he had a cult fringe following: JD Salinger, Saul Bellow, Allen Ginsberg, Jack Kerouac, Norman Mailer, Sean Connery and William Burroughs all believed in the OEA. 'Your intrepid reporter, at age 37, achieved spontaneous orgasm, no hands, in an orgone accumulator built in an orange grove in Pharr, Texas,' Burroughs famously wrote in *Oui* magazine. The view that sexuality could function as a means to fight repression and social injustice was not a new one and I wondered if the Ecosex Convergence would be another iteration of this idea, played out against the backdrop of environmental collapse. Perhaps there was a sense that by casting the Earth in the role of lover, we might be encouraged to keep her alive.

Chuck parked the car and I scoured the forest for a flat piece of ground. Once I had pitched my tent, just big enough for me and my backpack, I lay down and pulled out Wendell Berry's *The Unsettling of America*:

> While we live our bodies are moving particles of the Earth, joined inextricably both to the soil and to the bodies of other living creatures. It is hardly surprising, then, that there should be some profound resemblances between our treatment of our bodies and our treatment of the Earth.

I was astonished by the overlap between Wendell Berry, the author-farmer-environmentalist from Kentucky, and the sex-positive ecosex movement. Intersectionality was everywhere. As I read, I could hear laughter and birdsong and a woman having an orgasm in the woods nearby.

At supper that evening, I sat with Chuck and a handful of others at a wooden picnic table. Rain was falling and we sat on towels, coats, plastic bags, whatever we could find. It turned out we were all fairly new to ecosexuality. Over courgettes and asparagus cooked in tahini someone brought up the idea of consent – how could having sex with the Earth ever be consensual?

I said, 'Well who said you had to do anything *to* the Earth? Maybe you could let it do things to *you*.'

They fell silent. One of them said, 'You are so right! Like being rained on.'

'Hey, I like that,' someone else replied.

The idea which seemed to be floating among us was that ecosexuality was a fairly open-ended pursuit. It relied on energy transfers between plants and humans as much as a physical exchange. We all agreed that being barefoot at the beach and enjoying the waves wash over your toes could be an ecosexual experience. The movement aims to raise awareness of our relationship to the Earth and to bring a sense of humour to eco-activism.

A woman passed around some Ayurvedic seeds for

us to scatter over our food, to help our energy flow. The guy on my left told me he was really into sacred clowning, a form of performance art which plays with the character of the fool or trickster, whose job it is to reveal the corruption inherent in power by using humour and a sense of the absurd. Chuck got excited at this idea. It turned out they were in the same pathwork, involving some 'jester work'. I zoned out but came back to the conversation when the guy on my left announced that the court clown could 'like fuck with the King and Queen'. I headed to the only dry place – the inside of my tent – and made some notes until it was time to convene in the dome for our evening's entertainment.

The dome was a Buckminster Fuller-style geodesic structure about twenty-five metres in diameter – large enough for all 175 attendees to gather with space to spare. Carpets and cushions were scattered around and colourful banners hung from metal struts. Sitting in chairs across from the entrance were the two women who had made Surrender possible: Lindsay Hageman and Reverend Teri Ciacchi.

Lindsay was living at the Windward Education and Research Centre, an eco-community occupying adjacent land. You could just about see the centre from here and their goats could be heard bleating throughout the campsite. Lindsay, fresh-faced, dark-haired and I would guess somewhere in her mid-thirties, smiled readily and had an easy but focused manner. You sensed when she put her mind to things that they got done. She began by welcoming us to the land, which she said was happy to have us here. She told us a bit about the Windward Community, 'an intentional community dedicated to loving the land and to loving each other. We embody ecosexuality every day!' Its members were aligned in their dedication to sustainable living and an open approach to sexuality.

Teri Ciacchi is a sexologist, priestess of Aphrodite, and holistic spiritual healer in the Living Love Revolution Church. An Eco Magicks practitioner, Teri also teaches Cliteracy Salons, Clitoral Revelations and Vulvic Explorations. Teri was about my age. She was an ample woman who had difficulty walking and rode a golf cart. Tonight a leopard-skin pillbox hat (just like the Dylan song) sat atop her turquoise hair with its pink fringe.

We removed our shoes before taking our places cross-legged on the floor. Rain was pounding onto the dome and the air was moist with sweat and wet, earthy smells. Teri asked if we wanted to make a joyful noise. People whooped. As an aside she said maybe folk shouldn't be naked for our first meeting as that would be 'just weird'. There was laughter. Then she invited us to inhabit our bodies by doing 'the Line, the Cross and the Circle'. We sat or stood up straight, our bodies establishing a vertical towards the sky. We were told to picture ourselves sending roots or 'a monkey's tail – whatever works for you', down into the ground. That was the Line. The Cross was formed by our outstretched arms and the Circle was made by rolling our heads.

Once we were grounded, Teri went on to say that we are 'languaging a lot about the figure 8'. At this point I lost her. I managed to write the following notes as she spoke: 'We're being portals,' 'We speak regularly with non-human living things,' 'the elementals', 'the fae'. Then she brought it all together, 'We've got to be in relationship with these things. What we want isn't more important than what they want!'

'We need to listen to them, to do what the Earth is telling us to do,' Lindsay added.

Teri finished off the idea: 'And with the same rapt attention as we do with someone we want to fuck.'

A lot of discussion around consent followed. Lindsay told us to repeat after her: 'We aim to have zero consent violations!' We repeated it and she said, 'That felt good!'

There were readings from the Surrender handbook by people in the audience. Once these were finished a person got up to tell us that we all needed to respect the shrines that were in the forest and in clearings on this land. 'It's really important that you don't move anything on a shrine as that can be very traumatic for the person whose object it is.' People clicked their fingers in response. Finger clicking is a signal of agreement resurrected from the days of the Beat poets by the Occupy movement, as a replacement for the more aggressive clapping of hands.

Once the housekeeping was out of the way, it was time for the ice-breakers. We were instructed to move our bodies like jellyfish: 'A school of them! Wiggle!' The two people leading the ice-breaker told us we were allowed to make eye contact with people around us – '*Questioning* eye contact'. Then we were to turn into lava and move like molten rock, before forming small groups of around six to eight people. One of the guys in my group looked like Larry David, with impossibly white teeth. He had approached me earlier and commented on my plimsoles. We had laughed at how cloth shoes are the worst shoes to wear in the rain – they stick to your feet and are impossible to take on or off. After our short chat about footwear, he had said, 'Hey, we should *interact* sometime.'

That small exchange made clear to me that I had zero interest in 'interacting' with this man. I hadn't always been like this. I was rapacious in my twenties and thirties and led by sex. Boyfriends accused me of being a nymphomaniac. I was wild and hungry for experience and had several boyfriends on the go at once. Being sexually faithful is something that only happened once I had a child in my forties. Sex for the sake of it has lost some of its appeal and I am surprised by how comfortable I am about this new phase in my life. It feels more like a gain than a loss. More like power than vulnerability.

In her 1991 book, *The Change*, Germaine Greer wrote about Karen Blixen (AKA Isak Dinesen), Madame de Maintenon (who secretly married Louis XIV at the age of forty-eight), and the author and art historian Anna Jameson (the subject of my failed PhD), all of whom found love later in life. 'It is simply not true that the ageing heart forgets how to love or becomes incapable of love,' Greer reminds us.

> Indeed it seems as if, at least in the case of these women of great psychic energy, only after they had ceased to be beset by the egotisms and hostilities of sexual passion did they discover of what bottomless and tireless love their hearts were capable.

We were instructed to sit on the floor, close our eyes, and cup our hands. The moderators silently walked around the room, placing edible objects into our palms: strawberries, cress, courgette flowers, tomatoes and grapes.

'Taste, lick, smell, use all your senses. Feed yourselves and each other!' The dome went quiet but for some 'Yums' and 'Mms' and the licking and smacking of lips. We opened our eyes and were asked to say our names out loud. The members of our small groups whispered them back to us. Then we were to make a gesture and a sound to go with it. I rubbed my stomach and said 'Yum'. Everyone in my group repeated this.

We chanted 'we' and 'me' until the energy in the room was raised to a potent level. Someone stood up and read the Mary Oliver poem 'The Plum Trees', which I hung onto as a return to the world I recognized. I slipped out before the cuddle circle got going.

Lying in my sleeping bag I prayed that the tent would hold out against the lashing rain and high winds. The swaying branches above me were making me nervous. I heard Chuck walk into a tent pitched about twenty feet from mine. I had met my neighbours earlier in the day while they were setting up their camp: two men and a woman, all beautiful, tanned, confident and in their twenties. Chuck announced, 'Tomorrow I'm doing sacred clowning!' The strumming on a guitar stopped and a deep voice replied, 'I love this world.' Chuck and Deep Voice talked about heading to the smoking lounge, a large tarp stretched above some chairs and a coffee table. It was the only place where smoking was allowed. I heard their tent unzip.

Someone else in the tent started strumming Deep Voice's guitar. There was more whispering. Then a guy practically shouted, 'If you spray it in your butt hole, you'll get high!'

More laughter. I finally worked out they were talking about 'weed lube', which another guy said was for your 'lady bits'.

A woman asked if it worked on your 'man bits'.

'I don't know,' came the reply.

Then the woman spoke again, 'I think my pussy always has the munchies! It's hungry *and* horny!'

I turned twenty in 1985. AIDS had just hit and the free, open life I'd been inhabiting in the early eighties seemed like a dream. It became cool to be celibate. Having sex with people was conducted under the spectre of people we knew getting sick and dying. These were sometimes the same people we had gone clubbing with, taken drugs with, kissed and had sex with. We were still into pleasure-seeking, but by then it involved some degree of sadness, fear or uncertainty and lots of condoms. None of this fear was apparent to me at Surrender. What did feature was a lot of talk about consent.

'We live in a rape culture,' one woman had said during the meeting that evening, 'so we need to create a consent culture.' We were going to be having a two-hour talk about consent the following afternoon. I could not imagine what you can say about consent for two hours, but even in my short time at Surrender I had become aware that I knew nothing about love and sex in 2017. I hadn't even heard of weed lube until now. I fell asleep that night to the sound of more rain, more laughter and multiple orgasms.

The following morning I woke to a downpour. My tent was starting to leak so I removed the dirty clothes from my backpack and lined my nylon floor with them. My mouth tasted horrible and everything smelled like mildew. I could see my breath. My will to stay was starting to crack.

Breakfast that morning was buckwheat porridge with cryogenic cherries. The woman next to me told a story about her friend who got cryogenically frozen 'for like a second' as a way of boosting her immune system. A few people chimed in saying they had heard it was good for you, but really expensive. The rain was falling into our buckwheat. I slipped away to brush my teeth.

It was the first day of my Eco Magicks pathwork and I was relieved to have a place to go, a place where I could sit and learn something and not feel inadequate. I'm at ease playing the good student. Those of us doing Eco Magicks were told to meet at the entrance to Lilith's Forest, near Inanna's shrine. Inanna is the ancient Sumerian version of Aphrodite or Venus, who represents love, beauty, sex, desire, fertility and war. Our group of about fifteen people was led by Teri, who wore a furry pillbox hat, purple leg warmers, Birkenstocks with socks, and a faux leopard-skin coat. Next to her was a pretty fifty-something witch called Melanie and a guy called Benjamin Pixie dressed in hand-tanned salmon leather, and what Teri referred to as his 'bee skirt', a concoction of black and yellow fabrics sewn in asymmetrical stripes. He was bearded, tattooed and pierced with tribal earrings. He had an alert animal intelligence about him.

There were brief introductions. We said our names and also the pronouns we would like people to use when addressing or referring to us. I said I was fine with 'she' and 'her'. Many people preferred 'they'. One woman said she used 'zhe', whose object form is 'zhim' and possessive form is 'zher'. It is an archaic non-gender-specific Chinese pronoun. The 'zh' is pronounced like the second 'g' in 'garage'.

We were given an alchemical potion called 'Saturn's Anchor or the Embodiment of Rooted Desire', intended to open us up. It had a pleasant, herby taste. I think I heard Benjamin say it had been made with ground elk antlers and dinosaur bones. He spoke like a prophet, in a quick staccato. He was passionate about the Earth and the honey his bees made, the mead he brewed, the skins he tanned. His brain was a rapid-fire machine and he talked about the natural world as if reciting poetry that had been dredged up deep from a bog or the inside of a tree. He was someone with the practical skills needed to live in the wilderness. He was someone I wouldn't mind being stuck on a desert island with.

Melanie was soft-spoken, with wispy reddish hair, pale skin and fine features. She was a High Priestess in the Sylvan Tradition of witchcraft, a branch which emerged in the 1970s in Northern California. Rather than identifying as a religion, with rules and dogma, this tradition of witchcraft sees itself as a way of life that honours nature – hence 'sylvan', a word relating to Silvanus, the Ancient Roman god of forests. Sylvans respect their connection to the Earth, reserving a particular reverence for forests, which are home to the 'fey'. These unseen beings are what most of us would call fairies. They act as messengers between humans and nature. An elderly gentleman in our group put his hand up and asked about the ritual of mixing semen with blood and drinking it. Melanie told us this was used in sangromancy – which is the casting of spells involving the use of blood – but that nowadays the concoction was more likely to be yogurt and pomegranate or cranberry juice. 'It's safer,' she explained.

We were asked to visualize a Sheela-na-gig, the Celtic female figure with a large, open vulva, to 'let her come to us'. The images in my mind were pathetic: the witch from my daughter's illustrated *Hansel and Gretel* followed by the animals in the Disney version of *Snow White*. I felt utterly deficient. Teri and Melanie discussed how important it was for us all to connect with our non-human ancestors and plants. 'They can guide you,' Melanie said. Teri added that our ancestors would have 'listened to plants', but that 'monoculture, monotheism and monogamy' had done its best to sever this communication.

In the dome that afternoon we gathered for the consent talk. It was 4 p.m. and people were dancing to loud, trancy house music. The rain was still falling and the air inside the dome was thick and damp. Teri was rapping into a mic: 'It only takes one individual to start a revolution!' from the song by the artist Deya Dova. Participants were hugging, lying on their backs with their feet flailing in the air. As the dome heated up, more people were stripping off and swirling in ecstatic, naked dancing. I sat at the edge of the dome next to a woman in a lawn chair who told me she was a Buddhist and who, like me, didn't seem keen to get up and dance. I didn't feel judged for not taking part – I felt ungenerous.

Lindsay and Teri were sitting where they had been last night. As we were about to begin, Lindsay announced she wanted to run naked in the rain. 'Well, do it then!' Teri cried. About a dozen people stood up and ran outside to feel the rain on their skin. The lectures began once everybody came back. There was talk of body sovereignty. The Jesuit philosopher Teilhard de Chardin and the writer and activist bell hooks were mentioned. There was a discussion about the colonizing of the very land we were sitting on. The presentations wouldn't have been out of place on a liberal arts college course called 'Gender and Ecology in Post-Colonial Times'.

We were encouraged to engage with the Earth and not to deny our part in its colonization, but to move beyond that thought by getting in touch with our own ancestors, with our own histories. Place, for obvious reasons, seemed to play a significant part in this movement. Knowing where we came from would help us feel grounded. A woman stood up to say she was raised by radical hippies and struggled 'with the idea of going back to the land. The global population is so high, we can't all go back to the land!'

'Solutions have to be place-based. It isn't "one size fits all",' replied Lindsay.

It was time for the consent talk. 'We are creating a new culture here. Part of its soil is consent. We're building it into the soil...' said one of the three people leading this presentation. Subtleties were outlined in various hugging techniques. When someone asks you for a hug are you expecting the two-second 'greeting-style hug' or one of those long constricting ones? They illustrated this with play-acting. They talked about the feeling that comes from someone's body when they are saying 'yes'. I was finding it strange that we had come to a place where this all needed to be outlined. How had we moved so far from being able to understand each other?

We were reminded to continually check in with ourselves and that 'consent for one activity is not consent for others'. The speakers warned us to be aware of 'pop-up boundaries', which were described as akin to 'stepping on a rake'. The difference between 'consent' and 'compliance' was explained. We listed situations that could get in the way of consent, such as being drunk, stoned, hungry or 'hangry' (the anger that comes from hunger) or being in a 'trance state'. Environmental factors, such as being in the dark, could also prevent full consent.

I could now see how this would take two hours.

If we asked someone to do something with us and they said 'no', we were given some appropriate responses, such as 'Thank you for taking care of yourself,' or 'Thank you for being true to your authentic boundaries.'

One woman stood up and said how sick and tired she was of her kids having to 'go kiss grandma'. Her kids didn't want to kiss grandma and it felt like coercion. She got some knowing applause.

Then Lilith's Forest was brought up. Lilith seemed to figure prominently among those gathered here. She has come down through myth and storytelling as a she-devil, a femme-fatale and a wild woman of the night. In Sumerian sculpture, she is portrayed as slender and large-breasted, often with the wings and feet of an owl. In medieval Jewish mythology, Lilith appears as Adam's first wife – before Eve – but she left him in protest at her subservient role. The Hungarian anthropologist and friend of Robert Graves, Raphael Patai, explored the origins and symbolism surrounding Lilith. In a 1964 article in *The Journal of American Folklore*, Patai wrote that Adam and Lilith 'could find no happiness together, not even understanding'. When Adam asked to lie with her, she replied, 'Why should I lie beneath you... when I am your equal?' When she saw he was

determined to overpower her, 'she uttered the magic name of God, rose into the air, and flew away to...a place of ill repute, full of lascivious demons. There, Lilith engaged in unbridled promiscuity.' She was still attracted to Adam, however, and returned to him as a lover after he had taken Eve for a wife. The Hebrew for Lilith can be translated as 'Night Hag' or 'Night Creature'. I can see how, with her enormous sexual appetite and her unwillingness to be coerced into sleeping with Adam, she fit the model of the ecosexual.

The earliest mention of Lilith is found on Sumerian clay tablets dating from around 2400 BC. Her epithet was 'the beautiful maiden', but according to Patai, 'she was believed to have been a harlot and a vampire who, once she chose a lover, would never let him go, without ever giving him real satisfaction'. Scholarship varies on whether the Sumerian Lilith is related to the Jewish mythological figure. She was a fairly common character in ancient literatures but doesn't show up in the western canon until Goethe's *Faust*, when Mephistopheles encourages Faust to dance with Lilith, the dangerous 'Pretty Witch' who ensnares young men with her beautiful hair by winding it around their necks. Although her provenance is disputed, Lilith's role in contemporary culture is to represent the free-spirited woman, the goddess of the night, the physical manifestation of mysterious, female sexual urges, the personification of women's erotic power.

Lilith's Forest consists of twenty acres of woodland set aside for consensual group sex or any kind of consensual sex play you can think of. But you must negotiate with your partners beforehand – a 'Negotiation Station' was set up just outside the forest for this purpose. If things escalated and you wanted to go further or try some new things, you needed to leave the forest and renegotiate before heading back inside. I had been told by a woman sitting next to me that there had been two consent violations last year. Nothing serious but enough for the organizers to make sure everyone felt safe.

The meeting came to an end after some more play-acting, exercises and questions from the audience. The rain had not stopped. I headed to my tent in my soaking wet shoes, coat and rucksack. Lying on my sleeping bag (the one thing that remained dry), I unzipped the front flap of my tent and squeezed out the dirty clothes that had been absorbing the water on my few square centimetres of floor.

The conversation around consent seemed logical and yet I felt saddened by it, as if it were missing a crucial ingredient. Consent, for me, de-eroticized desire. I thought about the thrill of sex in my twenties, of not knowing where I would wake up and with whom, of how wonderful it was to trust the person or people I was with to not go beyond what I wanted, and how sometimes I had gone beyond and was elated that I had. I can't imagine finding sexual fulfilment by negotiating every step, every move, kiss and touch. Some of us want to lose control and inhabit the unbounded mystery of bodies at play.

When we hook up with someone, we are hooking up not just with their body, but with their morals, their sense of decency, their ability to read our body language and understand our words. And here is my problem with consent culture: sex for some people needs to be spontaneous, dark, unwholesome, and with an element of surprise for it to be arousing. This self-policing in the arena of sex felt, to me, anathema to its essence. In discussions around sex today, there is rarely a mention of pleasure or desire – these are subsumed into 'yes' and 'no' answers, as if all the information you needed from your sexual partners could be found in a multiple-choice test. It all seemed bizarrely reductive in its efforts to be more open.

It is indeed crucial to steer clear of the non-consensual – too many women, including myself, have been violated by men. But paradoxically by placing the emphasis on consent, we are placing the responsibility onto individuals to avoid rape and abuse rather than seeing it as a societal problem of power imbalance. As I was thinking about all this, I realized I am old, romantic, and very out of step. Yet I still liked knowing that there are elements within myself and others that can surprise, enchant and disturb me. In fact, I *want* there to be these places inside myself.

While the rain drenched the thin nylon skin of my tent, I recalled an interview I had done in 2015 with the writer Sarah Hepola. We were talking about her book *Blackout*, which deals candidly with her alcoholism and its impact on her sex life and her writing. In the introduction, Hepola describes her route to becoming a feminist:

> Activism may defy nuance, but sex demands it. Sex was a complicated bargain to me . . . It was hide-and-seek, clash and surrender, and the pendulum could swing inside my brain all night: I will, no I won't: I should, no I can't . . . My consent battle was in me.

Here is the crux of the debate: *our consent battles are inside us.*

'Feminism today is about identity politics and consent. We didn't use the word consent in the 80s, and now it's everywhere,' she had told me during our conversation. When your consent battles are within you, how can they be legislated for?

Supper happened quickly. It was still raining and the ground under the picnic tables had become a small lagoon of mud. I was thinking of leaving the festival as the rain had penetrated all my belongings and the floor of my tent was slick with several millimetres of water. I had a word with Chuck about leaving the next morning and she looked distraught. She hadn't had any sleep and emitted that energetic glow from having been up most of the night enjoying herself. She wanted to stay and I could not bear to drag her away.

'OK,' I told her. 'Let's stay, but if the inside of my sleeping bag is wet by tomorrow morning, we're leaving.'

She agreed. She had forgotten to put a tarp over her tent and everything she had brought with her was lying in a pool of water, but she had other things on her mind and seemed amazingly unperturbed.

That evening we were back in the dome for a performance. It was a re-enactment of the Sumerian myth of Inanna and the Huluppu tree from *The Epic of Gilgamesh*, the oldest written epic dating from 1300 to 1000 BCE. Discovered in 1853 in the ruins of the library of Ashurbanipal in modern-day Iraq, the story of the young Sumerian hero-king Gilgamesh was imprinted onto twelve clay tablets in cuneiform writing and describes the king's relationship to the wild, sexual Inanna. Gilgamesh's refusal to be lured by Inanna plays a part in his journey from an arrogant, reckless young man to a hero-king who rules with wisdom. Excerpts from the epic were read aloud:

As for me, Inanna,
Who will plow my vulva?

Great Lady, the king will plow your vulva.
I, Dumuzi the King, will plow your vulva.

Then plow my vulva, man of my heart!
Plow my vulva!

As I listened to the words of Inanna with her female power, fertility and unabashed sexual desire, something very strange happened. I felt a warmth between my legs. I quickly left the dome and ran to the outhouse in the pouring rain and saw that I was bleeding. Not just spotting, which was how my period had fizzled to an end last year, but gushing. All this talk of nature, sex, ancestral pathways, the goddess Inanna, consent, orgies, orgasms and weed lube had brought back my period. I headed to my tent where 'just in case' I had packed a few pads. My head was throbbing. I lay down feeling impressed with myself that despite my reluctant mind, my body had decided to show me that it was listening.

The next morning, as I was walking to the outhouse, I realized I didn't have any tampons. I saw someone in the forest and approached them to ask if they knew where I might find some. This person smiled and said, 'Hey, I don't get my periods anymore. You can have these!' And they reached into their pocket and pulled out three tampons. I noticed the peach fuzz of a beard and the vague outline of breasts. There was no way of knowing whether the people I was meeting here had ever bled, are still bleeding, never did bleed, wanted to or not. We seemed to have moved beyond assumptions to do with our biology. There was something strangely touching about this, as if we were in the process of stripping away some of our communal skin to reach a very young and raw humanity. In this small exchange I was also made aware that one of the mechanisms at play was the deconstruction of a patriarchal system. So much of the emphasis here was on female sexuality and a respect for boundaries.

We gathered for our morning pathwork chanting 'Great Mother, Grandmother, Great Grandmother' to invoke our ancestors. Teri was stark naked but for a necklace and a robe falling open around her large, curvaceous body. She talked about how there was no escape from our ancestors: 'Their blood is your blood, their DNA is your DNA, their success is your success. We need to undo the mess in our bloodlines, to undo the harm being done to the Earth. We need to take on this work, to tend to the hungry ghosts.'

She then passed around one of her sacred oils. A few drops of it on our tongue would encourage safe passage from one realm to another. She spoke of epigenetic trauma: 'If you are doing ancestral work, there will be magic. If a spirit comes to you, ask them to identify themselves.'

We lay on the ground and Teri led us into what I

can only describe as a trance state by talking to us and inviting us to connect with our ancestors, to forge a path through our lineage. We were asked to visualize where we came from and to picture ourselves going back there. I imagined my mother's mother, whom I remember vividly. She was a tiny, very strict, red-haired womanfrom Belfast. I found myself in Ireland, travelling down her lineage. There was a path lined with straw. My body took on the shape of a St Brigid's cross. A woman called Maria was tending a fire in a hovel in the north of Ireland. Teri brought us back from our trance state and I was not sure what had just happened. I had never really thought about myself as Irish – the clichéd North American of Irish heritage always seemed sentimental and overplayed. Despite my father also being part Irish through his mother, I had ignored this facet of my background. I had always seen myself firmly as someone from the New World, from the suburbs, from a place where 'place' didn't really feature. A woman from our group began sobbing hysterically. She ran into the forest, naked, howling and screaming. Melanie comforted her and escorted her back to us and we completed our pathwork together. The session came to an end.

In my tent later I heard crickets. I looked out and saw swallows circling overhead. The weather had turned. Earlier in the day I had been told about the Venus Lounge, which served coffee – the canteen where we ate was not only vegan but caffeine-free. Things were looking up.

The next morning I headed straight for the coffee drinkers. The caffeine hit felt illicit but welcome. It seemed my fellow caffeine addicts were my age and older. A guy in his twenties showed up. He was dressed in zebra print leggings and a green velvet smoking jacket. If you were to blend a young George Michael with Puck from *A Midsummer Night's Dream*, and throw in some tribal piercings, you would get Thumbs. He described himself as a 'peripatetic communitarian'. All his belongings fit into his pickup and he travelled from one intentional or alternative community to another, offering his services. He told me he had just been to the Farm, well-known for being one of the longest running and most successful sustainable communities. It started in 1971 when eighty school buses and assorted vehicles brought 320 idealists to a cattle farm in central Tennessee. The banner on their band bus read, 'Out to Save the World!' Thumbs had also spent time at Twin Oaks in rural Virginia, which was founded in 1967 and is now home to ninety adults and fifteen children. The millennials Thumbs knows are all on the move and experimenting. It is as much a seeking to find their place as a survival tactic. They are looking for ways to live on a planet whose background hum is one of mass extinctions, including our own. They are trying to find stability in a society with no centre. Thumbs was smart and articulate and, like many of the twenty-somethings I spoke with at Surrender, held two opposing ideas in his head: that there may not be a liveable planet in his lifetime and that he wants to have a productive life in spite of this. These are ideas I did not have to grapple with in my twenties.

After coffee, I headed to my third Eco Magicks session. We checked in with each other to express how we were feeling. Someone said they had a miscommunication with a spirit the night before. People nodded sympathetically. The lecture today was on deities. Teri started with 'the gods are living out their lives through us'. She reinforced that we 'need to choose the tradition from which we choose our gods. They can sometimes come to us over time.' After yesterday's vision, I was beginning to understand what they meant, though not intellectually. In my therapy sessions over the years, I have found it difficult moving between the pole of 'knowing' and that of 'feeling'. I have tried to imagine my thoughts being able to move down inside my body so they can be felt, and vice versa, to allow feelings to be transfigured into thoughts. This is akin to what was going on here.

We were led again in a guided visualization by Teri helping us to navigate through our ancestors. The ground, thankfully, was drier than the previous day. This time I saw a young woman giving birth in a hovel with a floor strewn with straw and a fire burning in the hearth. She was still in my maternal grandmother's lineage in Ireland – an unknown ancestor of my grandmother's. A man dressed in black, a priest perhaps, stood by the bedside. When the baby appeared, he strangled it for being born out of wedlock. He felt he was doing the young mother a favour, but the woman was distraught. Also by the bedside was Brigid. She was furious that the baby had been murdered, sacrificed for the sake of propriety. She had no use for propriety. Her pagan outlook was against this sort of hypocrisy.

Teri brought the meditation to a close and astonished me by knowing that I had seen Brigid.

'How did you know I saw her?' I gasped. She said I had mentioned it yesterday, but I didn't remember that. Much of what Teri told me about Brigid made sense of my vision: Brigid is the goddess of childbirth, straw, mother's milk, writing and the protectress of women. There were other things from my past that came to light, such as the fact my mother had wanted to call me Brigid, but my father had won with Joanna. So many things surfaced that I needed to untangle. And then I wondered if I was going crazy.

The question of how sexuality and environmentalism were linked was niggling at me. Where would the 'eco' circle overlap with the 'sex' one in a Venn diagram? I could now see that ecosexuality was a multifarious, many-tentacled beast. It involved fucking in the woods, a cuddle pile in a tent, naked forest bathing, a sensual massage, a breeze up your skirt, a vision quest, or feeding an altar with semen and menstrual blood. Its close links to paganism gave it a strong mystical dimension. This was where the 'ancestral work' came in. Ecosexuals want to get close to the Earth, honour its fecundity, explore and share the Indigenous rituals around it, but want to do so without appropriating them.

After my pathwork, Teri sensed I was shaken and confused. She said she'd be happy to talk to me about my experience later in the smoking lounge. That evening, after supper, I headed up there. She was holding court, chatting to a few people about hydroponics and permaculture, herbal tinctures and the history of BDSM. A woman was talking about how she had some health issues and was too physically weak to dominate her partner, that this was causing friction in their relationship. Another woman was passionately advocating for a pathwork dedicated to sex workers. I waited for a lull in the conversation and Teri turned to me as if to say, 'And, so?'

I blurted out that I was shaken by the fact that I seemed to know how to go into a trance state without being told how.

'You've never done it before?' she asked.

I shook my head.

'Wow. And you saw all that?'

'Yes,' I replied.

'You're a natural!' she laughed.

I then told her what I have never revealed to anyone before: throughout my life I have been approached by people – often strangers on the street – who tell me I am psychic. My eighth-grade science teacher in Ottawa, Mrs Peat, took me aside one day and told me that she had been born with a 'second sight'. She could tell I had been too. I mentioned how Mrs Peat knew I was the seventh child and that I had been born on 7 May. Teri laughed again.

'I often know things are going to happen before they do.'

'What have you done about it?' she asked.

'Nothing.'

'Why?'

'Because I don't believe in it. I am a rationalist,' I said.

Teri encouraged me to do some work on my ancestors, to get to know them and to get in touch with the sides of myself I haven't wanted to in the past. She firmly instructed me to make a shrine to my forebears. I was finding it hard to understand how I could have been sucked into this way of thinking. I had had enough talking for one night. The circuitous conversations around me had scrambled my brain. I didn't want a cigarette. I didn't want a hug or a cuddle or to be humiliated or spanked. I wanted my bed. I walked to my tent under the stars. They were bright tonight and the air, finally, was warm.

On the last day of Surrender, I witnessed ten people marry the Earth. Some spat into the ground and lay in the mixture of soil and spittle; others writhed in the dirt; and others still, like Thumbs, had written moving elegies to the planet, outlining the actions they would perform to honour the Earth. One young woman wore a bridal gown and read her vows aloud. She felt she might never meet a human she loved as much as she loved the Earth. Devoting herself to its wellbeing seemed the most sane and loving act she could think of.

After the ceremonies, we gathered to dance. The sun was beating down and I stood outside the circle under the shade of a Douglas fir. Some of the dancers were ecstatic. Many were naked. There was drumming, chanting. As people scattered in the woods for a last fuck, cuddle, or romp, I realized that what was going on here really was quite radical. What I had been living these five days was not some nostalgic hankering after the past, but a desire to imagine and create a different future.

Most ecological movements look back. Some communities model themselves after an agrarian idyll from a hundred and fifty years ago: the life of the homesteader growing their food, keeping goats, making their own soap and keeping bees. Some communitarians go even further back, to our Palaeolithic ancestors with their migration, their foraging, replanting of seeds and brain-tanning hides as their baseline for the Good Life. What all rewilders, off-gridders, ancestral skills practitioners and those seeking to live in harmony with the planet seemed to have in common was a nostalgia for a world that once existed but was now lost.

The striking thing about the Ecosex movement is its insistence on looking forward. In their eyes, social change is needed to envision a planet fit to be lived on. Their focus on consent is perhaps necessary for the uncharted waters they are diving into. Nostalgia is replaced by excitement over what the world *could* be. Who cares what it once was. Ecosexuals are not trying to recreate some lost Eden, but are instead imagining a whole new one with a new kind of society better suited for survival. They all drive cars and most of them rely on technology – a Surrender Facebook page exists – but most of them, though not living off-grid, are concerned with environmental issues. It is an approach that stands out from the others. Unlike so many ecologically based movements, this one is not misanthropic – it celebrates humans, rather than wishing them dead for their ecocidal ways.

Chuck and I left the Convergence together. Exhausted. Filthy. Elated. She was glowing from having had sex and physical connections for five days. I was buzzing from new thoughts, new angles from which to look at my relationship to the Earth. I had made it through, got my period, came to understand more about the movement, opened up, and didn't die. I wasn't sure what I would do with my 'ancestor work' but I wasn't going to dismiss it altogether as I once would have. I was almost two weeks into my three weeks away from London, where I had left behind my roles as mother and wife. I was happy here, moving through this landscape with Chuck. I have always been more at home being nomadic than I am being settled, floating rather than landing.

In Klickitat, a fifteen-minute drive from the Ecosex Convergence, Chuck and I passed the charred remains of a house. Broken and burnt furniture sprawled on the front lawn, reminding me of that Raymond Carver short story 'Why Don't You Dance', except in this case it was clear why the inhabitants' belongings were laid out

as they were. I heard later that someone had lost their life in this fire. We were trying to find the apartment of Brian, a film-maker friend of a friend who had invited us to stay on his floor. I spotted a nineteenth-century block of flats with an old enamel arrow hanging on the outside. It looked like artists might live here. We parked up and knocked. No answer. Chuck suggested we try the back balcony atop a wooden fire escape and sure enough there he was having a smoke.

Brian jumped up to greet us and apologized profusely for not being able to put us up. He was younger than I expected and handsome in a boyish way. His building, he told us, was infested with bedbugs. So we left our backpacks in the car – we didn't want to risk being infested – and spent the afternoon with Brian exploring Klickitat and visiting an old mill where we took turns sipping from a bottle of not very cold white wine.

Chuck and I had alternative accommodation. Priya, the woman who had greeted me at Surrender and slipped a necklace of shell around my neck, had invited us both to celebrate the summer solstice with her. She lived in White Salmon, Washington, about thirty minutes from Klickitat. The ease of this trip was making me feel buoyed. Everything was falling so easily into place: meals and beds and our movement across hundreds of miles had been seamless. In White Salmon, Priya installed us into a small turquoise trailer on her

front lawn. Guests were showing up throughout the evening carrying Tupperware containers of chicken wings and bowls of salad. About a dozen people had gathered on her little porch. Priya then led us around the block to another back yard where the midsummer solstice ceremony was to begin. After ecosex, it made perfect sense to mark the longest day of the year with blessings around a fire in a Wiccan ritual. The sun turned the sky orange and we watched the twilight at first dapple the top of Mount Hood only to eventually shroud it in darkness.

When we returned to Priya's kitchen, the table was piled with food and wine. I ended up talking to a man who lived in an intentional community – a multi-generational cooperative – just north of Seattle. Originally from Germany, he had swapped his security, healthcare, state pension – all that European stuff – for life in a community which focused on shared skills and sustainability. He had felt called by the land of the Pacific Northwest and felt free there. I asked him what happens when someone gets sick (my fear of US healthcare borders on the irrational) and he replied, 'We sing.' I admired the poetry of that idea and perhaps singing for some of us is what we need when we're facing death. But others might need the chemo, the hip replacement, the blood pressure pills. I couldn't get his answer out of my head. I was becoming someone who could see the benefit of more singing and fewer drugs.

The next morning Chuck and I hugged Priya good-bye. There was a small ancestral skills gathering called Saskatoon Circle about six hours north of White Salmon that I had heard about through the rewilding grapevine. It had been founded by Katie Russell around nine years ago, before she had started her Buffalo Bridge project. I hadn't planned on going and hadn't bought tickets, but I didn't feel my adventures with Chuck were over yet. We had tents, a car, money for a tank of gas, the sun was shining and there was no reason not to carry on.

I gave Chuck the lowdown on Katie and Buffalo Bridge, about the scraping of hides and the ancestral skills subculture. She was intrigued and totally up for it. This was the embodiment of the freedom she had been out to find.

I had no idea where this gathering was taking place, but I managed to find a number for Joshua Dodds whom I had met at Buffalo Bridge. He was now working as a site hand at Saskatoon Circle. He sent me a welcoming message with directions. The drive through the central spine of Washington State was a combination of stunning landscapes, agricultural fields and scrubby towns. We passed the turn-off to Chuck's home town. She sighed and told me that this trip was changing her, making her look at her roots differently. She was seeing this land with new eyes.

We arrived at Saskatoon Circle and parked up on a grassy field as the sun was just dipping below the

mountains of the Cascade Range. We were in the Methow (pronounced met-how) Valley which I had been told over the years was one of the most beautiful places on Earth. It reminded me of Montana, with its mountains, its cloudless blue sky and air smelling of grass and honey. There was a large circle of flags in a clearing and beyond that were wall tents with chalk boards leaning against them listing the classes and activities that would be taking place. In the centre of the waving flags was a fire pit the length of four bathtubs and twice their width. Katie was surprised to see me but was very welcoming. I asked her if we could stay for supper and we agreed on a hundred bucks for Chuck and I to eat supper with the hundred or so participants, pitch our tents and do some classes the following day. In our post-ecosex state we stuck out: Chuck, in a flowing salmon-coloured dress, was still dizzy from her week of sexual exploration and I looked like a middle-aged school teacher who hadn't washed in eight days. The place was filled with tanned limbs and bare midriffs between layers of buckskin. It was like a rave in Goa circa 1992 but with deerskin outfits instead of silk sarongs. The men had beards, there were a lot of dreadlocks and everyone had a project which they whittled, carved, tanned or hammered around the fire pit.

Katie rang the dinner bell and announced tonight's menu: bear stew.

I spotted Finisia holding her bowl at the front of the staff dinner line. I made a beeline to her. We hugged. I was overjoyed at seeing her again.

'Come to the front!' she said, gesturing to the two people about to serve her from a table heaving with food. 'You're an elder! C'mon!'

I didn't jump the queue, but I did quickly introduce her to Chuck. Finisia eyed her up and smiled. 'She's cute.' We arranged to meet at the fire pit once we'd filled our bowls from our respective lines.

Along with the stew, there was corn bread, carrots and salad. I was starving and got some of everything, even the bear meat.

I sat and ate with Finisia. She had met Katie Russell for the first time here, and another female ur-rewilder, Lynx Vilden, also happened to be at this gathering. The three women were the Wilderwomen of the West and they were together here for the first time.

After supper there was a talk on the science of being human. The guy giving it was very chirpy and had a way of speaking that reminded me of Malcolm Gladwell or Alain de Botton: all fast connections and pop-references. The only fact I took away with me was that our intestines are somehow descended from lamprey eels.

As the sky darkened, people started gathering around the fire pit to practise their skills. Kids were running around naked in the sun's last blast of heat. Teenagers sang and played fiddle and guitar. A man was handing out 'ash cakes' – dough baked in the fire – to the children. I heard 'hash cakes' and immediately thought of Joan Didion's essay 'Slouching Towards Bethlehem', in which hippies give LSD to a five-year-old. But we live in different and far more wholesome times.

Finisia had slipped away for her last spliff of the night and I stuck around the fire trying to make conversation. The atmosphere was not very expansive. I wasn't wearing the right clothing and I didn't have a project to work on, so I sat and stared into the flames. Eventually I headed to my tent where I tried to sleep.

I woke to the sound of hammering and peered outside. It was a stunning morning. The air was hot and the sky was a polished blue, like a stone. I had not seen such skies since Montana. I had set my alarm early so I could join a bird-watching group but for some reason it hadn't rung. I noticed a small gathering in a distant field and walked to them through very tall, wet grass. I was an hour late for the birders who had all brought folding chairs. I sat in a very wet patch of dewy ground and listened with them. I did not hear any birds. Then I remembered my dream: Finisia was throwing horseshoes, trying to hook them onto a post. She was wearing one of those buckskin bra-type outfits which revealed her midriff. Her nut-brown stomach was smooth and I was saying to everyone, 'See how beautiful she is!' Fin was laughing.

I got back to the camp in time for breakfast and signed up for a 9 o'clock tincture-making class taught by a sturdy Canadian called Jenna. She was a clinical herbalist from British Columbia who would be showing us how to harvest and process balsamroot, a plant traditionally used to cure chest infections, colds, sore throats and to boost a weak immune system. We started by taking a few drops of a tincture she had made earlier. It immediately sent heat down into my chest and its strong pine taste warmed my tongue.

Balsamroot is in the sunflower family and all parts of it are edible: the roots are a starch, the seeds are like tiny sunflower seeds, the young leaves and flowers can be eaten in salad or ground to use as a salve for skin problems. Fresh roots can be peeled and eaten raw. Its sap works as an expectorant.

We walked up a hill overlooking the camp where the arrowhead-shaped leaves of the balsam plants were plentiful. We collectively chose one that looked good and took turns digging it up, careful not to harm the roots. The plant we had chosen was not only the length of my forearm but had a twin. It was double root that looked like a voodoo doll for a wrinkly human.

We took it back to camp where we sat on the ground in Jenna's tent, blissfully shaded from the hot sun. She talked us through the whole process of making tinctures and the amounts of plant matter to alcohol while we chopped the root as finely as we could. She gave us

each a small bottle of tincture as a gift. I left thinking that if I were to give up writing, I would like to take up tincture making.

I bumped into Finisia who, as a member of staff, had been served a bowl of steamed blue potatoes and goat meat. I hadn't realized that lunch wasn't included for us commoners in the deal. Chuck and I had a few rice cakes and almond butter but not much else. I sat in the shade with Finisia, near where she had set up her sleeping mat. She offered me her bowl telling me she wasn't hungry, even though I knew she was. We took turns eating her blue potatoes.

I headed to my afternoon session, which Finisia said she would come to. It was a walk with someone called Seda, a young, slender pixie of a man who had been on the hoop with Finisia and had edited her book, *Growing Up in Occupied America*. As we walked up a dry, grassy hill, Seda told us that in the language of the Methow Native Americans, 'Methow' means 'Sunflower Seeds'. We found some *lomatium ambiguum*, which are edible, but not the tastiest lomatium. Seda's voice was quiet and calm. We stopped occasionally to take a sip of water and to look behind us at the view, which stretched for miles over the Methow River and the surrounding hills.

Eventually we came across my favourite Native First Food, the *fritillaria pudica* or what Seda called a Spring Beauty. This was once an important staple for the people of this land. The plant itself is no more than a few inches tall, topped with a small bell-shaped flower giving it one of its other names, 'Yellow Bell'. By this time of year, the flower has turned brown and its petals have curled outwards. If you dig up the roots, you will uncover a white disc made up of rice-like grains. This is its bulb. Eaten raw straight from the ground it tastes like a starchy rice-flavoured cookie. Like all good things, however, this plant is being dug up at a much faster rate than it is being planted back. Seda was keen to emphasize the planting of seeds as opposed to the act of foraging as the end product of our walk. From the moment a bit of the fritillaria bulb hits the soil, it takes around five years for a flower to grow. These plants are both hardy and delicate. Seda recounted being out with Finisia. When they came upon some fritillaria, she told him to kneel down and dig like crazy. By disturbing the roots you help them propagate.

Finisia hadn't come on the walk after all. Her health had been bothering her. Just after I'd met her in 2016, her hips had started giving her grief. She was no longer able to ride nor could she chase after her horses. She had given them away to Josh, whom I'd met at Buffalo Bridge. She has a base in California where she is staying with a friend. This stationary life has stolen some of her fire. Sedentism is what she has been fighting her whole life. Finisia's migratory existence had been an act of resistance as much as an act of giving to the Earth. For thirty-five years she has been living and preaching this life and trying to get people to share it with her. She was always seen as the freak, the outsider, yet her visionary approach seems to be finally catching on in the mainstream.

In a September 2017 issue of the *New Yorker*, John Lanchester writes, 'It turns out that hunting and gathering is a good way to live.... The lives of most of our progenitors were better than we think.' How Finisia and Lynx Vilden and Katie Russell would howl if they were to read this. The 'progenitors' Lanchester mentions are our Palaeolithic ancestors who migrated and followed their food source as opposed to relying on domesticated plants grown in one place in large monocrops, mainly cereal. This is stuff Finisia has been saying for decades, yet no one would listen. Peter Michael Bauer, too. So many of these fringe outliers are now having their cries taken up by academics and writers – but is it all too late? We can't all live as hunter-gatherers. And simply adopting the Paleo diet by eating steak flown into LA from Argentina isn't going to work either. The tragedy in all this is that for the sort of life Finisia has been living, we need to eliminate greed and envy. Tribal societies had myriad ways of keeping social groups on an equal footing. Finisia is still to this day appealing for people to join her in the planting she can do with the use of her second-hand truck. Michael and a handful of others are carrying on her work and living on the hoop. And there are Native Americans quietly doing the work as well – the work of their ancestors. But why are there not more people joining in? If I were in my twenties would I jump in? I am not convinced I would have the guts to leave 'civilization'. I am still too enthralled by its call, too domesticated to break free.

I stuck close to Seda as we walked. There was something detached about him, poetically detached, not arrogantly so. He seemed to see and hear things most of us are not able to, as if he were tuning into a different frequency, an animal one, a plant one. We found more lomatium, the staple for anyone on the hoop. We spotted some bitterroot, familiar to me from Montana. Seda told us that Finisia had been given a recipe by a Native Elder for what she called 'Tutti Frutti': dried bitterroot roots ground into flour and mixed with berries and a bit of fat. Others, like Lynx apparently, boiled the roots and ate them like noodles, but Seda found them too 'mucilaginous' to eat that way. We ended the walk in a forest where the shade from the searing afternoon sun briefly cooled us.

After the plant walk I managed to find Chuck. Like me, she was feeling somewhat alienated. We were not ancestral skills practitioners and despite having sympathy for and an interest in – and in my case a burgeoning obsession with – life lived as close to the Earth as possible, we decided to leave the following morning. Katie generously agreed that we could stay for another supper before heading out. Her husband had built a giant spit especially for the roasting of a huge side of beef. This, with some beets, sweet potatoes, kale salad and corn-bread would be dinner.

I sat with Finisia, chatting and smoking, on a buf-falo skin which had been left around the fire pit. Lee Whiteplume, the conservation officer for the Nez Perce whom I had met at Buffalo Bridge, stopped by to say hello. He had never met Finisia before. They laughed when they were introduced, as they had no doubt heard much about each other. It moved me to see these two worlds come together around the fire: chaos meeting order, the visionary trans-poet connecting with the family man. Harmony Cronin joined us – it was her buffalo skin we were sitting on. She was a member of Buffalo Bridge but hadn't been there the year I vis-ited. She had been travelling with the Sami in northern Sweden, learning how to sew reindeer hides. On her blog I found the following,

> To me, it makes sense to do what human beings have been doing the longest. The disastrous experiment of agricultural domestication has disabled our physical and mental health, our environment, and severely disrupted our biosphere.

This could be a quote from Lanchester's *New Yorker* article.

Cronin is a pretty, elfin young woman – think Cate Blanchett in deerskin. I'd seen her in photos from

Buffalo Bridge so I recognized her immediately. We'd spoken on the phone when I was living in Missoula and had emailed a bit, but I knew she wouldn't know who I was so I introduced myself.

'Oh, you're the *journalist*,' she said. All the fearfulness and reticence I had felt at Buffalo Bridge resurfaced.

She offered me a sip of mead made of osha – a kind of wild lovage – and balsamroot. It was strong, sweet and delicious. We made small talk about the food at Saskatoon Circle, about Katie's baby – Harmony was excited at the next generation being brought up with these skills and this knowledge around them. I admitted to her that I had felt weird eating bear meat. It wasn't just because I prefer being a vegetarian, there was something about their status as predators, their huge size – the mythology around them had made me uncomfortable. Lee Whiteplume chimed in saying his 'people don't eat that stuff'.

I sensed Finisia's melancholy about not being able to live the life she knows is right, her incredible sadness at having given her horses away – without horses she is close to powerless. We talked about her health and her future now that she could no longer travel thousands of miles every year on horseback. Instead she was planting fruit trees where she was living in California. She would keep sharing her knowledge however she could. I told her about my week at the Ecosex Convergence, worried that she would find it indulgent. It turned out she knew Teri Ciacchi. 'Of course I know that son-of-a-bitch!' she laughed.

Many years back they had been in a sweat lodge together. The purpose of a Native American sweat lodge, which is heated like a sauna or steam bath, is to purify oneself, to cleanse spiritually. By some fluke, Fin and Teri found themselves in one together. She then told me a story about trying to get funding with Teri for a project but I couldn't quite follow it. She talked too quickly and made too many detours. I was surprised that Fin didn't immediately write off ecosexuality as a waste of time. But, then again, she is amazingly plugged into the gender debates raging around the blogosphere and university campuses. Transitioning was both a political act and a personal choice for Finisia. Although she identifies as a woman, she finds identity politics self-indulgent and a distraction from the real challenges facing us all: the climate apocalypse. In her view, anyone who is not giving back to the planet is ecocidal. She couldn't care less if you've got a penis, never had one, had it removed or are having one surgically built. Nor does she care about pronouns. It's the planet she cares about.

I told her about my journey through my ancestors at the Ecosex Convergence.

'I think I come from a bog in Ireland.' I paused. 'Maybe that's why I moved to England in the first place. All that damp green ground.'

'Huh,' she replied and looked thoughtful as she lit up. 'A bog. Makes sense.' She fixed me with those grey eyes. 'You look like you come from a bog. Now you just need to find which bog,' and then she howled.

In *A Book of Migrations*, Rebecca Solnit writes, 'There are senses of ties that go back past the immediate family and home, to vaguer, more mythic things, to that ancestor in the people and the landscape.' Like Solnit, however, I worry about how these connections can sometimes be framed. How does one settle in a place when one has never had a connection to its land? The landscape I was born into was manmade: tarmac, sidewalks, strip malls, parking lots, Dairy Queen and McDonald's. Despite only just coming to some sort of connection with my ancestors, I am aware that I am so much more than bits and pieces of my forebears' DNA, more than a mystical pull backwards towards them. I am also created by the streets I have walked and the people I have met on those streets and the things I have felt, heard and said. As Solnit writes, 'To truly go back where we came from, I would have to be dismembered and divided among many lands.' I, too, would have to be divided and dismembered. I do not come from one land; I come from many, which makes this nativist idea of being connected to place problematic. I am torn between finding my place and not believing that such a thing even exists.

* * *

I'd had no contact with Jason or Eve for weeks. I was enjoying the freedom. Motherhood had come to me late in life, at the age of forty-two, after many miscarriages and a couple of terminations and a lot of soul-searching. I had wanted a child and yet I was a reluctant mother. I didn't like the idea of creating another human to consume the Earth's resources and I worried that I would be terrible at it. I am not a patient person and I like having time to myself. Both of those non-qualities did not bode well.

When I gave birth a strange thing happened: I disappeared. I don't mean I literally vanished, although the body I knew had been altered beyond recognition, but my 'self' no longer existed. The first part of this erasure came with the birth itself. My labour went on for fifty-four hours. I had hoped that my body would know what to do, but it didn't. The pain was unbearable. I kept vomiting and yet I was expected to push a baby out. The entire process was pure trauma. Eventually my daughter arrived. I remember exactly what I felt as she came out of me: relief. A sense of letting go overwhelmed me. I then thought about the stages I had often heard mothers talk about: the weaning from breastmilk, the potty training, the first time a teenager stays out all night, the empty nest that follows. I realized that motherhood was a continuous 'letting go'. This was just the first step.

I was also reminded of things I'd read about motherhood and how so many women describe it as a 'splitting open' – not simply physically but metaphorically. In *Natal Signs: Cultural Representations of Pregnancy, Birth and Parenting*, Ara Parker asks, 'Why had I not been told more about this initiation into being? Not my child's, but my own!' She compares the moment of giving birth to that of being

> like a dry log under the axe. I had died and been reborn in that instant of my daughter's birth. . . . The world itself was changed, *split open*. From this place life emerged anew. . . . In no time at all, life and death were one. . . . Where were the philosopher mothers to guide me into the sacred nature of this psychologically critical rite of passage?

I experienced depression for the first time in my life following my entry into motherhood. I could not join mother and baby groups. Singing *'The Wheels on the Bus'* in my local library with forced jollity simply compounded my feelings of isolation and loneliness. I did find some solace in Rachel Cusk's *A Life's Work*, in which she reveals her ambivalences around being a mother. After outlining so beautifully in her precise, elegant prose how she found being a mother excruciatingly difficult, the book ends with her pregnant with her second child. I was devastated. I felt I had been lied to. *It couldn't have been that bad, if she is about to do it all over again*, I screamed to myself.

When I got home after giving birth, I collapsed on the floor in what would become my daughter's bedroom. I had not prepared a room for her, nor had we bought a pram or any paraphernalia. I was too superstitious to have any baby things in the house. I remember telling Jason that it would be unbearable to have a baby room without a baby. I couldn't shake the feeling that she would die as soon as she came out of me. There must be a word for this very specific worry. It felt so reasonable at the time.

From that first day at home, I wanted to be on my own. I did not want my baby near me and I genuinely worried that I may have made a huge mistake. I felt traumatized by the whole experience. My entry into motherhood had been ugly and brutal. The only thing that seemed to work was breastfeeding. After my daughter arrived in the world, the midwife had put her on my stomach and she wriggled like a worm up to my breast and immediately started to drink. I had no idea what I was doing, but she seemed to know exactly how to do it. Her mammalian instincts were incredible to witness.

Despite being healthy and a good eater, my daughter did not sleep. My exhaustion – I was living on as little as an hour of sleep a night – contributed to my existential malaise. I was no longer in control of my life. I could not eat when I was hungry or sleep when I was tired, and those daily baths I had been told to take to help my stitches heal never seemed to happen. The person I had been for over forty years had been subsumed into this child's needs.

In his 1983 essay 'The Bad Mother: An Archetypal Approach', the psychologist James Hillman states that a child displaces its mother's imagination:

> as the child is growth, she [the mother] becomes static and empty...her sense of future and hope is displaced on her actual child; thereby postpartum depression may become a chronic undertone....Her thought processes become restricted...so that the ghost voices and faces, animals, the scenes of eidetic imagination become estranged and feel like pathological delusions and hallucinations.

Estranged from myself and feeling static and empty – that was me for almost two years. Those terrors were eventually usurped by the fullness of being a mother. Now that Eve is older, I have returned to myself. I am not one of those women who can't imagine life without my child. I can imagine it very well. In fact, I am living it now out in the American West eating bear meat around a fire with strangers and seeking out nomadic rewilders. I am seeking them out perhaps *because* I can imagine life among them if I had not had a child. Or maybe I am simply telling myself this because it flatters me. I will never know.

* * *

I asked Finisia if she was still in touch with Michael. When I had been with them a year ago, they had left each other on bad terms. Since then, I had noticed some slagging matches between them on Facebook, but the acrimony seemed to have dissipated. Finisia was taking comfort in knowing that Michael was doing the hoop, living the life she had helped him embrace and was taking it one step further. Not only was he replanting, he was documenting the plants and animals he came across during his wildtending. He was making graffiti out there in the wilderness, writing messages that would take years to bloom. He had written the name of his sweetheart in biscuitroot all over the West.

'You should go after him,' Finisia told me. 'You really should. He's doing it. He's doing the real thing.' She took a drag of a spliff and shook her head.

We hugged and said our goodnights. I probably wouldn't be seeing her in the morning. Some contact improv dancing began around the fire pit with people falling, rolling, touching, moving around each other. Lee joined in, to much laughter from his friends and family. The fire circle was enlivened. Music started up somewhere in the darkness beyond the flames. I felt more alienated than ever and desperately sad that Finisia was no longer travelling on horseback – she drove up here in a truck funded by a crowdsourcing website that I gave twenty bucks to. It seemed all wrong.

The next morning Chuck and I packed up. She told me she had had a chat with Finisia while I had been out on my walk with Seda. Finisia insisted Chuck was really a boy. 'Those eyelashes,' she repeated, 'they're boy eyelashes!'

'I kept telling her I'm non-binary, but she wouldn't have it!' Chuck said sounding mock-frustrated. 'She is convinced I'm a boy!' We laughed and threw our stuff in the car.

'Where are we going?' Chuck asked. I wasn't sure if she was tired of this trip or coming down from the high of ecosex, but there was weariness in her voice. We admitted to each other that we had felt alienated from the crowd here, our lack of ancestral skills being an obvious snag in the fabric of this gathering. I felt deficient and aware of my lack of ancestral knowledge.

We made the short drive into Twisp, Washington (population 920). It was exactly how I pictured it: tidy, quaint, well to do. Half a million dollars will buy you a house. We went straight to the Cinnamon Twisp Bakery. Like most of the millennials I've come across, Chuck was gluten-free. This being Twisp, they could accommodate her. I got a gigantic confection of yeasty dough, butter, sugar and cinnamon, with an enormous mug of coffee.

I messaged Michael and was surprised to get a very quick reply. He was somewhere called Cyrus Horse Camp near Madras, Oregon. It was a seven-hour non-stop

journey from Twisp. I asked what I could bring him. 'Fresh meat,' he replied. I wasn't sure I would find much of that and told him as much. Plus it was thirty degrees outside and we had no cooler or air con in the car. He replied with a short comment about not pushing my vegetarian ways in his direction. Point taken. I found a deli in Twisp and the only meat-based product that would survive the drive was a ten-dollar salami stick of organic turkey. I bought it.

'So, do you want to meet a rewilder?' I asked Chuck. 'Someone who lives on horseback planting the wild gardens of the West?'

'Sure,' she replied. Her energy was back.

We packed a bit of food for ourselves and headed into her Subaru. Michael sent us the GPS coordinates and we were off.

The drive was one of those classic Western road trips. We passed impossibly beautiful empty hotels with signs that made me want to cry, that seemed to encompass so much of the recent history of the West, with its shiny dreams and its inevitable busts. Abandoned ghost towns like Shaniko appeared out of nowhere. Despite its thirty-six inhabitants, the town looked more like a film set than a place people lived. There were defunct drive-ins leaning into long grass, roadside diners whose windows had fallen out, exposing formica tables and red leather banquettes to the elements.

We passed the turn-off to Antelope, a sleepy town

of forty-seven people, mainly ranchers, agricultural workers and retired folk. This little outpost made the news in 1981 when the nearby Big Muddy Ranch sitting on hundreds of kilometres of dry, overgrazed land was purchased by a religious movement from India. Overnight it became the Rancho Rajneesh after its leader the Bhagwan Shree Rajneesh. The story of the Bhagwan and his thousands of followers or 'sannyasins' is still talked about here. People remember the followers of the Bhagwan clad in their bright maroon and coral outfits building their enormous city in the desert.

In the early eighties, Rajneeshpuram, as the community was called, was home to 5,000 sannyasins. They had their own fire department, police station, water reser-voir, beauty salon, casino (the Omar Khayyam Lounge and Card Room), a bank (the Rajneesh Financial Ser-vices Trust) and an airport for the Bhagwan's private jets.

Before organic gardening had hit the mainstream, Rajneeshpuram had created the template for an ecologically sustainable community in the desert. According to Hugh B. Urban, the author of *Zorba the Buddha: Sex, Spirituality, and Capitalism in the Global Osho Movement*, the commune included

some 60 acres of vegetables, 900 acres of dry land grain crops, 100 beehives, 2,800 chickens, 100 ducks, 20 geese, a flock of peacocks, and 2 emus. At its peak, the ranch was producing 3,000 gallons of milk and 1,500 eggs a day, roughly 90 percent of its own vegetables, and even included a vineyard that would produce some 20,000 bottles of wine. Not only was all of the farming organic but the community's sewage was biologically treated and purified for irrigation. Finally, 70 percent of everything used on the ranch was recycled.

Pretty impressive for a patch of overgrazed desert ground.

As Rajneeshpuram grew, so did its hold on the tiny town of Antelope. Animosity flared when the Bhagwan began buying up houses and local businesses. By 1982, there were three sannyasins on the city council. They even managed to elect one of their members as mayor of Antelope and took over the school system. A local group called the 1000 Friends of Oregon decided they'd had enough with the Bhagwan and his followers, their orgies and the free love. The federal government caught wind of Rajneeshpuram's arsenal of weapons and ammunition, the bioterror campaign in which members infected salad bars with E. coli poisoning 750 people across Washington state, their programme of surveillance, their plans to assassinate politicians they regarded as enemies and the Baghwan's expired visa. By 1985, the Rajneesh community had collapsed.

Twenty-five sannyasins were charged with

conspiracy to eavesdrop electronically and many more were charged with offences ranging from immigration fraud to attempted murder. The Bhagwan, who had changed his name to Osho, escaped in the middle of the night on one of his private jets heading for Bermuda. He was arrested during a stop in North Carolina. He reached a plea bargain agreement and was fined 400,000 dollars and was allowed to leave the country voluntarily. He died in Pune, India in 1990. The ranch is now called the Washington Family Ranch and is a summer camp for evangelical Christians. The desert here no longer blooms. In the place of organic vegetables, pristine turquoise swimming pools glitter under the hot sun. The 'Big Muddy' water slide, a zip line, skate park and all manner of good clean family fun are available here for people who want to get closer to God in the Oregon desert.

Chuck and I drove along the narrow two-lane Highway 26 south from Madras, Oregon towards Cyrus Horse Camp. We could smell smoke and then noticed to our right a discreet wildfire working its way along the brush. The air was blue and hazy. A few volunteer firemen were assessing the flames. We slowed down to ask if we could turn off the highway onto the dirt road we thought would take us to Michael. The fire was heading in the same direction but they didn't think there was any danger, so we carried on. There were no signs, we had no GPS, and our phones had no signal. But so far, Chuck and I had not taken a wrong turn. Listening to our guts had been working.

As we started to drive uphill away from the fire, the track sent up clouds of dust into the desert. From the lushness of Twisp, Washington and its rivers and pine forests to the deserts of Oregon in a day – the West is a place of extremes. I stared out at the strip of horizon, a fine dark line between the sandy earth and the blue dome.

Michael was standing in a corral stroking the nose of a large auburn horse while two smaller ones nibbled on some grass nearby. He hopped over the fence to wave us into a small flattened parking area next to his tarp. When I stepped out of the car, he welcomed me with a hug. I noticed immediately how calm he was compared to the last time I had seen him.

The Horse Camp overlooked a large body of water, the Haystack Reservoir, and beyond that, hazy ripples of blue and purple mountains disappearing in the distance. The air was scented with creosote and sagebrush. The sun was touching everything with that golden hue you only get in the West. The light here is not like the light anywhere else. Something to do with the enormous sky, the Earth's tilt and the aridity in the air. The dryness seems to polish everything to the edge of its being – the minty sage and the red-ochre soil against the expanse of sky and bare earth. Nothing in this landscape is extraneous. Everything is intentional and necessary. And all of it breathes if we let it. 'Westward I go free,' wrote Thoreau.

I must walk toward Oregon, and not toward Europe. And that way the nation is moving, and I may say that mankind progresses from east to west ... Every sunset which I witness inspires me with the desire to go to a West as distant and as fair as that into which the sun goes down. ... We dream all night of those mountain-ridges in the horizon, though they may be of vapor only.

I was in that West made of vapour only.

Michael told us he had some friends showing up. He didn't go into detail. I was expecting a couple of thirty-something rewilders in buckskin, seeking a connection to nature, and keen to do some planting of seeds. I was not expecting the Christian couple who showed up with two supermarket roast chickens and a glowing Jell-O salad. Beth wore a stars and stripes Western-style hat and Mick was dressed in worn jeans and a checked shirt. She was a nervy fifty-something, constantly puffing on a cigarette. He was quiet and thoughtful and had one of those slow, measured, spell-binding voices.

Beth and Mick had come upon Michael while he was walking with his horses along a highway. Enthralled by his project of rewilding, they decided to support him. When we met, Beth and Mick were working out how to get a horse trailer down to Michael so they could drive him north across the Columbia Gorge. The slippery metal grates on all the bridges make it impossible for horses to cross on them. Michael was heading up into Washington – to Twisp – to spend the winter. He'd never met Katie and the Buffalo Bridge gang and asked me what they were like. I told him they would welcome him – he was very much one of them. All the rewilders I'd been meeting, from Buffalo Bridge to Ecosex, spanned thousands of miles, and yet the overlaps and coincidences kept cropping up. This was a network moving underground like mycelium, under the radar, but very much alive.

We converged around the picnic table which sat between Michael's tarp and the horse corral. There was an unblocked view of the mountains in the distance. Mick regaled me with tales of his stepmother who had been a witch and tried to kill him. He'd had four wives, raised six kids, struck it rich and lost everything several times. One of his ex-wives, according to him, had spent her life trying to get her hands on whatever savings he might have left. He and Beth have a small cabin near Sparta, Oregon but while they're on the road, they sleep in their van with their dog. They don't look like they're rolling in money and yet they had taken on Michael and were passionate about supporting his rewilding.

Like so many people I have met in the West, you simply cannot superimpose Left or Right, Democrat or Republican onto them: Beth and Mick defy categorization. They believe in God, make their own honey and are virulently anti-Big Pharma. Mick told me about another guy they were supporting whom they'd met outside a McDonald's in Baker City, Oregon. He'd bicycled almost 2,000 kilometres from Tucson, Arizona pulling his dog Dexter behind him in a little trailer. When Mick saw the guy feeding a burger to his dog, he felt a strong tug. He knew that this man was going hungry in order to feed his animal. They started talking and eventually Mick hired Chris to do some work

on his house. In return for labour, Mick offered him three square meals a day, some ground on which to pitch his tent, and access to the house for showers and cooking. Chris was not only escaping difficulties with his marriage, but, as Mick told it, he was trying to get Dexter to the ocean before he died. Apparently Dexter had grown up near the sea and it was Chris's mission to get him back there one last time.

While Beth and Mick were telling me this story, a text came through to Mick's phone. Chris had set off from their house, several hundred kilometres from the coast, because it looked like Dexter was 'passing'. Beth and Mick called him back and arranged to meet him at their house the following day to take him by car to the coast so the dog didn't die before smelling the salty waves.

That evening we shared what food we had and sat in a small circle next to Michael's horses. We witnessed the setting sun lavish the land in purples and pinks and oranges. Once it was dark, the only light was the red dot at the end of Beth's cigarette; the only noise, the occasional stomp of a horse. The soundscape for so much of my time in the West seemed to come from horses. The talk turned to the yearly Rainbow Gathering, which was happening nearby in Oregon's Malheur Forest from mid-June to the end of July.

The Rainbow Family of Living Light, as it is technically called, is a loose-knit group of individuals from all walks of life who have been congregating in different national forests since 1972 for a couple of weeks around the Fourth of July. The Rainbow Family was born out of the late 1960s and early 1970s counter-culture, with its roots planted firmly in anarchic utopianism. The gatherings, run by volunteers (called 'focalisers'), do not involve any money. Rainbow people share, barter and trade for food and anything else they might need. The only stipulation for joining the Rainbow family is 'having a bellybutton' – all genders, orientations, religions, races and belief systems are welcome. Every gathering takes place in a forest, or 'natural cathedral', and is made up of various camps: the Jesus camp, the Faeries, the Krishnas, Kid Village, the meat-eaters, the abstainers, and the heavy-drinkers. 'A Camp', which consists of anarchic alcoholics, sits at the entrance to the gatherings. On the fourth of July, there is some silent meditation, but as the meetings have grown in size, the Rainbow people have also come in for criticism. Native American groups have seen the New Age adoption of Native American rituals and beliefs by Rainbow members as cultural appropriation that verges on racism. Environmentalists believe that the growing numbers of Rainbow members – sometimes up to 30,000 – invading places of natural beauty and ecological sensitivity can often lead to irreparable damage to the land where they congregate. There have also been outbreaks of dysentery from bad sanitation, violence, copious drug-taking and over the years several deaths. Like Finisia, who knows a lot of Radical Faeries, a subculture that overlaps with the Rainbow people, they call the civilized world 'Babylon'. For the most part the Rainbow Gatherings manage to remain committed to their belief in radical equality, respect for diversity, personal freedom and peaceful congregation. Mick had heard that this year's gathering was going to coincide with the eclipse of the sun, so there would be at least 40,000 people, if not more, camping nearby in a fragile desert ecosystem. I was immediately reminded of Denis Johnson's dazzling 2000 essay 'Hippies', which takes place at a Rainbow Gathering in Washington state:

You hear wildly varying figures, eleven different guesses for everything – 4,000 feet elevation, 6,700 elevation, 8,000 elevation. Claims of anywhere from 10,000-50,000, as far as attendance. But let's say 10,000 or more hippies touring along the paths here in the American wilderness... Yes! They're still at it! – still moving and searching, still probing along the avenues for quick friends and high times, weather-burned and dusty and gaunt, the older ones now in their fifties and a whole new batch in their teens and twenties, still with their backpacks, bare feet, tangled hair, their sophomoric philosophizing, their glittery eyes, their dogs named Bummer and Bandit and Roach and Kilo and Dark Star.

'Hippies' can be compared to Didion's 'Slouching Towards Bethlehem' for its insights and contextualization of the counter-culture. Johnson, however, reveals more about himself. He confesses to ripping off his friend by ingesting all the magic mushrooms they've pooled their money to buy. He links this betrayal to his dying car, his ageing friends and the confusion, chaos and rot at the heart of so much 'searching'.

Mick said he'd already seen some Rainbow People around the place. 'The thieving has already started!' he claimed. 'And there will be impact here on the land forever from so many people.'

'But, they're just people who are lost,' Chuck replied. She had been very quiet as we talked of the Rainbow Gathering. 'How do you know they're thieves?' she asked and started to cry – perhaps seeing herself more as one of them than as someone living in 'Babylon'. Mick, a kind soul, backtracked and started telling me about the articles he'd written for his local newspaper. We didn't mention the Rainbow People again.

As I fell asleep that evening, I heard coyotes and at one point in the night something small rustling in nearby bushes. Maybe a fox or a hare, a woodrat or a weasel. It was too tiny to be anything scary. In my deep sleep I had nightmares about London.

I woke early and watched the sun rise behind the horse corral.

Over breakfast, Mick and Beth asked how I knew

Michael. I told them about meeting him last year with Finisia.

'Oh, wow!' they exclaimed giving each other looks.

Beth covered her face with her hands and Mick shook his head before launching into a story about the time Finisia and Michael stayed at their house. This would have been around the time I had first met Fin. One evening she emerged from her bedroom stark naked saying, 'Who wants to see a tranny dance?'

They were not amused and kicked her out.

'I'm more the fine sandpaper and she's the coarse stuff,' Michael said in his usual understated way.

I couldn't hold in my laughter at the image of a naked Finisia in all her middle-aged, post-op glory. After all, I had dreamt of her midriff.

We sipped our coffee as Michael handed around a Ziploc bag containing what looked like crushed, moist granola bars, his 'pinch cakes' made with yampa, wocus (a pond lily whose seeds are used like flour or oatmeal) and piñon nuts mixed with currants and gooseberries and stuck together with honey. To gather and process the ingredients had taken him a full year. Each small bite was probably equivalent to a week's worth of his time.

Mick and Beth left that morning and I realized I was all alone at Michael's camp. I headed off on a walk up a trail that slowly snaked uphill. I passed some logs

pierced with bullet holes. Spent cartridges were scattered like confetti on the ground. The sky was a painful blue and the air so still, dry and hot it was hard to imagine anything was capable of moving through it. In the distance a couple were riding on horseback, their horses gingerly stepping over the sagebrush. I stopped every now and then to take in the view. The sun was searing and I could feel the atmosphere thin out as I got higher. I found an outcrop on the edge of the path where I sat and gazed at the reflection of sky in the reservoir with the snow-capped Mount Hood, whose shape reminded me of Hokusai's Mount Fuji, in the far distance.

I wandered back down to Michael's camp. After about an hour, Chuck and Michael returned. Chuck was avoiding eye contact with me. I sensed something was up. I did an informal interview with Michael about the hoop. He was grateful for Finisia's knowledge, despite their differences. He told me about his Swedish girlfriend, whom he'd met online. She was the daughter of nomads and also a model. It was her name he had been planting in biscuitroot so that in five years it will be blooming all over the West. They were talking about children, which surprised me. When I had first met Michael, he had been adamant that he did not want to bring more people into the world. He and his sweetheart were planning to meet in Seattle and ride together to Twisp this September, where they would spend winter camp. He showed me photos of her on his phone. It was odd to be here in the wilderness in Oregon looking at modelling photos of a woman in Sweden. Worlds colliding.

We headed out to do some digging. I was wondering what might be growing here in this high desert. Sure enough we found a lot of biscuitroot and yampa. We gathered seeds for Michael to plant as he travelled north. As we wandered through the creosote under a huge sky, Michael mentioned that he had been consulting for some reality TV programmes on the West for the Discovery Channel. He only needed to work on one more show to get an equity card. Finisia had told me when we first met how she had been approached by television companies from New York. They had said they wanted a reality series about her and other rewilders, in the vein of the recent slew of popular Alaskan reality TV shows. These generally feature characters struggling with the hardships of living in remote places, where the land was portrayed as an adversary. Finisia had told them to bugger off. The land was not the enemy and she wouldn't take part in something that described it this way. Unlike Finisia, Michael inhabited the modern world. He ran an Instagram account and a Facebook page called Walking with Western Wildflowers, which he uses as a teaching tool to spread his knowledge of plants and ancestral skills. His fine-sandpaper touch is more likely to entice people into living as he does than

Finisia's rougher, more extreme approach.

The three of us had dinner together and were fairly quiet. I sensed something was going on with them. As Chuck and I were heading to our tents for the night, Chuck turned to me and said, 'I need to tell you something.'

I thought I knew what she was going to say. 'Oh, yeah?'

'I think I'm in love with Michael.'

'OK,' I replied. 'That's complicated.'

'He showed me the source of a spring and we put our faces into it. It was amazing!'

'Wow,' I said.

'It was ecosexual!' she exclaimed, opening wide her big blue eyes. 'Is that OK?' she asked, suddenly sounding worried that she might be somehow upending our arrangement.

'It's fine,' I replied. 'But it's complicated for you because we're heading off tomorrow.'

She looked down. 'I know. I'll drive you back to Portland but I think I'll be returning to see him.'

I was moved by this. I could see my twenty-five-year-old self. I would have considered doing exactly the same thing.

We hugged and then fumbled in the dark to our respective beds. As I was falling asleep I heard her tent unzip. I wondered if she was going out to stargaze, to take a pee or to visit Michael.

Michael wouldn't let us leave until he had cooked us a proper breakfast. Bacon, eggs, toast and thick, strong coffee. He would be heading up to Twisp soon and had put the word out that he needed a yurt or a tepee and somewhere to keep his horses. I had heard that Lynx was selling her yurt. I offered to put them in touch. We talked a bit more about Twisp and his trip up there. One of his horses had hurt her eye and he'd had to take her to a vet. He was hoping it would be healed for his journey. Then I watched Chuck and Michael hug. Michael is so self-composed, self-sufficient. He was difficult to read. We drove off leaving him with any food he might be able to use. I wanted to stay longer. I was beginning to see how this life could pull me in forever.

In the car, I turned to Chuck. Her face was full of excitement. She let out a huge laugh.

'Oh, my god, he is amazing!' she said.

After ecosex, Chuck had been receiving texts from a guy she'd met there whom she was also hoping to see again. She liked him a lot. Now there was Michael. I remembered being in my twenties. Giving my heart to people and the excitement of it all. Waking in strange beds. I was vicariously enjoying her enthusiasm.

Chuck had already planned to meet up with Michael again. 'He'll be at Cyrus Horse Camp for a while longer,' she told me.

I asked if he had mentioned his girlfriend in Sweden.

I could tell by how she looked at me that he hadn't. 'What?'

'Oh God,' I said regretting I'd mentioned it.

She wanted to know more.

'He met her online. Her father is nomadic and she's a Swedish model and they're planning on living together this winter.'

'He didn't tell me,' she said.

We drove in silence for some time.

Our conversation picked up again. We were heading back to Portland, only a three-hour drive from Madras, though it felt like it was on the other side of the planet from where we had just been. Chuck didn't seem too upset about Michael. There was a wonderful easy-come-easy-go side to her nature. I would miss her.

In Portland I stayed with Jane and Mark, the same friends of friends I had stayed with before. I was filthy and smelled of sweat, old food and woodsmoke, but I was getting used to my itchy, greasy hair, my dirty fingernails, my pungent odour. I marked the end of my journey by having a shower. Watching the bits of grass in the brown water circle the drain made me sad. The smell of soap was unpleasant. I was already mourning the scent of my sweaty, sun-touched skin.

It was early afternoon but I was tired. I lay in bed in an attic room painted a deep red, where the heat had been collecting all day. The temperature outside was around thirty-eight degrees. In this room it felt hotter. Next to the bed was a small table and on it I found a copy of Barry Lopez's *Crossing Open Ground*. I wondered if Mark or Jane had placed it there to welcome me from the wilderness. In his essay 'Landscape and Narrative', Lopez talks of the interplay between the interior and the exterior landscapes. How the 'shape and character' of one's inner landscape are

> deeply influenced by where on this Earth one goes, what one touches, the patterns one observes in nature – the intricate history of one's life in the land, even a life in the city, where wind, the chirp of birds, the line of a falling leaf are known.... The interior landscape responds to the character and subtlety of an exterior landscape; the shape of the individual mind is affected by land as it is by genes.

The call to home then is as much about one's closeness to the Earth and the pull towards the land of one's ancestors as it is about our mind's work, the people we meet: the place where things align to tell us we belong.

I was taken out of my reverie by Jane and Mark's dog Avery walking across the living room floor, his nails clicking on the hardwood. Then some voices. Supper was being made. It was so hot, I was sweating even as I lay perfectly still on a white sheet. I was missing the wilderness. I knew these sounds I was hearing. They were the sounds of a city. I had my bearings in cities. I can always find a coffee, a glass of wine, a copy of *The New York Times* and the book whose review I had just read in the pages of the Book Review section. I am not lost in cities but I am left searching.

Soon I would be on a plane which would take me back to London. I felt unbearably miserable at the thought. I had reconnected here with a stranger: myself. I didn't feel I'd had enough time with her. And I hadn't answered one of the questions I had set out to: where do I belong?

Before I left Portland, I made a dash downtown to Powell's Bookstore and found a second-hand copy of *Crossing Open Ground* for $5.95. It fit nicely in my pocket. Heading back to London, I thought about the Welsh word *Hiraeth*, which roughly translates as 'the longing for a home you can't return to or which never existed'. It isn't necessarily a home in the physical sense but more of a sense of place and the feeling attached to it. I had been thinking about this in my relation to London. In all my twenty-five years of living there, my pulse would quicken, my blood would flow faster and I would be filled with excitement at the thought of returning. But the flight from San Francisco with Jason and Eve after our two years in Montana and now this one from Portland filled me with sorrow and gloom. I had been utterly changed by my experiences in the West. For the second time in my life, I was not looking forward to landing at Heathrow.

Jason and Eve greeted me with hugs and cards that Eve had been making me over the weeks. Despite their warmth, I felt strangely cold and distant. I didn't want to be here but I didn't know what to do about it. It would be crazy to jack it all in to live in a tent in the American West. There's the whole healthcare issue. There's the lack of stability. The lack of jobs. There were a million reasons not to up and leave. I was thinking about all this and working through it in my mind. Meanwhile, I was aware that I was being a moody bitch.

My menopause seemed to have flattened. No more bleeding. But the sweats were vicious. An inner fire was raging inside me. I tried to let my body do what it needed to, calmly and without fighting it. I was vehemently against the hormones used in hormone replacement therapy, most of which are made from the urine of tortured, pregnant mares. The bio-identicals seemed too expensive, too poorly researched. Besides, I wanted to hear what my body was telling me, even if at times I struggled with what I was hearing. I would learn to embrace my 'inner hag', as Germaine Greer suggested in *The Change*.

The dirt and the noise and traffic and the bad air were all weighing on me. I wanted to escape back to Missoula. Jason wanted out, too. Eve didn't. We were spending evenings talking about how to migrate West again. Our conversations were not going well. We would have to give up so much. We were caught between our practical reality and our desire to flee. Then a piece of the West showed up on my doorstep. The one person I hadn't had a chance to spend time with was coming to Britain.

Many of the eighteen participants who had come to learn ancestral skills with Lynx Vilden wore the trademark rewilder outfit of buckskin and sat on sheepskin rugs. There were flasks made of wood and plenty of hand-carved spoons and bowls stashed neatly on shelves in the small hut where we stored our utensils. My industrial-era enamelware was out of place, violating the aesthetic. I was looking at people's feet. Some of the shoes were obviously hand-stitched. There was jewellery crafted out of leather and bone, and sweaters full of holes, fastened with buttons made from deer claws. A few of us city-dwellers wore clothing that shouted 'civilization' and 'sweat shops' and I was grateful not to be the only 'civ' here.

As if from nowhere, Lynx bounded barefoot like a cat towards us. I had first heard of her when I was living in Montana and had met her briefly at Saskatoon Circle but didn't get much of a chance to speak with her. Yet here she was in Dartmoor, in the west of England, teaching a week of ancestral skills.

Lynx Vilden is revered among rewilders in the

American West for living as our Palaeolithic ancestors did. Her knowledge is vast. Rumour has it she can get a fire started in thirty seconds using only two sticks. She is tall and thin with chiselled cheekbones, spiky blonde hair and eyes the colour of a mountain lake. Born in 1965, Lynx is exactly my age but looks like Brigitte Nielsen's younger Stone Age sister.

The camp where we had gathered hugged the north-eastern shoulder of Dartmoor National Park on several acres of private land whose owner was keen to get more people involved with seeking ways to live off-grid. There were no buildings anywhere to be seen and our week would be spent entirely outdoors, living as close to the land as possible. Although it was April, we would be bathing in a stream. We would forage and eat local food. We were surrounded by craggy forests, meandering rivers, giant boulders – this is as wild as it gets in England.

After we'd pitched our tents, tarps and hammocks, Lynx silently motioned with her hands for us to gather. We were to follow her to a nearby patch of flat ground where she instructed us wordlessly to take off our shoes. She was holding a hand drill, a flat piece of wood known as a hearth, and a stick, known as the bow. She motioned for one of the participants to hold the bottom of the bow onto the hearth while she spun it. Lynx then signalled for us to gather some dry grass. It took maybe forty-five minutes for us to take turns holding

the hearth and spinning the bow to get enough heat for the grass to light. Witnessing fire appear from two bits of wood is to witness something primal and ancient.

In Hesiod's *Theogony*, written around 700 BCE, the wily shape-shifting Prometheus stole fire from Zeus. In retribution for this theft, Zeus created Pandora and filled her with every earthly charm. When Prometheus's brother took Pandora as his wife, all manner of ill-fortune previously unknown to mankind was unleashed – everything but hope. Roughly two hundred years later, the playwright Aeschylus re-imagined Prometheus. His theft of fire, rather than unleashing punishment, was responsible for bringing us civilization, for granting us mastery over nature, for creating the arts. From Hesiod to Aeschylus another vivid line can be traced reaffirming the trajectory that so many rewilders believe in: pre-agricultural humans knew what was right and good. Once we began to revere culture and our mastery over nature, the rot set in. To my eyes, watching two sticks make fire is like witnessing birth.

We followed Lynx. I was not used to walking barefoot over hard April ground. The pine needles, twigs and rocks hurt my soft city feet, but this added to the elemental sensation of being close to the Earth. Lynx lit a larger fire with the bundle she had carried and we sat in a circle around it. Our week of living outdoors on Dartmoor had officially begun. Dusk was settling. A wind picked up and I straightened my legs so my bare feet could catch some of the warmth from the flames. We passed around a talking stick and told each other what 'miracle' had brought us here.

Back at camp, Katie, the cook, had a large pot of venison stew waiting for us. The meat had come to us from Bob, a local deerstalker. Any worries about the animal's welfare were put to rest. We would be eating Paleo all week.

After dinner, we were to tell the group what we had been passionate about when we were seven years old. I talked of my upbringing in the soulless Canadian suburbs. Most of the participants told tales of playing in streams and catching frogs. Canadian suburbs were designed for cars, for life with sunken living rooms, dry bars, rec rooms, where everything was tinted by the glare of TV and the sound of canned laughter. I hated growing up in those suburbs and now I was feeling as I so often do, somewhat disappointed, even a little cheated that my childhood had not been spent in the woods but rather in a place where soil was called 'dirt', where lawns were mowed to a buzzcut every few days and where bees were swatted to death for fear they might ruin the barbecue. I had no connection with the place I grew up in. This has always rankled me. My birthplace has left me empty-handed of stories, unlike the ground I am sitting on now with its hauntings and Druids, ghost stories, songs and rituals involving stone, bone, moss, fertile swathes of soil and rain-soaked forests.

The next day I tucked my knife into a cloth bag with some non-Paleo bread and cheese, a bottle of water, my journal and my copy of *Crossing Open Ground*. We began a silent walk: each one of us was led to a spot to sit alone for an hour or so. From my rock I could see a decaying, moss-covered stone wall. Fallen trees were criss-crossed with ivy. Fat bees buzzed around me but what I noticed most of all were the birds: wood pigeons and the quick trills of what I thought might be a wood warbler. Sunlight struggled to make its way to the floor of the forest through the branches of very tall oaks. Where I was sitting, the air was cool.

Our assigned task had been to gather 'vegetal matter with a utilitarian value for the whole group'. This way of thinking was so foreign. We have all become so individualized, so atomized with our own phones, computers, social media accounts and living spaces. Lynx, by contrast, was trying to revive the idea of the tribe. I had bristled when I'd heard this word being used earlier in the day. I had felt it was a word one needed to earn, that in this context it was somehow fake or pretentious or a case of cultural appropriation. But now, alone in the woods, I was beginning to understand that a tribe can be formed when we rely on others for our food and shelter, warmth and companionship – even temporarily.

I was also starting to see the landscape as active rather than passive – for what it could do rather than as a collection of named objects. Barry Lopez captures this idea in his essay 'Landscape and Narrative' when a black-throated sparrow lands in a paloverde bush: 'the resiliency of the twig under the bird, that precise shade of yellowish-green against the milk-blue sky, the fluttering whir of the arriving sparrow' – these are what he means by 'landscape'. It is by watching the landscape that one learns it, not necessarily by knowing the names of things. Or put another way: should the naming of things arrive in tandem with our observation and understanding of the interaction of these things?

I spotted some fiddleheads. My mother used to buy small packs of these velvety green ferns at vast expense from the supermarket in Ottawa. She would unwrap them from their clingfilm, lift them from their Styrofoam tray and then soak them, boil them and sauté them in butter. We would savour the two or three on our plate as if they were gold. I harvested a few to bring back to the group. I looked around for something else I might be able to share. I pulled off a hunk from a charred stump. We could draw with it. Then I spotted a bone. This could be a ladle or a spoon. I put that in my bag and topped it up with some young nettles. We could use these for tea. My inadequacy was making me manic. Just then I saw members of the group approach.

I took a breath and joined the line. Some of them had bulging bags and I wondered what foods and implements they had conjured from these woods.

We walked silently across fields and through forests of bluebells. Eventually we came to Blackingstone Rock, a 75-foot-high, Christmas-pudding-shaped tor of pure granite flecked with shiny feldspar. Running up the back of the tor, like a spine, was a metal ladder. We climbed to the top where the wind whipped and the views over Dartmoor spread out on all sides.

The Dartmoor chronicler William Crossing believed that in an attempt to settle an argument, King Arthur and the Devil hurled a giant quoit at each other. As the quoits hit the ground they turned to stone, creating two tors, Blackingstone Rock and Hel Tor. Blackingstone Rock is pockmarked with small circular basins, which were Druidical altars. Like a cat, Lynx curled into one for a nap.

England has little wilderness left, but here in Dartmoor, in England's 'West', you can get lost. There are no predators, however. You have to go up to Scotland for wild cats. Wolves and bears are also being considered for reintroduction into the United Kingdom. But this place, with its granite tors, altars, and ancient-looking flora is as close as I could get for now to the trance visions I experienced at the Ecosex Convergence. I remembered Teri telling me to make an altar, to listen to the call of

my mother's ancestors in Ireland. Is this partly what I am doing here? Getting closer to my 'bog'?

While living in Montana, I was keenly aware that much of the land in the American West is stolen land. Not only did the American government in the nineteenth and early twentieth centuries attempt to sever Native Americans from their land, their language, their rituals and their culture, but they tried in earnest to eradicate them through assimilation and through a systematic genocide. It is impossible to ignore this as one moves through the West. The signs of injustice are everywhere if you are willing to look. Probably the most visible manifestation came in the form of the protests at Standing Rock in North Dakota.

In 2014, the US Army Corps of Engineers granted authorization to begin digging a 1,186-kilometre oil pipeline called the Dakota Access Pipeline (or DAPL), which would bring crude oil from the Bakken oil fields in North Dakota, across three other states – South Dakota, Iowa and Illinois.

It's worth noting that the pipeline had originally been designed to run past North Dakota's state capital, Bismarck, but the strength of nimbyism won that battle on the grounds that its proximity to municipal water sources would make it a potential danger to the town's drinking water. An alternative route was chosen which would bring the pipeline 800 metres from the Standing Rock Indian Reservation and its water sources. The pipeline would also snake through farmland, sensitive natural areas, wildlife habitats and, crucially, under the Missouri River and Lake Oahe – the ninth-largest lake in the US and the primary source of drinking water for the Standing Rock Sioux Tribe. It would also be nudging dangerously close to crucial underground aquifers. Any cracks or breaches in the pipeline would have serious consequences for drinking water for an enormous region and a large population.

The fears of the tribal members fighting the pipeline are not unfounded. In 2010, Michigan's Kalamazoo River had close to a million gallons of tar sands crude oil dumped into it from a burst pipeline owned by the Canadian firm Enbridge, resulting in a clean-up lasting more than five years and costing over a billion dollars. The river is still contaminated, because water cannot ever be cleaned up. Montana's Yellowstone River has also had its share of crude oil dumped into it. In 2011, ExxonMobil Corp's pipeline ruptured releasing more than 1,000 barrels of crude oil. And again in 2015 – 1,200 barrels of Bakken crude oil leaked into it.

Before granting permission to the DAPL pipeline, federal law required the Army Corps to review and assess any potential environmental impact from this project because some of the land and water the pipeline would be crossing falls under federal jurisdiction. However, in the initial environmental assessment, the maps utilized by Dakota Access and reviewed by the

Army Corps did not indicate the proximity of the proposed pipeline to tribal lands. In fact, the environmental assessments omitted the very existence of the tribe in their analysis, in direct violation of US environmental justice policies. The company behind DAPL, Dakota Access LLC, a subsidiary of Energy Transfer Partners LP, also worked their way around having to conform to the Clean Water Act and the National Environment Policy Act by using a permit process that treated the pipeline as a series of small construction sites.

Standing Rock Sioux elder LaDonna Brave Bull Alland established a camp in April 2016 as a centre for cultural preservation and a gathering place for spiritual resistance to the pipeline. Over that summer the camp grew to thousands of people. Brave Bull's great-great-grandmother, Mary Big Moccasin, had survived the bloodiest conflict on North Dakota soil between the Sioux Nations and the US Army on this very land, when an estimated 300 to 400 Sioux were killed in the Whitestone Massacre. The protests at Standing Rock were a continuation of the fight against land appropriation – a fight that has been going on for over 150 years.

In the independent, non-profit *Yes!* magazine, Brave Bull explains how the camp at the confluence of the Cannonball and Missouri Rivers had once been the site of a whirlpool that created large, spherical sandstone formations. The river's true name is River that Makes the Sacred Stones. 'The stones are not created anymore,' she writes, 'ever since the U.S. Army Corps of Engineers dredged the mouth of the Cannonball River and flooded the area in the late 1950s as they finished the Oahe dam. They killed a portion of our sacred river. I was a young girl when the floods came and desecrated our burial sites and Sundance grounds. Our people are in that water. This river holds the story of my entire life.'

Protests came to a head in the winter of 2016 when police used firehoses to unleash freezing cold water onto protesters, who claimed rubber bullets, tear gas and concussion grenades were also fired at them. Hundreds of people were injured. The situation at Standing Rock went viral, and the outside world started to take notice, when dogs were used to attack protestors, some of whom were silently praying. By October 2016, 140 protestors had been arrested. President Barack Obama was slow to take action but he did request a halt to the building of the pipeline until all tribal concerns had been heeded. This was reversed in January 2017, when the newly elected President Trump signed an executive order allowing the pipeline's construction to proceed.

I could not look out at the Missouri river or at any land in the West without feeling that somewhere in its recent history blood had been shed by people trying to protect it. Arguments over land are ongoing. By building this pipeline, the government and Energy Transfer

345

Partners LP are discrediting the Fort Laramie Treaty of 1851, which was signed by eight tribes and the US government. It clearly states the ground in question belongs to the Sioux. For the past 150 years, tribes have been in court challenging those who refuse to honour these and similar treaties. More often than not, the energy and mining companies and corporate interests win out. This is the ground under your feet in the American West. And it is impossible not to feel the grief and struggle in the soil.

In Dartmoor, the wilderness may not be so vast or awe-inspiring but there are no reminders of recent genocide. The rewilding movement in the United States looks back to when human animals were a minority, when resources were bountiful, to the time before the Europeans showed up, which for me was a difficult task to master. I was so aware, when I lived there, that the land in the American West was not mine. In England it seems – to me at least – that rewilders see the land as connected to stories, songs and myths. The wildness here is one of imagination, it is internal. As a foreigner in Britain and the United States, I was swimming once again in that liminal space between places. I did not belong in Dartmoor either.

We headed back into the forest, quieter now, feeling the effects of the sun-warmed stone on our backs. Lynx instructed us to gather two dry sticks and eight switches of hazel. People were running into the woods, knives and folding saws at the ready. I was already lost. A couple I had spoken with earlier noticed my anxiety and patiently showed me what hazel looked like and offered me the use of their saw.

Once we had our sticks, we headed back to camp. Katie, the cook, had prepared fried pollock with mashed swedes, parsnips and celeriac. I was hungry. In my effort to lighten my backpack, I had taken out a lot of my food. Hunger was something I had forgotten how to live with. I was shamed by this.

As I tried to sleep that night, I heard two owls hooting to each other in a call and response. They were marking their territory with this conversation taking place high in the treetops. I fell asleep with a burning desire to understand them. It was only when they stopped their hooting around 4 a.m. that I woke. It was the silence that had roused me. A very faint light crept over my tent, almost like a shadow. I felt I was suspended in that fleeting moment between night and day, between the animals of the dark and those who emerge with the light. I was inhabiting a precious liminal moment. At fifty-two, I was suspended between youth and old age and this sense of being between things seemed to be the frequency I was tuned into. The word 'liminal', from the Latin *limen*, means 'threshold'. I was feeling it everywhere. A strange sense of total and utter wellbeing consumed me, as if I had connected to something infinite. Then the birds of the morning took over and the woods around me filled with sound. Life could continue for another day. I realized that perhaps the only place for me is one that exists between places.

The following morning, we were to find a partner and forage for our lunch. I was paired with Lynx. We walked together down a lane away from the camp. Lynx had seen some very young, green spruce buds. She showed me how to remove the brown husks from the lime-green almond-shaped buds. Their taste was sharp, astringent, lemony. She spotted a curved slice of fallen tree bark to put them in. It made the perfect receptacle, which in New York or London would add about twenty pounds to the price of a meal in a restaurant ('served on a hand-harvested spruce board infusing the buds with the taste and smell of wilderness').

With her survival skills, Lynx shared similarities with the Preppers or survivalists I have met – people who prepare for serious social, economic or planetary disaster. They stockpile food, water, ammunition and medical supplies in the hopes of being able to survive any catastrophic eventuality. Religious survivalists are preparing for a kind of biblical Armageddon, but the variety of non-religious Preppers is incredibly wide-ranging, from those who believe that bio-terrorism will finish us off to those who see natural disasters as the endgame. Many buy gold and silver, believing in its inherent worth, for when the economy crumbles

and cite the stock market crash of 1929 as the basis for their fear. But essentially they all value self-sufficiency and train their focus on outliving whatever disasters might show up.

Instead of filling her bunker with bottled water and ammunition, Lynx has prepared in another way. Like Finisia, she can live in the wilderness by hunting, gathering, making bows, arrows, clothing and whatever else she needs; she does not have to escape the wild in order to survive it. Many Preppers, who see themselves surviving the oncoming collapse by storing up on man-made supplies, have a deep fear and a mistrust of government. A bunker lined with tin cans and bars of gold is finite, whereas Lynx can survive indefinitely and pass on her skills. Both schools of thought share a mistrust of the system, but their approach could not be more different. I don't feel I can exist at either end of these extremes, but Lynx, Finisia and Katie Russell all share a sane view of the Earth as something to tend with a vision of a future on the planet. I don't think the Preppers imagine much beyond their own survival.

We all placed our foraged food onto a picnic table. The colours were spectacular. We silently took turns tasting every plant, taking in the smells, flavours, textures: stitchwort, garlic mustard or jack-by-the-hedge, gorse flowers, pink purslane, primrose, violets, landcress, pennywort or navelwort, dock leaves, hawthorn leaves and spruce buds. It was like eating a fairy tale.

That afternoon we were to begin weaving our baskets. This is what the sticks were for. I broke into a sweat. I had only ever made that one basket in Portland, which was a mess. Lynx showed us how to strip the bark from our hazel switches, how to bend them and tie them into a U-shape using animal hide as string. I felt my body move in sync with the making of my basket: I bent to make the wood bend, my muscles contracted when I tied the struts together. While the deer hide soaked, I stood, relaxed, watching it soften in the water. This work was three-dimensional, tactile. There were smells and sounds – it was the antithesis of the flat, backlit screens so many of us spend our days staring into. It was this physical dimension I had been craving without knowing it. Maybe this basket would not betray my urban neuroses.

On our second to last day, there was a snow flurry, which was unusual for April. As the snow got heavier, we took shelter in the lodge, the one structure with a partial roof. We watched in wonder as the grove of beeches was bleached white. A wind whipped the flakes around us. Lynx announced we would walk out onto the moor with what we could fit in our baskets and camp without tents. Many of us laughed, thinking she was joking. Silence descended as we realized she was being absolutely serious. I wasn't prepared to camp in the snow. An elderly gentleman from France came over to me and whispered, 'This is too much!' He was on the verge of a very Gallic rebellion.

'Let's see what the weather is like tomorrow,' Lynx said as a way of placating us.

The following morning the inside of my tent was a golden pink. I stepped out onto crispy, white grass. We had agreed that if it wasn't raining we would head off for our night of wild camping. It had dipped below zero but the skies were clear, so I got packing. We hiked out late morning walking through blue-bell meadows, crossing streams on bridges of fallen granite slabs and we said hello to the inhabitants of the few small towns we passed through. They stared at our buckskin and hazel baskets strapped to our backs. We were filthy and excitable and giggled like children at the disconnect between us and the villagers with their Lidl bags, heading home to their running water and televisions.

After about three or four hours we came to a wall of Herculean boulders. We scrambled up. On the other side was a tiny patch of flat ground, just big enough to cradle a fire and our bodies around it. We set up camp and Katie heated up some leftover stew made from Chunko the lamb, whom we had been eating through-out the week. She added nettles and threw a few garlic heads into the fire along with some sweet potatoes. We ate with our hands and there was something wonder-fully primitive about being here, eating like this from the land. We sang, we laughed, we chatted. The group was one unit now.

After dinner, I was told the temperature would again sink below freezing. I moved my bivvy bag from between two slabs of rock to a spot next to a woman with a surplus of blankets. We agreed to ignore the ticks on our patch of soggy ground. I went to bed before the others. Maybe because I am the youngest of seven children, I feel comforted falling asleep to the faint murmur of voices. When I was young, much of my education came from this late-night eavesdropping. I wondered if this had been an attempt to recreate tribal life in those cold, atomized suburbs.

I listened to the laughter and the crackling of the fire. I watched the stars above me. I never wanted to leave. I was suspended here. We all were. This was the discovery I made: we are all living liminal lives. Denying this is part of the madness. The only real thing is the liminality of life, the moments when we can inhabit fluidity, accept the threshold. We are just passing through. Why should we expect anything other than being between places and times and states of being? I realized as I was approaching my fifty-third birthday that I probably would never join the hoop. I may not ever live totally wild, despite the craving to do so. But I did know that these two 'wests' had changed me. I would be seeking to give myself over to wildness however I could.

I let my tears quietly fall. There was that familiar tickle as the salty water slid along my cheekbones into my ears. This was right. I should be crying. I was comforted by the black sky above me. I had lived another day. We had all lived another day. This felt like the miracle it was. Sleep came to me before the group had dispersed for the night. My dreams were more vivid than they had been since leaving Montana.

I got back to London very late the following night. My ten-year-old daughter was still up. She ran to hug me. 'You smell of dead animal,' she said, excited at this meaty version of her mother.

My husband, Jason asked, 'So, are you a new person?'

Me: 'Um, Yeah.'

Jason: 'Will I like this new person?'

Me: 'I don't know.'

Jason: 'Do *you* like this new person?'

Me: 'I have no idea.' I cast my eyes around this familiar, yet utterly foreign kitchen.

Of course I had no idea.

How could I?

This new person had yet to return from the wild.

Finding the ending for this book has been the most challenging part of writing it. I find it hard to imagine that a night will come when I am not dreaming of those mountains and the people in these pages, many of whom are now friends. They are part of my life and of a wider world I have come to care deeply about. Michael Ridge is carrying on hoop culture. He wintered in Twisp, Washington near Katie Russell, Joshua Dodds and some of the Buffalo Bridge people. A few more have joined him. Chuck has been out with him this summer in Hell's Canyon, Idaho. Chuck became close to someone we met on our travels and is now pregnant with his child. Her baby is due this summer. Lynx felt a calling to the North and was considering moving to northern Sweden but decided to stay in Twisp with her animals and the community there. Finisia, who is not well enough to be on the hoop, is living in California with a friend. She made it to pine nut camp this autumn and she travels in her battered old truck when she can to participate in rewilding and replanting. Last I heard she was going to be at Saskatoon Circle again this coming summer. Hoops, circles, the planting of seeds, the tanning of hides, honouring the land – it is all being carried on quietly in the margins.

The other day I happened to read about the trapper Jason Maxwell and his marriage to his fiancée, the equally enthusiastic trapper, hunter and writer, Angela Montana. The date they chose, 15 September 2018, is the opening day of the general wolf- and bear-hunting season. An online publication described the furs and wolf traps hanging on the posts at the altar and the last bull elk Jason's grandfather shot before passing away several years ago hanging front and center on the altar they built. Don't forget the MAGA onesies with the US flag on the back and the red, white and blue themed everything... and a five-tier wedding cake comprised of every Little Debbie and Hostess snack cake you can think of with a cake topper of a bride and groom back-to-back, each aiming AR-15s.

But the touch that has stayed with me, that embodies so much of what is wrong about the West, was this: 'In addition, a couple of camo-clad friends showed up straight from hunting in the mountains with the back of their pick-up containing their first bear they tagged earlier that evening! How awesome is that?'

When we first arrived in Montana in that summer of 2014, Jason announced he wanted to make an unlikely literary pilgrimage to Idaho. The author Denis Johnson, who died in 2017, was living in Idaho's panhandle up near the Canadian border. Jason and I had talked about his book *Jesus's Son* when we first met. Jason was the only person I knew who had wanted to see the obscure Canadian film adaptation. Over the years we had read and shared Johnson's books with each other. If one were being corny, you could say he was 'our' writer, the way some couples have 'their' song. The nearest town to Johnson's home was Bonner's Ferry, Idaho (population 2,500). We made a beeline there from Missoula one weekend, just after we'd moved into our first rental house. About three hours into the four-hour drive, we crossed a long bridge over the earring-shaped Lake Pend Oreille at Sandpoint, Idaho (population 7,365). It's a long bridge – over three kilometres – running partially alongside a handsome iron railway bridge built in 1905.

'This reminds me of the bridge in Marilynne Robinson's *Housekeeping*,' one of us remarked. I can't remember who.

A quick look online revealed the town of Fingerbone, where *Housekeeping* is set, was indeed based on Sandpoint, the town Robinson grew up in. Our Idaho literary pilgrimage was offering us more than we'd bargained for.

We got to Bonner's Ferry just before Bonner's Books, the independent bookshop, closed for the day. They had every single Denis Johnson book, all of them signed. In a fit of nerdish completism, Jason bought the one Johnson book he didn't have, *The Stars at Noon*. We got talking to someone in the shop, who told us about the Boundary County Fair. 'It might not be your thing,' she said, 'but there isn't much else going on here.'

The following morning was hot and very still. The wildfires were far away, the wind was not blowing in our direction and the air was clear. We drove to the fairgrounds, just on the edge of town. Wooden buildings were lined with neatly arranged trestle tables laden with local vegetables, baked goods, jars of preserves, all being judged for their size, shape, taste and colour. Prize-winning pigs, goats, cows, sheep and rabbits sported fancy rosettes and ribbons, while kids and teenagers mucked out the stables and groomed the animals. This was all very familiar to me having grown up in Ottawa where every summer we would traipse to our very own county fair called the Central Canada Exhibition or the 'Ottawa Ex'. But there were differences here.

One building, devoted to taxidermy, was lined with stuffed animals. There was also a huge box of pelts for kids to play with. In another exhibition hall, a long pre-fab structure the length of several shipping containers, we were greeted with smiles by a towering, clean-cut father of six. He explained why Obamacare, or the Affordable Care Act as it is officially known, was such a terrible idea. When he heard Jason's accent he told him how much he loved listening to the goings on in the UK Parliament in *Question Time*. From the very beginning of our time in the West, the place surprised me and undermined my expectations.

Then on to the next stall: the National Rifle Association. They were raffling off a long-barrelled gun, the kind that sits on a tripod. It was as tall as Eve. The guy manning the booth asked me if I had taken

Eve to the Bonner's Ferry shooting range yet. I admitted that I hadn't.

'How old is she?' he asked.

'Seven,' I replied.

'The perfect age to start firing a gun,' he said cheerily.

I could feel Eve's hand tighten in mine. I thanked him and we walked on, passing dozens of banners with haloed foetuses and messages about 'murdering babies'.

Right at the end of the hall were three middle-aged men wearing casual shirts tucked into their jeans. They looked like American *soixante-huitards* with their grey hair and expressive faces – the sort of people you might want to share a beer with, who had a few stories up their sleeves. It turned out they were the only Democratic representatives at the fair. We stopped to take a look at the literature they had on offer. One of the three guys, a small friendly-looking man, noticed the Denis Johnson book under Jason's arm.

'Hey I know that guy,' he said excitedly.

It turned out Jerry Shriner was Johnson's car mechanic and was also running for office in Idaho as a Democrat. One of the other three Democrats asked where we were from and then told us he'd married his first wife at the Kensington and Chelsea registry office. Another spoke of his years on the Magic Bus. I asked if they were ever lonely being Democrats here in this very red state and one of them piped up, 'I've got Jerry to hold my hand.'

We wandered the fair in a slight state of disbelief. Christian families in nineteenth-century clothing admired the livestock – the girls with hair neatly braided wore long dresses made puffy with slips and light crinolines; the men and boys wore cowboy hats, white shirts and trousers with braces. On a trampled, once grassy lawn next to the buildings were more tables piled with the usual cupcakes, popcorn and balloons. Local firefighters handed out safety stickers. A miniature train, called the Redneck Railway, ferried small children around.

Then we stumbled upon the Oath Keepers' booth, manned by a couple of large, smiley guys in baseball caps offering glasses of water with their literature. Like everyone else we'd met here, they were friendly and happy to talk. Founded in Montana in 2009, the Oath Keepers are a Patriot group who focus their recruitment on current and former military personnel, police officers and firefighters – although in reality anyone can join. The Anti-Defamation League describe them as 'extremists' whose views closely resemble those of the 'militia' movement, whose adherents believe that the United States is collaborating with a one-world tyrannical conspiracy called the New World Order to strip Americans of their rights – starting with the right to keep and bear arms. The Oath Keepers swear to 'defend the Constitution against all enemies, foreign and domestic', and do so 'under God'. Their oath is 'to the Constitution, not to the politicians', they 'will not obey unconstitutional (and thus illegal) and immoral orders, such as orders to disarm the American people or to place them under martial law and deprive them of their ancient right to jury trial'. They have been known to show up at protests in military gear openly carrying weapons and ammunition. They did so in August 2014 in Ferguson, Missouri (an open-carry state) when riots broke out after a police officer shot and killed Michael Brown Jr, an eighteen-year-old African American man. We had just arrived in Montana when the rioting started, and the ripples from those riots and from the ones that followed when the police officer was found to have acted in self-defence and was acquitted of all charges had been one of the things that had originally unmoored me. The violence I felt everywhere around me in the US had taken me by surprise. I think my escape into the rewilding communities was partly my attempt to escape this violence.

The last thing we stumbled upon at the Boundary County Fair was a spitting competition. Large men in baseball caps and a few women queued up to take turns seeing who could spit the furthest. Crowds fist pumped and cheered them on. We'd seen enough for one day.

There are worrying rumblings in the West that have picked up in velocity and power since we left. The various anti-government Patriot movements, of which the

Three Percenters are a part, have gained in momentum. Just a few years ago, the people I was meeting at county fairs wearing Patriot regalia were happy to talk to me, to share their beliefs, which mainly revolved around their love of guns, liberty and the Constitution. They home-schooled their kids, went to church and taught their children how to be God-fearing, resilient and self-sufficient. Would they be so welcoming to us now?

The ideology shared by these groups appears to be metastasizing in a more sinister way. Members of these movements have been emboldened by the loudest voice in the land. Donald Trump's rhetoric around race, minorities, women, the selling off of public lands, the disdain for the concerns of Native Americans and his bulldozing of any environmental regulations is bolstering Patriot movements. No longer do many of these patriots hide their racism, their anti-semitism – they flaunt it.

The pull Jason and I feel towards the West is not because of these issues, but it is related to them. In the West, there is still so much to fight for. Half of the American West is made up of public lands. These are under threat. I have slept in the desert. I have dug for life-giving roots in ground that once looked dead to me but whose heartbeat I can now hear. I have seen first hand the destruction of rivers and attempts at their reclamation. On a canoe trip down the upper part of the Missouri river with Jason, Eve and a few friends we paddled through a torrential rainstorm. At night, while hail lashed the outside of our tent, the inside was lit up like a disco with flashes of lightning. We didn't know what it was at the time, but we heard what sounded like a jet taking off nearby. When we reached 'civilization' after this trip, we were told that sound was a tornado touching down a few kilometres away. Boxcars had been overturned and power lines had been shredded across the northern part of Montana. We had been in a tornado on the banks of a river, nowhere near a road, without any signal and far from any kind of help. I have felt the power of this land. *I have been prey.*

I have witnessed that western light gather in intensity and sharpness as it moves across the landscape towards me. The vastness, the inscrutability of so much space, performs an act of initiation. It does things to you that cannot be undone.

I am also having to inhabit London and its lack of light and space. The liminality I experienced in Dartmoor will be my salvation. For now I will have to exist with my feet planted here and my dreams existing elsewhere. I will navigate both. I have faith that I will eventually touch down on land that wants me there. It's been one year since the Ecosex Convergence and my final period, which means I am on the other shore of menopause. I have avoided hormone replacement therapy and have let my body do its wild raging as it needed to.

By writing about my two years in Montana, I am attempting to call back the person I was, to reclaim her and the ground she walked on and make sense of the unexpected trajectory of her journey. By looking back I can see connections I couldn't have imagined. Reclamation has been a recurring theme in my writing. I almost called this book *Reclamation* but realized at the ecosex festival that *Surrender* would be a more accurate title. Sometimes all we can do is surrender, to our circumstances, our desires and fears, our need for escape, our failures, our pain, our inner wildness, our domestication and in turn surrender to whatever essence is at the centre of our very beings. I yearn for the land of the West. I want to obey Finisia's words, to 'kneel down and dig'. My conversations there are not finished. There is so much more to say. And I have much more listening to do.

Illustrations

Readings

Edward Abbey, *Desert Solitaire*

Eve Babitz, *Eve's Hollywood*

Rick Bass, *The Nine Mile Wolves*

Wendell Berry, *The Unsettling of America*

Mary Clearman Blew, *Bone Deep in Landscape*

Nadya Burton, ed., *Natal Signs: Cultural Representations of Pregnancy, Birth and Parenting*

Claire Dederer, *Love and Trouble: A Midlife Reckoning*

Annie Dillard, *Teaching a Stone to Talk, The Writing Life, Pilgrim at Tinker Creek, The Abundance*

Timothy Egan, *Lasso the Wind: Away to the New West, The Immortal Irishman*

Gretel Ehrlich, *The Solace of Open Spaces, A Match to the Heart*

Ralph Waldo Emerson, *Nature*

Germaine Greer, *The Change*

Emma Harris, *Rambunctious Garden: Saving Nature in a Post-Wild World*

Kathleen Jamie, *Sightlines*

Denis Johnson, *Seek*

Jacqueline Keeler, *Edge of Morning: Native Voices Speak for the Bears Ears*

Karen L. Kilcup, *Fallen Forest: Emotion, Embodiment, and Ethics in American Women's Environmental Writing, 1781-1924*

Paul Kingsnorth, *Confessions of a Recovering Environmentalist*

Winona LaDuke, *All Our Relations: Native Struggles for Land and Life*

Patricia Nelson Limerick, *Something In The Soil: Legacies and Reckonings in the New West*

Rosalie Little Thunder, 'The Sacred Buffalo' in *Rethinking Columbus: The Next 500 Years*

Barry Lopez, *Crossing Open Ground*

Finisia Medrano, *Growing Up in Occupied America*

John Muir, *A Thousand-Mile Walk to the Gulf, My First Summer in the Sierra*

Roderick Nash, *Wilderness and the American Mind*

Michael I. Niman, *People of the Rainbow: A Nomadic Utopia*

Katha Pollitt, *Learning to Drive and Other Life Stories*

Marilynne Robinson, *Gilead*

Rebecca Solnit, *Hope in the Dark, A Book of Migrations*

Wallace Stegner, *Where the Bluebird Sings to the Lemonade Springs*

Mark Sundeen, *The Unsettlers*

Henry David Thoreau, *Walden*

Frederick Jackson Turner, *The Significance of the Frontier in American History*

Terry Tempest Williams, *Refuge: An Unnatural History of Family and Place*

Kathryn Winograd, *Phantom Canyon: Essays on Reclamation*

John B. Wright, *Montana Ghost Dance: Essays on Land and Life*

Acknowledgements

Excerpts from this book have appeared in different forms in the following publications: 'Congregation, Total Chaos and Greed: On Trapping Wolves in Montana', 'Stories Made of Water' and 'The Sparrow and the Twig' appeared on the Dark Mountain blog; 'The Hoop' was published in *The Tahoma Literary Review*, 'The Scavengers' in *Orion* Magazine and 'Surrender: Who Will Plough My Vulva' in *Cutbank*'s Spring 2018 issue.

I am also grateful to all the people within these pages who opened themselves up to me, gave me rooms, beds, spaces under their tarps, lifts in their cars, and most importantly their time. I am forever indebted to Finisia Medrano for igniting my concept of giving back to the planet more than I take and for her love, knowledge and dedication to the earth. And to Michael Ridge for his generosity and his continuation of hoop culture. I am also indebted to Lynx Vilden, Joshua Dodds, Peter Michael Bauer, Katie Russell, Lee Whiteplume, Archie Fuqua, Harmony Cronin, Alexander Heathen, Paul Parson, Ilona Popper and Keith Aune whose knowledge of land and ritual has enhanced these essays. I would like to thank Cathrine L. Walters and Chuck for their smarts and willingness to ferry this non-driver around the West. For their hospitality Mark Eifert, Jane Wilcox, Priya Hendrick, Betty Bell, Bruce Bell, and Brian Spellman came up trumps (shame about the bed bugs). Thank you to Jon Jost for reminding me that it's possible to make work against the odds and for putting me in touch with so many people who helped me with my research. To all my friends in Missoula, who are far too numerous to name, thank you for giving me and my family not only a soft landing but more love and support than is reasonable: Kevin Bell, Sasha Bell, Diane Benjamin, Michelle Bryan, David Allan Cates, Lulu Delphine, Rebecca Durham, Michael Fitzgerald, Catherine Jones, Jason Kelly, Jack Lawson, Gita Saedi, Courtney Saunders, Prageeta Sharma, Andrew Smith, Mike Steinberg, Sally Weaver and Garth Whitson. Thank you to Lorna Scott Fox for reading many drafts of these essays and always having impossibly intelligent things to say and thanks to Dinah Wood for always being my ally and to Andrea Mason for continuing to wield her pen and for urging me to do the same. And thanks to Nick Hunt for publishing some of these essays on the Dark Mountain blog and for reading a first draft of this book and encouraging me to continue with it. A huge thank you to Jacques Testard and Fitzcarraldo Editions for seeing value in this book. Thank you Guy Robertson of the Mahler & LeWitt studios for making my residency in Spoleto such an incredible experience. And of course my biggest thank you of all to Jason and Eve for sharing in some of these adventures and for giving me the freedom and encouragement to explore the ones I had to do on my own.

DINAH WOOD

JOANNA POCOCK is an Irish-Canadian writer living in London. Her writing has notably appeared in the *Los Angeles Times*, the *Nation* and on the Dark Mountain blog. She was shortlisted for the Barry Lopez Narrative Nonfiction Prize in 2017, and won the 2018 Fitzcarraldo Editions Essay Prize for *Surrender*.